WINE

Rod Phillips is a wine writer who lives in Ottawa, Canada. He is professor of history at Carleton University, where he teaches courses on alcohol, food and European history. He has published in wine media such as *The World of Fine Wine, Wine Spectator, Vines Magazine* and the guildsomm.com website, and he is wine writer for *NUVO Magazine*. His books on wine include *The Wines of Canada* (in the Classic Wine Library, 2017), *9000 Years of Wine* (2017), *French Wine: A History* (2016), *Alcohol: A History* (2014), and *A Short History of Wine* (2000). His books have been widely translated.

WINE

A social and cultural history of
the drink that changed our lives

ROD PHILLIPS

infiniteideas

First published in 2018 by
Infinite Ideas Limited
www.infideas.com

A CIP catalogue record for this book is available from the British Library

ISBN 978–1–908984–89–0

All web addresses were checked and correct at time of going to press.

Front cover image showing detail from The Wine of Saint Martin's Day by Pieter Bruegel the elder (1568) courtesy of FineArt/Alamy Stock Photo

All text photos and illustrations courtesy of the Wellcome Collection except image on page 68 courtesy Carole Reeves.

Typeset by DigiTrans Media, India

Printed in Britain

CONTENTS

INTRODUCTION

Wine has an extraordinarily complex and rich history that extends across most of the world. It has been made on every continent, except for Antarctica, for hundreds or thousands of years. It sometimes seems, from the perspective of the early twenty-first century, that there is no place on earth that lacks a wine industry. Although there are climatic limits to the locations where sustained and successful viticulture can be practised, entrepreneurs and would-be vignerons seek out small areas with marginally suitable mesoclimates to try their hand at growing grapes and making wine. Moreover, the recent phase of climate change has shifted the boundaries long accepted as suitable for viticulture and has opened up possibilities for growing wine grapes where it used to be not only marginal but impossible. Wine is now made commercially in all states of the United States, except Alaska, and in many parts of northern Europe, including England, Ireland, and Denmark.

Climate might dictate the extent of sustained and successful wine production but the only restraints on sustained and successful wine consumption are those imposed by laws. Civil and religious authorities have historically established regulations for the production, sale, and consumption of wine. Today these limitations range widely in their forms. They include regulating wineries, setting minimum legal drinking ages, licensing bars and restaurants, controlling the hours of wine sales, and restricting the drinking of wine in public. These limitations usually apply to beer and spirits, too, of course. In some places, wine and other alcoholic beverages are not restricted but banned. A dozen Muslim-majority countries, such as Saudi Arabia, Iran, and Kuwait, prohibit the production, sale, and consumption of alcohol entirely. The

Constitution of India declares that 'the State shall endeavour to bring about prohibition of the consumption, except for medicinal purposes, of intoxicating drinks' and Prohibition is in force in three states and one territory in that country. These examples represent exceptions to the near-global reach of wine today.

Wine, then, is a nearly ubiquitous beverage, just like beer and distilled spirits and a little less so than water, tea, and coffee, and there are times when their histories intersected. For example, when coffee, tea, and chocolate (consumed initially only as a beverage) were introduced to wine- and beer-drinking Europe, there were debates as to which were more or less healthy or harmful, regardless of whether they contained alcohol or not. Water, the sole universal beverage, was for some centuries regarded as so dangerous in some parts of Europe (and later in North America) that physicians advised against drinking it and recommended rehydrating by drinking wine and beer instead.

But it is arguable that the history of wine is that much more complex because of the cultural, social, and medical values that have historically been attached to it. Stressing the richness of the history of wine is not to diminish the histories of water, tea, and coffee, or of the other alcoholic beverages. Beer, distilled spirits, cider, mead, and fruit wines have fascinating histories, and I have written about them in my general history of alcohol. I am particularly aware of the occasional tensions between beer and wine lovers. Some years ago, when I was writing a weekly wine column for Ottawa's main daily newspaper, my editor asked me to write a column on beer for Canada Day, on the ground that beer was Canada's national drink. I complied, but I compared the complexity of beer unfavourably with wine, a move that generated angry letters to the editor from partisans of beer who demanded that I be fired or, at the very least, be prevented from writing about beer ever again. I responded the following week with a *mea culpa*, explaining that I would not have been so casually dismissive of beer had I known that beer drinkers could read.

To avoid another episode of that sort, I have tried to keep beer out of this account of wine, but it has crept in from time to time, as have distilled spirits and other alcoholic beverages. The reality is that when we discuss behaviour and attitudes as they relate to wine, we often have to bring other alcoholic beverages into the narrative. It would be misleading to pretend that wine was the only drink that had religious associations in many ancient cultures where there were beer gods, too. If wine was often in the past credited with having medicinal properties, so were beer and distilled spirits. And when we look at the ways men and women had different associations with wine, it is frequently their different associations with alcohol more generally that is at issue.

This, then, is a measured history of wine that places wine in various contexts but does not pretend that wine has been the world's most important and history-changing commodity. There are books that, facetiously or not, place certain foods (such as potatoes) front and centre in the broad sweep of history. This is a problem common to many biographies, especially of minor figures whose importance must be inflated and distorted by their biographers simply to justify their writing about them. The history of wine needs no such manipulation. The subtitle of this book, referring to the way that wine 'has changed our lives' might sound like a world-historical claim, but it recognizes that the readers of this book are more likely to be people engaged with wine to an extent that it has made an impact on their lives.

This has been an interesting book to write in that, unlike most histories, it is organized by theme rather than chronologically. It has made me think about wine differently, starting with the question of which themes were the most important. Some, such as health and religion, were obvious. Others, such as crime and landscape, were less so. It also brought to light the limitations of dealing with wine thematically in that it is impossible to isolate themes from one another. The medicinal properties attributed to wine are not only a matter of health, but stray into food and wine pairing in the chapter called 'wine and the table', and into ways of describing wine in 'wine and words'. Similarly, the discussions of food cross over to issues of health in 'wine and wellness' and, through the idea of terroir, into 'wine and landscape'. Overall, though, it is a very viable way of looking at the history of wine, and it allows readers to consume the book in discrete pieces more easily than a chronological history does. Here you can start reading any chapter without missing anything.

I have also had to digress from talking directly about wine in a number of places in order to provide background, so some paragraphs might appear to head off in uncertain directions. Discussing wine thematically risks ripping it out of its wider context, and it is important to include the framework within which wine is located. We can only understand the role of wine in medicine when we understand the dominant paradigms of the human body. We need to understand eighteenth-century English class relations to appreciate why upper-class men took to port, which had been a middle-class drink, with such gusto. Similarly, changing notions of gender help us appreciate why some wine writers began to call some wines 'feminine' and other wines 'masculine' and why there has been a reaction to the practice.

As in my other books, I owe a massive debt of gratitude to the historians, scholars in other disciplines, wine writers, and journalists who have written the material I have drawn on for this book. I have listed those I used most in the bibliography, but there were of course many more. I would especially like to thank Kolleen Guy, of the University of Texas at San Antonio, who is the author of an important history of champagne. Kolleen is now writing a book on terroir, provisionally titled *Eating Landscape*, and she generously allowed me to use parts of the draft. Once again, it was a pleasure to work with Infinite Ideas: Richard Burton, Rebecca Clare, Kate Santon and Kim Stringer. As usual, my friends and family had to listen when I needed to think through some things, but at least I provided them with wine as I did so.

Rod Phillips
Ottawa, December 2017

1

WINE AND WELLNESS

In November 1991 the American television program *60 Minutes* broadcast a feature in which French researchers claimed that wine was responsible for what was called the French Paradox: that although the French diet was heavy in saturated fats (especially animal fats, butter, and cheese) which should have led to high rates of heart disease, France actually had relatively low rates. Consumption of saturated fats by the French was much higher than in the United States, where vegetable fats were more widely consumed, but the incidence of heart disease was much lower in France than in the US. Some French scientists and nutritionists who studied this apparent contradiction concluded that resveratrol, a compound found in wine – especially in red wine – had the effect of neutralizing the effects of this diet. In 1990 French wine consumption (73 litres per capita) was far higher than in the United States (8 litres), and at that time about 75 per cent of the wine consumed in France was red.

Whether wine is or is not responsible for the French Paradox has been vigorously debated ever since, as have other aspects of the paradox – including the question of whether the incidence of heart disease really is relatively as low in France as was thought. But from a historical perspective, what was remarkable was not the claim that wine has medicinal or therapeutic properties but that such a claim was so controversial. For thousands of years physicians stated without fear of contradiction that wine was a healthy drink, one that was not only generally beneficial to physical and mental wellbeing but also helped combat countless specific ailments. Only from the later 1800s, about 150 years ago, did doubts begin to grow in the medical profession about the health benefits of wine, and even then the belief in wine's medical properties persisted much longer in some countries – notably in France. There had never been any doubt that heavy or excessive wine drinking was harmful, but by the mid-1900s a general consensus had emerged that even moderate wine consumption was either therapeutically neutral or actually harmful to human health. The link between wine and lower rates of heart disease set out by the French Paradox researchers – their suggestion that wine could actually be good for you – was novel to many people who had grown up with the idea that alcohol was harmful or never thought for a moment that it might be good for them. It was great news for wine drinkers (and the wine industry), and is said to have led to an immediate increase in the consumption of red wine in the United States.

WINE AND ANCIENT MEDICINE

For thousands of years before the French Paradox was described and explained by French researchers, physicians had been recommending drinking wine as a way of maintaining good health and curing illnesses. In addition, they had included wine (often as a solvent) in potions and medicines designed to deal with a wide range of ailments. As we might expect, the prevalence of wine in physicians' remedies at any given place and time varied according to its availability and importance. In ancient Mesopotamia and Egypt, all social classes, from rich to poor, drank beer, but only the well-off also drank wine. Grain for brewing grew quite widely in those places, but grapes for wine could be cultivated only in the mountains to the north of Mesopotamia, and in the Nile Delta and some oases in Egypt. Supplies of wine were limited, it was far more expensive than beer, and it was consumed only by the rich and powerful.

It is not surprising, then, that wine played a minor role in the medicine of these societies. In one important Egyptian medical papyrus (the Hearst Papyrus, dating from about 2000 BC), wine was called for in only twelve of the 260 prescriptions, about the same number as milk (eleven). On the other hand, twenty-seven prescriptions included the more widely consumed beer, and twenty-four required water. Beer-based remedies in Egypt included beer infused with coriander, bryony (a flowering plant), flax, and dates (for stomach problems) and grated coriander and other plants steeped in beer which was then strained and drunk (for blood in the faeces). Among the remedies that include wine, we find 'pig's blood and wine to be drunk immediately' (to cure 'rumbling within the body'), powdered dung in wine given orally for one day (to get rid of trembling in the fingers), and a generic mixture of herbs plus dill mixed into wine (to deaden the pain in any limbs). Another medical papyrus, this one from about 1550 BC (the Ebers Papyrus), includes remedies such as the finely ground testicles of an ass mixed into wine to deal with epileptic episodes, and bitter apple, honey, and wine to cure depression.

The full range of medical sources from Mesopotamia and Egypt lists hundreds of remedies that included wine as a way of dealing with ailments and conditions as varied as earache, loss of appetite, jaundice, and asthma. A Babylonian medical text shows that wine was even part of a cure for wine, or at least for the effects of enjoying more wine than was advisable: 'If a man has taken too much wine, if his head gives him trouble, if he forgets his words and his speech becomes confused, if his thoughts start wandering and his gaze becomes fixed, to cure him take licorice … beans, oleander … and at the approach of evening mix them with oil and wine; let the patient take this potion the next morning before the sun has risen and before anyone has kissed him, and he will recover.'

This is an early example of the 'hair of the dog that bit you' remedy for a hangover, meaning that the headache and nausea brought about by drinking too much could be cured by drinking more of the alcohol that was their cause. The term is said to have originated in the notion that a dog bite was best treated by placing a hair of the offending dog on the wound, but it might also have come from the use of animal hairs in a number of ancient remedies.

Wine was used by physicians beyond the civilizations of north-east Africa and western Asia. It was highly valued in Chinese medicine, and the Chinese character for medical treatment contains the elements of the character for wine. The earliest Chinese medical and pharmaceutical works cite wine as an important medicine and medium for cleaning wounds, and as a means of circulating medicines throughout the body. In the Taoist period wine was an ingredient in elixirs designed to promote longevity.

Yet although wine was more or less widely recommended as an ingredient in potions everywhere it was produced, it was not central to the medical writings in places where it was a marginal beverage, produced in small volumes, and consumed only by the elites. That was the case in Mesopotamia and Egypt, where – as noted – beer was far more widely consumed. But when knowledge of viticulture and winemaking reached ancient Greece and Italy, wine quickly became the principal fermented beverage. In fact it was virtually the sole fermented beverage because beer was not consumed in those societies and mead, made from honey, was only a minor drink. Wine of varying kinds and qualities was consumed by all social classes in Greece and Italy, and beer all but disappeared from influential European medical texts until the Romans began to colonize ancient France and other beer-drinking regions of Europe.

WINE AND THE HUMORAL THEORY

As viticulture was being extended to the Greek islands and mainland, from about 2500 BC, physicians began to develop a new theory of the body that not only became the dominant paradigm of Western medicine for thousands of years but also gave wine a central role in maintaining health and curing illnesses and diseases. Elaborated by such influential Greek physicians as Hippocrates and Galen, this paradigm was known as the humoral system because it taught that the human body was essentially composed of, and governed by, four liquids or 'humours': black bile, yellow bile, blood, and phlegm. These humours were said to exist on two axes, moist–dry and cold–hot. Blood, for example, was moist and warm, while black bile was dry and cold, and each humour contributed its character to the overall composition of the human body and each person's physical health and emotional temperament.

A person with a healthy body and mental state was someone whose humours were balanced, but this did not mean that all four humours ought to be in the same proportion and strength in every body because certain categories of people were, by nature, dominated by particular humours. Women were said to be naturally more moist than men because the moist humours (blood and phlegm) played a more important role in their bodies. But everyone (female and male) was naturally warm when young, although they began to cool as they aged until, when they died, their bodies became totally cold. Within these general tendencies defined by gender and age, each individual had their own subtly peculiar balance of humours.

The humours in a person's body also influenced temperament: blood promoted a sanguine (happy and optimistic) character while yellow bile (also known as choler) led people to be choleric (ill tempered). To this extent, the balance or proportion of each humour in the body was reflected not only in someone's health but also in their emotional character. We retain these humoral notions when we describe people as ill humoured and good humoured, and say (more rarely) that people are phlegmatic, choleric, sanguine, warm, or cold. The axis of temperature also related to sexuality, as warmth (which was particularly associated with youth) also indicated sexual passion. Thus we say that animals go into heat and describe sexy women and men as hot.

According to the humoral system, a person was physically and mentally well when the humours were appropriately balanced, given their age and gender, and a disease or ailment of any kind indicated that the balance of the humours had been upset. The task of a physician, therefore, was to discover the appropriate relationship of humours in each patient's body and to ensure that they remained in the right strength and proportion to one another. Illness occurred when the humours lost their natural balance and the physician's task was to rebalance them. Thus a fever accompanied by sweating indicated that the warm, moist humour (blood) was exercising too much influence over the body, and it was necessary to raise the strength of the cool, dry humour (black bile) to counteract it. Clamminess, on the other hand, suggested that the moist, cold humour (phlegm) was too powerful and that the dry, warm humour (yellow bile) needed to be boosted. It was a delicate balancing act and the physician needed to ensure that the process of balancing did not result in a new imbalance. To complicate matters, the time of year had to be taken into account: the warmth of a hot summer, for example, might need to be counteracted by cooling influences.

Wine was integral to medical solutions because physicians using the humoral perspective looked primarily to their patients' diets – the food and drink they consumed – both for the explanation of illnesses and for their cures. Specific medicines, mixtures of herbs and other substances, were widely used as short-term correctives, as were bleeding (when bodies were believed to have excess blood – when blood was thought to be too dominant an influence), and purging and emetics when the body needed to be cleared of other excesses. But having a diet that ensured the right humoral balance was the key to long-term good health and physicians modified their patients' diets in order to correct imbalances. For this purpose, all foods and drinks were given a value on the cold–hot spectrum: some were cool and others were warm, both in varying degrees. The value related not to the physical temperature of the food itself (which, clearly, could vary whether it was consumed raw and cold or freshly cooked and warm) but to the supposed effect of individual foods on the humours. In this system, water, fish, beer, and most fruit were considered cold in that they boosted the cold humours, but meat and wine were considered warm.

As a warm substance, wine proved to have many curative properties and it was a staple in the medical dispensary of classical physicians. But wine was not thought of as simply wine. The Greeks differentiated wines according to the grape varieties they were made from, where they came from, and by style: white, dark, new, old, sweet, thin, and heavy. Hippocrates wrote extensively on the ways that various types of wine could help digestion. 'Dark and harsh wines,' he noted, are more difficult to digest, 'and they pass well neither by stool nor by urine, nor by spittle'. On the other hand, 'soft, dark wines … are flatulent and pass better by stool' and 'harsh white wines pass better by urine than by stool'. White wines and thin sweet wines 'pass better by urine than by stool; they cool, attenuate and moisten the body, but make the blood weak, increasing in the body that [the other humours] which is opposed to the blood.' The range of wines available on the Greek market – wines of many different styles and grape varieties, coming from various regions of Greece, the islands, and Egypt – was a veritable pharmacy on which physicians could draw to deal with their patients' varying needs.

Beyond the role that wine could play in balancing the humours, it was recommended by physicians for specific purposes. The link between wine and digestion became a principle of Western medicine for thousands of years. In the New Testament, Paul advises Timothy, 'You should give up drinking only water and have a little wine for the sake of your digestion and the frequent bouts of illness that you have.' In fact, classical descriptions of individual wines, far from focusing on flavours and tannins as modern descriptions tend to do, often included notes on their medical properties. Athenaeus, for example, described a wine produced near Alexandria as 'excellent, white, pleasant, fragrant, thin, not likely to go to the head, and diuretic'.

Wine was also considered a general pick-me-up and a cure for sadness or depression. The Greek poet Euripides wrote that Dionysus, the wine god, had invented 'liquid wine as his gift to man', and 'filled with that good gift, suffering mankind forgets its grief; from it comes sleep; with it the oblivion of the troubles of the day. There is no other cure for misery.' But Euripides was not simply recommending drinking to the point of losing consciousness ('filled with that good gift … comes sleep') as a way of forgetting one's troubles. The humoral understanding of the body taught that melancholy was associated with black bile, which was cold and dry. Wine, a warm and moist food, would help counteract the influence of black bile and rid the drinker of sadness.

The physicians of the ancient world attributed many positive effects on physical and mental wellbeing to wine, but they insisted on what we would call moderation, and they were clear that excessive consumption of wine was detrimental to health. Among the effects of heavy drinking, Seneca and Pliny the Elder included memory loss, identity confusion, impaired speech and vision, narcissistic self-indulgence, antisocial behaviour, a distended stomach, halitosis, quivering, vertigo, insomnia, and sudden death. Excess was a relative concept, of course, and athletes, for whom physical fitness was important, were warned off wine except in small volumes (they were also advised to avoid desserts and cold water). Philostratus noted that athletes who drank too much wine 'have an excessive paunch … and too much drinking is discovered by a fast pulse'.

It is noteworthy that although beer was more important than wine in the medical texts of predominantly beer-drinking societies such as Mesopotamia and Egypt, Greek and Roman texts rarely mentioned it or did so negatively. Pliny thought beer was good for the sinews and in the first century AD the medical writer Celsus placed beer above wine in nutritional value. But most Greek and Roman physicians thought beer had a negative effect on health. The Greek herbalist Dioscorides, who wrote soon after Celsus, thought that beer was a diuretic that harmed the kidneys and sinews and caused flatulence, headaches, bad humours, and elephantiasis. A number of classical writers added that drinking beer made men effeminate.

Because the humoral system remained the primary paradigm of the body from the ancient period to the eighteenth century, wine remained central to medical theory and practice. In fact, within this system of attributing warm and cold values to beverages and foodstuffs, wine occupied a special place because whereas foods and other drinks had a single value of coldness or warmth, wines of varying styles were attributed different degrees of warmth. By the Middle Ages, sweet and rich wines were treated as warmer than lighter, more acidic wines, but some writers produced more nuanced scales of warmth. In the mid-fifteenth century the Paduan physician Michele Savonarola wrote that 'small' wines are warm in the first degree, small but more powerful wines are warm in the second degree, wines made from Grenache, Malvasia, and certain other grapes are warm in the fourth degree, and eau-de-vie or brandy (which, he pointed out, was made from wine) is warm in the fourth degree. Intuitively this sounds like a gradation based on alcohol content, but alcohol was not a recognized compound in the fifteenth century and there was no way of calculating the level of the active ingredient in intoxicating beverages.

It is more likely that Savonarola's ranking of wines by their degree of warmth was based on perceived strength, which would have included alcohol, but might also have included acids and fruit intensity. Eau-de-vie would certainly be stronger and warmer to the senses than a low-alcohol wine with flavours of low intensity. It is not clear quite why Savonarola specified three or four grape varieties for his third degree of warmth, but perhaps it reflected his experience of these wines as seeming to have a strength (or 'bigness') that was midway between small wines and eau-de-vie.

As a warm and moist food, wine enhanced the influence of blood, the warm and moist humour, and this helps explain why wine and blood were so closely associated. Some physicians believed that wine was transformed into blood when it entered the body. The appearance of red wine was certainly similar to blood – more similar than any other beverage or food – although most red wine made in the Medieval and

Early Modern periods was claret, a light and fairly translucent red, rather than the more intense and opaque colour of blood. The similarity in the colours of red wine and blood would explain why physicians sometimes specified red wine and sometimes white. Blood and wine also came together, of course, in Christian doctrine, where wine represented the blood of Christ in the Eucharist, and in other significant ways (see pp. 73–4). The humoral connection of wine and blood, which was already well elaborated in the early centuries AD, might well underlie this particular aspect of Christian doctrine.

As a warm food, wine could be prescribed to correct a body that a physician deemed to be too cold. Thus old people, who were cooling naturally but perhaps cooling too quickly, might be recommended to drink more wine to slow or arrest the ageing process. One proverb put it this way: 'Old age does not want games but rather wine, heat, and fire.' On the other hand, children and young adults were generally advised not to drink wine because they were, by nature, warm; the addition of more warmth through wine would lead to their becoming overheated to the point that their sexual passions would be aroused. Allen Grieco points to the 'telling metaphor' of Baldassare Pisanelli, a physician of sixteenth-century Bologna, that allowing children to drink wine 'adds fire to fire on top of kindling wood'. Pisanelli elaborated that young people should avoid wine because it disturbed their minds: they 'have a warm and fervent nature' and when they drink wine they 'run the risk of becoming powerfully impassioned in the spirit, and in the body furiously excited'. Fear of precocious sexuality was clearly a prominent part of this prohibition.

Fear of sexual arousal was also a reason why St. Benedict, whose rules of monastic behaviour became an important model for monasteries throughout Western Europe, declared that 'wine is no drink for monks'. Meat was also thought to arouse passions of the flesh that threatened monks' chastity and its inclusion in monastic diets was also discouraged. But as far as wine was concerned, Benedict continued that 'since, nowadays, monks cannot be persuaded of this [abstaining from wine] let us at least agree upon this, that we drink temperately and not to satiety'. In practice, monks were permitted no more than about a quarter of a litre of wine a day, but Benedict noted that monks who abstained from wine would have 'a special reward' – presumably in heaven.

Medieval and Early Modern medical texts stressed the importance of wine and reinforced the distinction between wine as a beverage and wine as a medicine. When used for medical purposes, wine might be consumed even in circumstances where its use was not recommended as a beverage. One fourteenth-century book, *Liber de Vinis* (*The Book of Wines*), was devoted to the therapeutic uses of wine but the author, Arnaldus the Catalan, did not exclude children from its beneficiaries. Indeed, some wine-based cures were designated specifically for children suffering from specific ailments. Trotula of Salerno proposed treating a child who had a severe cough with hyssop and wild thyme cooked in wine or with grains of juniper in wine.

Similarly, although most monastic orders urged their members to abstain from wine and allowed only a small ration to those who could not manage without it, monks who were ill were given more generous allotments. Wine was not simply a beverage in these cases, but a medicine. More striking was the argument advanced by some Arab physicians that even though Muhammad had forbidden the consumption of wine as a beverage, it might be taken by ailing Muslims when it was the only remedy that might save their life. Wine had been counted as a medicine by Arab physicians before the advent of Islam, and it remained in Arab medical texts. Although there is still a debate whether a Muslim might take wine (or any alcohol) when life depends on it, most Islamic scholars argue that alcohol is forbidden in any circumstances.

We must, then, make careful distinctions among drinking wine simply for pleasure, drinking wine as a means of hydration, and taking wine as a medicine. Clearly, any drinking session might satisfy more than one of these purposes, as drinking wine past the need to rehydrate became a matter of pleasure. Even then, there is the question whether drinking wine was necessary to rehydrate when water would do just as well or better. But Allen Grieco has suggested that in the Middle Ages and Early Modern period the line between wine as beverage and wine as medicine was not at all sharply drawn, and that notions of choosing the 'right' wine – which today would depend largely upon the occasion and the food being served – were generally based on humoral principles.

THE MEDIEVAL AND EARLY MODERN PERIODS

By the seventeenth century there was widespread anxiety in Europe about the safety of water, some – perhaps much – of which was contaminated by industrial, animal, and human waste. Physicians in many parts of Europe advised against drinking water and records of water drinking sometimes pointedly note that it did no harm. When the Pilgrims arrived in New England in the early 1600s they panicked when their beer and wine supplies ran out, and were surprised to discover that the water in the local streams could be drunk safely, unlike the water supplies they had left behind in England. There had been no such fears in the Middle Ages. To do penance for their sins, men and women were often ordered to forgo wine and beer, and to drink only water, but the Church clearly did not intend them to risk their lives by drinking polluted water. We could look upon drinking some water and some wine each day (perhaps as diluted wine) as a balanced approach to hydration that included beverages that were both cold and warm on the humoral scale.

Wine was not only drunk as a tonic and a medicine and used as the base solvent for preparations to be drunk, but was also applied externally to wounds, where its alcohol acted as a mild antiseptic. Even though Medieval and Early Modern wines probably had alcohol levels of only about 10 per cent, they were the most effective antiseptics available until distilled liquids (such as brandy), with much higher alcohol levels, became more widely available in the 1500s. Hippocrates wrote that 'no wound should be treated with anything except wine' and, although his rule was not followed by all physicians and surgeons, wine remained the mainstay of wound management for nearly two millennia. In the thirteenth century, just as the technique of distilling wine and other fermented liquids was becoming known in Europe, a textbook on surgery (*Cyrurgia*, by Teodorico Borgognoni, the medically trained bishop of Cervia) insisted on wine as the best dressing for wounds. Wounds were to be washed and cleaned with wine, then dried and closed. Old wounds were moistened with wine so that the edges would stick together better, then covered with a bandage soaked in wine.

The treatment of wounds was especially important on the battlefield where, until firearms became widely used in the fifteenth century, most wounds resulted from close-combat cutting weapons or from penetration by arrows and lances. First-aid instructions included the removal of barbed weapons so as to do least damage to the tissues, and the use of wine to clean wounds. Firearm wounds were more complicated because of infections caused by the bird-dung nitrates and lead in the bullets, but wine remained a treatment of choice. Ambroise Paré, a sixteenth-century French surgeon, described treating a patient who had been wounded in the knee by an arquebus, an early long gun: 'I made injections into the depths and cavities of the ulcers, composed of aegyptiacum [a compound of verdigris, vinegar, and honey] dissolved sometimes in brandy, other times in wine. I applied ... over them a large plaster [of compounds] ... dissolved in wine ... Then I made him drink wine moderately tempered with water, knowing that it restores and quickens the vital forces.'

The advent of distilling and the widespread production of brandy and other types of high-alcohol spirits lowered the profile of wine as an antiseptic, even though brandy was distilled from wine. We do not know the alcohol level of distilled spirits before the nineteenth century but they were clearly much higher in alcohol than the base wines and grain-based liquids they were made from, simply because of the process of distillation. These spirits were generically known as *aqua vitae*, or water of life (eau-de-vie, in French) and, as the name suggests, they were quickly associated with health. Distilled spirits gave the drinker a warm feeling and, glass for glass, had a much more rapid intoxicating effect than wine.

Being that much stronger than wine, brandy and other distilled spirits were attributed all manner of therapeutic benefits, including reversing the ageing process itself and prolonging life, as well as being a remedy for such age-related conditions as poor memory and greying hair. The higher alcohol content of spirits made them that much more effective than wine as an antiseptic. Containing less water, spirits could be used to clean wounds and leave them dry because the alcohol evaporated quickly, whereas wine had to be mopped from a wound after cleaning it, so as to leave the wound dry and ready for closing. Their higher alcohol also made distilled spirits a more efficient solvent in medical preparations.

The production of distilled alcohol in Medieval Europe was initially limited by law to monasteries and pharmacists, and because distilling was for a short time associated with alchemy and magic, it was banned in France and possession of distilling equipment made a capital offence. From the fifteenth century physicians began to include spirits more and more in their remedies and treatments but, although spirits might have superseded wine in some respects, wine retained an important role in medicine for many centuries afterwards.

From the Middle Ages until the early 1700s, a long period when Europe was struck by episodic outbreaks of plague – including the Black Death of the later 1300s, which wiped out as much as a third of Europe's population – wine was intrinsic to many suggested remedies. In 1348 the medical faculty of Paris recommended 'a clear, light wine' diluted with one-sixth water as treatment for anyone suffering from the plague. In the 1590s, Queen Elizabeth I recommended a preventative to the Lord Mayor of London: a spoonful of sage, rue, elder leaves, red bramble leaves, ginger, and white wine to be taken morning and evening for nine days. In his *Treatise of the Plague* (1603), the English physician Thomas Lodge recommended victims of the epidemic drink a powder of various ingredients 'in good white wine or in the winter time with claret wine'. Poor people who wanted to avoid the plague should take 'twenty leaves of rue, two common nuts, two dried and fat figs, a little salt, mix all together and take every morning a morsel, and drink a little pure white wine after'.

As this suggests, wine with other commodities could be a prophylactic as well as a remedy, and it was also recommended simply to maintain good health so that the body would be better situated to resist illnesses and diseases. But it had to be drunk in moderation. Thomas Lodge fell back on humoral principles when he advised on the best way to 'warrantie the body from all evils'. The rule, he wrote, was sobriety – moderation in all things, including alcohol consumption. He cited Hippocrates and Galen to support his view that the most common 'error and folly … in the time of infection and pestilence' is 'to overcharge themselves with wine and fill their stomachs before they go out in the morning'. Nor should wine be drunk without food, because the heat of the wine opens the veins and arteries and makes them more receptive to the diseases circulating in the air. But wine with modest meals was good: 'In use of wine, claret and white (nor over hue coloured, but tempered with good water) are very fit to be drunk at meals and no otherwise.' It is noteworthy that Lodge recommended claret, the light red wine (mostly from Bordeaux) that was popular in England and warned against 'over hue coloured' wines, the deeper red wines that were sometimes referred to as 'black wines'. Most French wine at this time (in the early 1600s) was light red with white and dark red wines being made in much smaller volumes.

Wine was considered nutritious in its own right – more nutritious than 'milk, eggs, corn, fruits, or the like', according to the seventeenth-century English physician, Tobias Whitaker. Wine drinkers, he wrote, were 'fair, fresh, plump, and fat' (a positive set of attributes at the time), unlike beer drinkers, who 'look like apes rather than men'. Like his colleagues, Whitaker warned that excessive drinking undid all the good that wine conferred: 'by the excessive quantity [of wine], you will add so much oil to the lamp as shall extinguish it'. Too much wine in the body 'inflames the blood, debilitates the nerves, and vexes the head', preparing the ground for 'deadly diseases' that included apoplexy, dropsy, palsy, and gout.

'Champaign Driving away Real Pain: Wine cures the Gout, the Colic and the Phthisic, Wine is to all men the very Best of Physic.' A group of merry patients discard their medicines in favour of wine. Aquatint by Theodore Lane and George Hunt, 1827.

Some physicians suggested that certain wines were suitable for working folk and others for the better-off and more refined. In the seventeenth century the French physician Jean Liebault wrote that 'red wine nourishes more than white or claret and it is more suitable for those who work hard'. As for vignerons and farmers who toil on the land, black (deep red) wine was preferred 'because once digested by the activity of the stomach and work, it gives more solid and plentiful nourishment and makes the man stronger in his work'. These black wines made the blood of their drinkers 'thick, melancholic, and slow-flowing', but that was appropriate for peasants who were known to be crude, not too bright, and slow in thought and action. But they were not suitable for nobles, bourgeois, and the clergy, who were lively and spiritual. Liebault advised them to stick to claret (light red) or white wines, which passed easily from stomach to liver, produced rich blood, and rejuvenated the heart and the brain.

The effects on health of the temperature of wine were also discussed by physicians, especially in the Early Modern period (1500 to 1800) when many people drank their wine warmed, either by placing it near the hearth or by plunging a heated metal rod, sword, or burning stick into the wine. Jean-Baptiste Bruyerin Champier, physician to François I of France, did not approve of warming wine – but he wrote in the mid-1600s that drinking it from a cool cellar was no better. Cool wine damaged the throat, chest, lungs, and stomach, corrupted the liver, and could cause instant death. Wine stored in a cool cellar should be brought to ambient above-ground temperature for a few hours before being drunk. Bringing wine to 'room temperature', then, has medical origins.

Yet there was no consensus on this. A few decades later another physician, Laurent Jaubert, wrote that when wine was being administered to a young person (itself a controversial practice), it should be cooled. If a cellar was not available, the wine should be cooled in a fountain or a stream. The reason Jaubert gave – that warm wine would overheat young blood – was a departure from the principle that any food's position on the cold–hot spectrum of the humoral system referred to its effect on the humours, not to its physical temperature. In the humoral system, wine was more or less warm, no matter what its serving temperature. That was the very reason, remember, that Baldassare Pisanelli discouraged giving any wine, warm or cool, to children – because it added 'fire on fire on top of kindling wood'.

These notable exceptions apart, wine was almost universally counted as a good thing, and not only by the physicians and their upper-class patients. Many proverbs of the time, passed through cultures at all social levels, refer to wine. 'In summer when it's hot and in winter when it's cold, wine gives you energy', went one seventeenth-century French proverb. Another advised that 'if you don't drink wine after raw vegetables, you risk being ill'. As for pears, which were considered hard to digest and feminine by shape, a wine chaser was called for: 'if pears are not followed by wine, they will soon be followed by the priest'.

Wine not only kept people healthy and warded off illness, it was essential to the sick. There is no end to the conditions that wine – by itself or as a base for compounds – could not cure. It is hardly surprising, then, to see it becoming a necessary supply in hospitals. When Louis XIV founded Les Invalides, the military hospital in Paris, in 1670, he exempted it from paying taxes on the first 50,000 litres of wine ordered by the authorities. By 1705 the exemption was raised to 800,000 litres, so much did the inmates need wine therapy. Wine was dispensed at meals three times a day (officers got a more generous ration than men in the ranks), and although wine in this context was a recognition that it was part of the daily diet, it was considered especially important for people who were ill. Much later, at the beginning of the First World War, the wine producers of Languedoc-Roussillon donated 20 million litres of wine to the government for distribution to military hospitals where, they said, it would boost the morale of the wounded and hasten their recovery and recuperation.

This belief in the healing properties of wine persisted through to the eighteenth century. In 1753 the American preacher Jonathan Edwards proposed a number of remedies for his sick daughter. They included a dead rattlesnake (he apologized for being unable to provide one) and ginseng (which he could). For the ginseng Edwards wrote, 'Try steeping it in wine, in good Madeira or claret; or if these wines are too harsh, then in some good white wine'. But he added a cautionary note that he was afraid 'the heat of 'em might raise a fever' and suggested diluting the wine with water 'to abate the heat of it'. Wine was employed as a stimulant and as a life saver. In the 1790s in Rouen, Normandy, a group of women rescued a neighbour who had been beaten unconscious by her husband, and 'gave her some wine to restore her senses'. From the

1770s, when abandoned infants were transported from the French countryside to city orphanages – they were carried, three at a time, in backpacks worn by men who made the journey on foot as quickly as possible – the children were often fed only wine. The purpose might have been to sustain them or make them drowsy, or both, and it suggests that the couriers themselves drank wine as they made their way through the countryside.

It is easy to accumulate recipes for potions, pills, and applications of wine alone or wine used as a base for other substances. Some were herbs, leaves, spices, and roots, while others evoked (if we can make the distinction) magic and superstition: the eyes of crabs, the flesh of a viper, or the moss that had grown in the skull of a man who had died violently. Wine was common to thousands of medicines that were prescribed by various authors for conditions as varied as scorpion stings, fevers, leprosy, haemorrhoids, late menstruation, and kidney stones. Beyond that, wine promoted health and repelled illness, the point made in the title of a 1638 book by the English physician Tobias Whitaker: *The Tree of Human Life, or, The Blood of the Grape. Proving the possibility of maintaining human life from infancy to extreme old age without any sickness by the use of wine.*

The challenge is to make some general sense of all these recipes and therapies and to some extent that task was achieved by the publication of a series of pharmacopoeias during the seventeenth and eighteenth centuries. This was a period that saw the accumulation and organization of knowledge in the great encyclopedias, the codifications of laws, and the drawing up of constitutions. The pharmacopoeias did the same for medicine, in that they were systematic compilations of remedies. There had been many similar compilations before, going back as far as the Tang Dynasty in China, but the new generation that began to appear in the 1600s standardized measures and the names of ingredients, limited the number of ingredients, and offered more precision about their effects. Between the 1600s and 1800s, as the pharmacopoeias brought some order to the chaotic range of remedies on offer, national pharmacopoeias began to emerge, and pharmacists became more professionalized.

As the various pharmacopoeias went through several editions, some of the more bizarre ingredients were discarded by the editorial committees.

It was a slow process and if the 1721 edition of the influential *London Pharmacopoeia* did not include moss growing on skulls, it still allowed for medicines with ingredients such as dogs' excrement and earthworms. But wine was never in danger of being written out of the physicians' arsenal. Perhaps that was unfortunate in some cases: an English pharmacopoeia of 1741 included a recipe that called for half a pound of hog-lice (alive) to be put into two pounds of white port wine for two days, then strained out and replaced by saffron and salt. Once filtered, the wine was to be taken twice a day for jaundice or dropsy.

During the Enlightenment there was no less sense that wine had medicinal properties. The *Encyclopédie*, the first attempt to bring together all knowledge, edited by Denis Diderot, summarized the medical writing on wine by Hippocrates, Galen, and others, and set out what we assume was the current (mid-eighteenth century) position. It gave special attention not only to the colour and weight of any wine, but also to its character. Wines with 'an agreeable smell, which is described as raspberry, are stronger than others. They restore strength more quickly and contribute more effectively to digestion; also they are more suitable for the old.' Among other things, this notion that any attractive aroma from (presumably, red) wine can be referred to as 'raspberry' reminds us that the attribution of fruit descriptors to wine has a relatively shallow history.

The *Encyclopédie* placed even more emphasis on the way the age of wine affected its therapeutic value. Young wines (which it defined as within one or two months of fermentation) were green, and drinking them led to diarrhoea and vomiting. (Millions of litres of wines such as these were shipped from Bordeaux to England from the Middle Ages onwards.) Middle-aged wines were between four and twelve months old, and these wines were at their peak for medicinal purposes, with all the components integrated. After one year, wines began to break down and become bitter, acidic, or harsh, and as such they were not good.

The *Encylopédie* also set out the therapeutic strengths of wines from various regions. German wines from the Rhine and Mosel Valleys were light, healthy, and diuretic – a good thing as we have seen, as it was important to keep the bodily fluids moving – and the wines of Alicante, in Spain, fortified the stomach. As for French wines, those made around Orléans in the Loire Valley fortified the stomach but tended to go to the head and easily intoxicated drinkers. Champagne had the same effect of making people light-headed but this was offset by its desirable diuretic properties, while the excellent wines of Burgundy were nourishing, good for the stomach, and tended not to go to the head. As for the best wine, the *Encyclopédie* declared that the 'big and dark' wines from Bordeaux (so not the clarets) were 'perhaps the healthiest wines of Europe'. They could be a little hard and austere, but they were good for the stomach, and although they were warm they did not go to the head. The particular emphasis in the *Encyclopédie* on wine 'going (or not going) to the head' suggests a new concern for intoxication and its effects in the Age of Reason.

It is worth noting that intoxicating propensities were attributed to the wines themselves, rather than to the volume of wine consumed. There was discussion of some wines being more 'aqueous' than others and some being 'warmer' than others, and we might take these terms as referring to alcohol levels – watery wines being lower and warm wines being higher in alcohol. To this extent the ability to intoxicate was partly intrinsic to any given wine, but drinking patterns were clearly also important: two bottles of Riesling at 9 per cent alcohol drunk in the same period as one bottle of Zinfandel at 16 per cent alcohol give roughly the same effect.

With the influential Enlightenment writers firmly committed to the medicinal properties of wine, it is not surprising that the following century saw little change in its status, especially in Europe. During the French Revolution, when Burgundy's prestigious La Romanée (later Romanée-Conti) vineyard was seized from the Church and auctioned off, the prospectus described the wine as reaching its peak between its eighth and tenth years, when 'it is then a balm for the elderly, the feeble, and the disabled, and will restore life to the dying'. The principles of the humoral system were tenacious.

THE NINETEENTH CENTURY

In the nineteenth century, wine remained central to national pharmacopoeias. The 1836 edition of the *London Pharmacopoeia* listed numerous recipes involving wine while, as one would expect, French versions were even more wine-centred: Antoine Jourdain's *Pharmacopée*

Universelle (1840) listed 164 wines. The first such compilation, this reflected a tendency towards more precision in matching specific wines to ailments. An example of this comes from a commission established in 1880 by the British medical periodical *The Lancet* to report on the medical uses of wine. The commission broke with tradition by arguing that wine was not needed by healthy people – although it did agree that it could be a tonic, preserving good health. Clarets were to the fore here because they had excellent tonic properties but lacked stimulant or sedative effects. Wine was, however, especially suited as a medicine for the ill. The most prestigious red burgundies, which lacked any sugar, were good for diabetics (rich diabetics) while the best white burgundies were much better as stimulants than the ports or sherries most often prescribed. Doctors, it seems, were expected to have a good knowledge of wine.

Many of the temperance and general anti-alcohol movements of the nineteenth and early twentieth centuries put the therapeutic properties of wine and other alcohols to the test. To those who held the most radical views – that all alcohol was pernicious to the human body and to the body social – it was incomprehensible that, whether it was consumed as a tonic or as an ingredient in medicines, wine could ever be good for anyone. That was certainly the position of most temperance movements in the United States and England. In France, however, the temperance movements generally focused on distilled spirits and to a lesser extent on beer, but they embraced wine as a noble exception. They saw wine not as contributing to the problem of drink, but as the solution to it. Rather than push for French people to give up drinking alcohol, they encouraged them to abjure spirits and beer and drink wine. In this general sense, they expressed the historic French belief that within the range of alcoholic beverages, wine was exceptional in that it was healthy.

For most of the nineteenth century and some of the twentieth, French physicians thought that the poor quality of distilled alcohol was more dangerous than heavy drinking. But most physicians exempted wine: it was not harmful, no matter what quantities were consumed. They argued that the alcohol in wine was qualitatively different from the alcohol in distilled spirits. Laboratory experiments on animals carried out by advocates of wine showed to their satisfaction that wine, and alcohol derived from wine, was less harmful than alcohol distilled from grain, sugar beets, potatoes, or other products. When phylloxera destroyed most French vineyards in the 1870s and 1880s, wine was in short supply and many drinkers turned to distilled alcohol, especially brandy and absinthe. Supporters of wine constructed series of statistics that showed increasing consumption of these drinks and a rise in alcoholic insanity. Needless to say, they drew a causal connection that underlined the safety and health benefits of wine. In *L'Assommoir* (1877), Emile Zola focused on the anxiety about alcoholism and has his hero Coupeau become a degenerate, violent alcoholic only when he ceases to be an abstainer and begins to drink alcohol. To make the scenario credible to his readers, Zola has Coupeau drink heavily and drink distilled alcohol, not wine. Bourgeois readers of *L'Assommoir*, which was published in the early phase of the phylloxera disaster, could see its message reflected only too vividly in the perceived social chaos that a shortage of wine had brought to French society.

Scientists who insisted that alcohol was alcohol, no matter what the source, and that it was dangerous even in small volumes, found it very difficult to dislodge the mainstream French medical belief that wine was exceptional. In the 1880s a commission headed by a senator produced a 300-page report, replete with statistics, maps, and other evidence, which concluded that distilled alcohol was to blame for the apparently rising rates of alcoholism, suicide, insanity, crime, and general degeneration in France, as well as the country's declining birth rate – long a concern of French governments. If wine was implicated, it was innocently: inadequate supplies of wine (mainly because of phylloxera) were driving people to distilled alcohol. Fortunately, the report concluded, it was only a temporary phase and alcoholism would disappear when France's 'former viticultural prosperity' returned. This was not only a French view. In Australia Dr Henry Lindeman, who founded a well-known winery, saw spirits as the cause of alcoholism and wine as an antidote.

The relationship of wine to alcoholism was especially problematic. Alcoholism as a disease was constructed in 1849 when a Swedish physician, Magnus Hus, first used the term 'alcoholismus' to describe a condition where regular and heavy use of alcohol led to adverse effects when individuals could not manage their personal and work lives. Alcoholism was described as a 'disease of the will', in that it sprang from a deficit of will, of moral strength, on the part of the alcohol drinker. It was thus a function of the relationship between alcohol and its consumer, which explained why some people who drank regularly and heavily became alcoholics while others who drank in the same way did not.

In the nineteenth century certain categories of people were believed to be generally weak-willed. They included women, workers, and the poor – women because they were women, while the lack of will on the part of workers and the poor was demonstrated by the conditions they lived in. This was problematic in France, where the medical profession accepted that distilled spirits could cause alcoholism but rejected the notion that wine could do the same. It was argued that although there were many drunks in France, there were no alcoholics. While some Frenchmen and women were confined in asylums and diagnosed as alcoholics, many persisted in arguing that this could not be true as they drank only wine and that they drank no more than a litre of that a day.

In Bordeaux, one of the heartlands of French wine, alcoholism was believed to exist only among dock workers and drinkers of absinthe, aperitifs, and brandy. Reputable physicians claimed that people who worked in the wine industry were never alcoholics, no matter how much wine they consumed. Emmanuel Régis, professor of clinical psychiatry in the Bordeaux medical faculty, argued that alcoholism appeared as a general problem only after phylloxera killed many of the region's vines and the shortage of wine drove wine drinkers to turn to the dangerous alcoholic beverages. He had, he said, never seen an alcoholic who drank only wine.

Whether or not wine contributed to alcoholism, there seems to have been a general weakening of the medical profession's support of alcohol as a medicine. To some extent this paralleled the rise of proprietary medicines such as aspirin and a host of other painkillers, sedatives, and antibiotics, all of whose effectiveness could be demonstrated in clinical trials. They were the products of scientific research and could be mass produced, and they were launched onto the market accompanied by testimonials, however exaggerated, as to their marvellous curative properties. Although wine was still praised as therapeutic, there was no hard evidence of its effectiveness and by the nineteenth century it was rarely any longer recommended for specific ailments – it was more often said to be 'healthy', 'hygienic', and 'a tonic'. As medicine became more specialized and as physicians focused on the physiological dimensions of their patients, rather than take the holistic view that earlier physicians had done – considering the physical and emotional conditions of their patients – the vaguely positive properties of wine were no longer as appealing. The wine inventories and alcohol budgets of some hospitals point to the decline of alcohol as a medicine. British hospitals, in particular, reduced their expenditure on wine steadily from the late 1800s.

Yet there were holdouts. In the late 1800s Francis Astie, a physician and editor of *The Practitioner* and a doctor in London's Westminster Hospital, published highly detailed instructions for using wine while also criticizing his colleagues for prescribing wine willy-nilly, without matching wine type to a patient's condition. Levels of alcohol, acid, and sugar, as well as ash content, made some wines unsuitable for some illnesses, he wrote, and physicians should not confuse fortified wines and light wines with about 10 per cent alcohol. Among his recommendations were burgundy for dyspepsia, old sherry for typhoid fever, and port for anaemia. As a general tonic he recommended half a bottle of wine a day, but the wine should be consistently the same, day after day.

There were hospital holdouts as well. One in Darmstadt, Germany, went through 4,633 bottles of white and 6,332 bottles of red Rhine wine in a twelve-month period in 1870 to 1871, together with sixty bottles of champagne, a few dozen bottles of superior white and red wine from Bordeaux, and thirty dozen bottles of port. A little later, in 1898, some three million litres of wine were served in Paris hospitals.

The French had more opportunities to press their case for wine as a healthy beverage during the First World War. While British troops were given rations of rum and Germans rations of schnapps, and while the Russian army was technically dry – although in fact fuelled by illicitly produced vodka – the French forces ran on wine. It was not only the supposed health benefits of wine that were at play here. Wine was part of the daily diet for soldiers from many parts of France, and during the war it also became part of the diet of soldiers from beer-, cider-, and spirits-drinking regions. There is no doubt that a daily ration of wine (a litre a day by 1917) boosted morale but wine also enhanced fitness, as the French military authorities noted: soldiers sent on a route march after drinking beer were slow, tired, and inefficient, while those who drank wine first completed the march easily, with energy to spare. The conclusion: a beer-guzzling army like Germany's would be no match for a wine-drinking army like France's. The result of the war bore it out, and a French military newspaper pointed out that although strategy and leadership were important in defeating Germany, the ordinary wine that soldiers drank played an indispensable role in the final victory.

If France is notable for its stress on the health benefits of wine up to the twentieth century, it is undoubtedly so because of the cultural and economic importance of wine there. Other major wine-producing countries, such as Italy and Spain, lagged behind the French in wine consumption; their wine exports were small and their wine industries were less important to their national economies. It is not necessary to argue that French physicians were deliberately falsifying or spinning evidence when they argued for the medicinal benefits of wine. But it is understandable that they were immersed in the traditions of their profession and shared the cultural values that held wine in such high esteem. To that extent, the positive value of wine to individuals and society was their default position, such that they needed powerful counter-evidence to disavow it.

But if French physicians were notable in their support of wine, their colleagues in other countries still held to the medical value of alcohol more generally. Perhaps nothing more demonstrated the persistence of physicians' reliance on alcohol as a medicine than the provision in the regulations governing National Prohibition in the United States (from 1920 to 1933) that distilled spirits (generally whiskey or rum) could be obtained and consumed if prescribed by a doctor. Beverage alcohol was condemned as the underlying cause of all the ills thought to beset America – insanity, marriage breakdown, crime, and sexual promiscuity – and the promise that Prohibition would purify the United States was underscored by its being called the 'noble experiment'. Congress was serious about keeping alcohol – especially spirits, but also beer and wine – out of the hands and stomachs of Americans, and it defined alcoholic beverages as any with more than 0.5 per cent alcohol. The exemptions were alcohol used in religious rituals and alcoholic beverages prescribed by a doctor. It was understandable that Congress would not want to interfere with the religious use of wine, which might have been viewed as an attack on the freedom of religion. But it was another to provide for alcohol consumption for medical reasons when there was, by the early

1900s, an open discussion on its therapeutic usefulness. Even though it was permitted as a medicine during Prohibition, alcohol was highly regulated. To write a prescription for alcohol, a physician needed a permit from a federal official and the prescription could be for no more than a pint of alcohol in a ten-day period (about an ounce and a half a day). Many doctors opposed these restrictions not only because they were against Prohibition in principle – the American medical profession was divided on the issue – but because it gave the government power over the way they practised medicine.

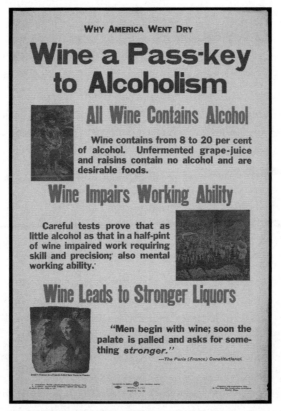

American Prohibition poster from 1920 warning that wine is a gateway to stronger forms of alcohol.

They also objected to the fact that the law referred only to 'liquor' (distilled spirits) and did not permit them to prescribe beer. (Wine was a minor alcoholic beverage in the United States at that time and producers of mass-market wine, such as the Gallo brothers, did not start business until the 1930s, after Prohibition was repealed.) Many prominent physicians demanded that their patients had access to beer and for a while doctors were permitted not only to prescribe beer, but also the volumes they thought appropriate for their patients for such ailments as anaemia, anthrax poisoning, and 'certain ailments of women'. But Congress closed the beer loophole after a year because it threatened to undermine Prohibition; American legislators were clearly at odds with the country's physicians. Many of the latter considered alcohol an important part of their patients' treatment, although wine was only a small part of the debate.

As in ancient Mesopotamia and Egypt, where wine was consumed by a very small minority of alcohol drinkers and played a minor role in medicine, so in the United States physicians placed emphasis on spirits and beer, the most popular alcoholic beverages. A 1922 survey of 53,900 randomly selected doctors showed that 51 per cent were in favour of prescribing whiskey, and 26 per cent thought beer was 'a necessary therapeutic agent'. Only 6 per cent argued in favour of wine, but one Texas physician reported the successful use of champagne in the treatment of scarlet fever.

Although doctors could prescribe only spirits, wine was used in many commercial, proprietary medicines, tonics, and 'restoratives' that were produced in unprecedented volumes in the United States before, during, and after Prohibition. In addition to fortified wine, their ingredients included beef and iron citrate (both used in popular Beef and Iron Wine preparations), as well as cocaine, opium, herbs, and bark. (These ingredients might seem strange but we should note that Coca-Cola, made from coca and cola nuts, was initially marketed as a 'brain tonic' and a remedy for headache, neuralgia, hysteria, and other conditions.)

One popular concoction was Triner's American Elixir of Bitter Wine, which an advertisement shows as having won medals at exhibitions in Brussels, Rome, San Francisco, Paris, and London. It was made from 'pure, mature California wine' and 'extracts of laxative, tonic, carminative and aromatic herbs' and was to be used 'in all cases calling for a safe evacuation of the bowels ... in loss of appetite, nervousness and weakness'. Of this Elixir's ingredients, the advertisement said that 'Red Wine strengthens the intestines and regulates their work. It also increases the appetite, stimulates and strengthens the body.' Consumers were warned to beware of imitations. The authorities administering Prohibition required wine-based tonics to be prepared so that their flavours made them unappealing, if not outright unpalatable, but sales remained strong as consumers looked for alcohol wherever it was available.

Wine as medicine came to the fore again in France during the early 1930s. There were bumper grape harvests in 1930 and 1931 but the opportunities to export French wine were limited. Much of Europe was affected by the Great Depression, and some of France's main wine markets had raised tariffs. Prohibition in the United States ended in 1933 but although there was a burst of buying (especially Bordeaux wines) as restaurants, wine stores, and individuals replenished their cellars, wine ranked low on the alcoholic preferences of Americans. Besides, the California wine industry started in earnest (so to speak – Gallo was founded in 1933) and soon began to cut into imported wine. Nor was France's domestic market buoyant. Although per capita consumption of wine, at 131 litres annually (compared to 41 litres today) was the world's highest, wartime mortality had cut deeply into the prime wine-drinking demographic of males and especially young males: regular wine drinkers were drinking a lot, but there were fewer of them.

In order to reduce the glut of wine, the French government embarked on a campaign to persuade its citizens to drink more wine and, of course, it needed to show that increasing wine consumption would be healthy. Eminent doctors formed an association called *Médecins Amis du Vin* (Physician Friends of Wine) which wrote letters to editors and newspaper articles in support of wine. Advertisements stressed its health benefits, with one claiming that the average life expectancy of a wine drinker was sixty-five years, compared to the fifty-nine years of water drinkers. Eighty-seven per cent of centenarians, it pointed out, drank wine.

The writings of Louis Pasteur, an icon of French science, were repeated and reprinted over and over to reinforce the health benefits of wine. They became part of the school syllabus because it was never too early for French people to learn that wine was, in Pasteur's words, 'the most healthy and hygienic of drinks'. The point was made that wine was good not only for the body but also for the mind: the great ideas of the Enlightenment were said to have come forth thanks to the influence of wine, while Louis XVI mismanaged the state's finances (and produced the French Revolution) because he diluted his wine with water.

Over the long term it is the French who have most vociferously championed the health benefits of wine. It should not be surprising, then, that if some circumstances should arise which pointed to wine being a healthy choice – notably the French Paradox – it should be in France. The French have historically been the greatest champions of wine (of French wine) and its health benefits. Throughout the course of history they have resisted divergent conclusions that were accepted elsewhere: when temperance movements argued that wine was as dangerous as any other alcohol, the French repeated Pasteur's words and even printed postage stamps declaring 'wine is the healthiest of beverages' and describing wine as a food. When some countries looked at alcohol as being harmful to military efficiency, the French army increased its soldiers' wine rations.

The French Paradox has spurred more research on the medical benefits of wine. At present the medical profession is divided, with some arguing that moderate consumption is associated with lower rates of some conditions, including heart disease and some cancers. The scope has widened, too, allowing white wine some benefits, while some research suggests that cool-climate reds and some red varieties have more of the beneficial resveratrol than others.

But medical views are divided on the issue and so, apparently, are wine drinkers. It is not clear how many wine lovers seriously believe wine is doing them good in a strict physical sense, although many surely believe that it makes them happier. The original French Paradox claim stressed the particular benefits of red wine, and sales of red wine in the United States are said to have surged. But since the early 1990s many of the French, the very people who were said to have been benefiting from wine consumption, have turned from wine to water. And those who drink wine are drinking less and less (78 litres per capita in 1995, 41 litres in 2014), and less of it is red wine (80 per cent in 1990, 50 per cent today). Why they would so abandon a drink that was apparently beneficial to them is another French Paradox.

Over time, wine has often been thought to convey not only narrowly physiological but also emotional benefits. Physicians from the ancient to the modern period have written that wine relaxed people who consumed it, relieved their stress and made them more sociable. The same was claimed of brandy when it first became commercially available in the 1500s. The author of a 1532 manual on distilling noted that it 'is good for the sad and the melancholy … it gives back strength and makes one hearty and happy'. This position is rarely heard from modern physicians, and if anything there is clear opposition to the idea that you might drink wine or any alcohol in order to forget your troubles and cheer up. But a physician who is embracing a holistic view of health might easily think that if drinking a moderate amount of wine made someone happy, then that could contribute to their overall wellness.

As always, this raises the issues of excess drinking and now, more than ever before, there is a fear that recommending wine drinking could lead to drinking far too much. Physicians in the past, if we can generalize, seem to have had more confidence in their patients. They warned against excessive drinking but that did not stop them from recommending wine for all manner of complaints, both physical and emotional. The external use of wine is another thing. Wine is sometimes said to be good for the skin, and spas specializing in wine treatments are becoming more and more popular. American spas offer such treatments as a Pinot Noir Body Polish, a Champagne Facial, and a Vineyard Bath.

2

WINE, WOMEN, AND MEN

'Claret is the liquor for boys; port for men,' Samuel Johnson said in the eighteenth century, 'but he who aspires to be a hero must drink brandy'. The association of these beverages with masculine nouns (boys, men, and hero) was not a case of encompassing both men and women within a common masculine form. The statement should be understood literally. It was men that Johnson was referring to as he associated alcoholic beverages of ascending levels of alcohol with men in ascending ranks of masculinity. Boys might drink claret, the light Bordeaux red which had an alcohol level of no more than 10 per cent, that Johnson thought was so weak that 'a man would be drowned by it before it made him drunk'. Men drank port, wine fortified with brandy, which probably at that time had an alcohol content of about 15 per cent. But heroes – real men, we might say – drank brandy, whose alcohol level was neither measurable nor regulated at the time, but probably fell between 30 and 50 per cent. Few are able to drink brandy, Johnson thought: 'That is a power rather to be wished for than attained.'

Historically, drinking alcohol has generally been viewed as the quintessentially male activity that Johnson suggests, and drunkenness has often been seen by men as a measure of their own and their peers' masculinity. In the eighteenth century, when port was the most popular drink for upper-class English males, some men earned reputations as 'three-bottle men' – men who could consume three bottles of port at a sitting and apparently be none the worse for wear. Samuel Johnson himself was reported (by James Boswell, who recorded Johnson's conversations) as saying, 'I have drunk three bottles of port without being the worse for it. University College has witnessed this.'

It is true that there was no standard bottle size for port or other wines in the eighteenth century, that some of the volume was taken up with sediment, and that there was less eau-de-vie in port at that time than there is now – making it lower in alcohol than the 20 per cent that is standard today. Even so, downing three bottles of port was an achievement of sorts, perhaps the equivalent of drinking three bottles of Barolo or Châteauneuf-du-Pape today. Yet some men felt constrained to better it and there are reports that a classical scholar at the University of Oxford was a 'ten-bottle man'. This is undoubtedly spurious, because anyone trying to drink that much at one sitting would almost certainly pass out before completing the challenge. We should probably be thankful there was no *Guinness Book of Records* for these port-drinking gentlemen to aspire to.

But if being able 'to hold one's drink' was a sign of the mature male so, paradoxically, was getting drunk, as Johnson's reference to drinking claret suggests. The boasts of young men about how drunk they got the night before have littered the historical record for hundreds of years. Getting intoxicated was as much a rite of passage for male university students in England in the sixteenth century and in the Netherlands in the seventeenth as it was for their counterparts on North American and European university campuses in the late twentieth century. These students might well have experienced intoxication before entering university, but getting drunk with fellow students signalled their transition to a new status.

Equally historically, women have had a completely different relationship with alcohol, in so far as we can tell from the dominant social attitudes – attitudes that we should remember were established, maintained, and recorded by men. At some times and in some places, women have been forbidden to drink wine or any alcohol whatsoever. But even when there has been no outright ban on drinking by women, men have been anxious about women in possession of alcohol – especially 'their' women, meaning their unmarried daughters and their wives. Women were advised (by men) to drink alcohol sparingly, if at all, and for the most part women were barred by law or custom from public drinking places such as taverns and alehouses until the twentieth century.

Given negative attitudes toward their drinking and their more limited access to alcohol, it is safe to assume that women drank less and drank less frequently than men. But there is little direct evidence of women's drinking patterns because actual historical consumption rates by gender are hard to come by. Estimates of per capita rates of consumption in the past are virtually useless as guides to drinking patterns not only because they do not differentiate by gender but also because abstainers and heavy drinkers are subsumed into the average. Whether they refer to the past or the present, what are called 'per capita wine consumption rates' (obtained by dividing the wine supply by the population of drinking age) really tell us only how much wine is available to each person, not how much each person actually drinks.

It is possible and even probable that, unable to drink in public places, women drank – perhaps alone, perhaps together – in whatever privacy their homes afforded. By doing so they would have escaped the surveillance that brings to light patterns of male public drinking: taverns and other drinking places often attracted the interest of the police and other authorities. We learn about men's drinking patterns from court records of tavern brawls, charges against owners who served drinks outside the legal hours, and investigations into crimes – from adulterating wine to theft from patrons – that were committed in public drinking places. Apart from occasional prostitutes and those reputed to have been, women were absent from such places, and so rarely appear in the historical record. It is probable, then, that even though women drank less than men in reality, their rate of consumption of wine and other alcohol is more likely to be concealed, or private rather than public, and is therefore under-represented in the historical record.

DRINKING IN ROME

Beyond the frequency and volume of drinking, different meanings were attached to drinking by women and men. Drinking by males was largely normalized and seen as no different from their other daily activities, such as eating, walking, and sleeping. It is not that all men in any society drank alcohol, or drank alcohol of the same quality and style. In ancient Rome, for example, all men drank wine but the elites drank regular wine, usually flavoured by substances such as sea water, herbs, and spices. For their part, the lower orders drank low-alcohol, pale, and largely insipid wines made either by adding water to the skins and other sediment that remained after the juice destined for elite wine was pressed, or by adding water to sour wine.

Yet if all Roman men drank wine of some kind and quality there were periods when Roman women were not only forbidden to drink any sort of wine – even the alcoholically anaemic styles consumed by the poor – but could be put to death for doing so. One story involved a Roman woman whose family condemned her to death because she opened a purse holding the keys to the wine cellar. Another story made a hero of a certain Egnatius Mecenius, who was said to have beaten his wife to death because she drank some wine; Romulus, one of Rome's founders, is said to have praised him for the deed. True or not, these are surely didactic stories that made the point that women should not drink wine and would take their lives in their hands if they did so. Romulus, indeed, is said to have declared that women who committed adultery or drank wine should be put to death because 'adultery was the beginning of madness, and drunkenness was the beginning of adultery'. (It is noteworthy that the act of drinking and the state of drunkenness were treated as the same thing.) If Romulus forbade women from drinking wine under pain of death, it made the prohibition foundational to Roman law, even if it was eventually attenuated. Some later writers, such as Valerius Maximus and Varro, nostalgically recalled Romulus's rule against women drinking as they surveyed what they perceived as the widespread immorality of their own times.

The practice of putting women to death for drinking wine might have disappeared but disapproval of women's drinking and the link between wine and adultery persisted. Pliny the Elder was among a number of commentators who blamed intoxication from wine for adultery and other offences. Other Roman texts discuss excessive wine drinking and adultery together, as if they were two facets of the same thing, without making an explicit causal connection between them. That connection underlay the fact that a wife's drinking wine was a ground for divorce for some time in Roman law.

Yet the negative view of women drinking wine seems contradicted by the fact that women were permitted to participate in the convivium, the Roman eating and drinking event that was a modified version of the Greek symposium. Women were not permitted to participate in symposia, although they might be present in other capacities, as servers, dancers, singers, and prostitutes. This tells us something about attitudes toward women drinking wine in ancient Greece, as does the fact that women were often portrayed as being drunk in Greek comedies, where drunkenness was the standard female vice. A number of Greek writers, all male, alleged that whereas men drank their wine diluted with water (a prerequisite at a symposium), women drank wine straight – with predictably negative consequences. Drinking wine this way placed women on the same level as barbarians, who were often defined by their drinking habits. Drinking wine properly – diluted, in moderation, and politely – was a key criterion of the civilized person and society. Greeks defined peoples such as the Thracians and Macedonians as barbarians in part because they guzzled undiluted wine to the point of intoxication. Greek women were often alleged to do the same.

Allowing women to participate in Roman convivia, in contrast, suggests a more inclusive attitude toward drinking wine, but that suggestion must be qualified by the stories of the killing of Roman women accused of wine drinking. In fact it is not clear how women and which women participated in convivia. Many sources and images suggest that the women present other than as servers were prostitutes, and their posture at the convivium – reclining alongside men on couches – is indicative of a sexual relationship. If there were indeed concerns about drinking wine leading to adultery, then the copious volumes available at a convivium made the occasion an ideal occasion for immorality – but the adultery would have been committed by any married men who were present, not by married women.

If wine drinking was widespread among all men but among many fewer women in Greece and Rome, it is likely that many men and women in Medieval and Early Modern Europe drank no wine (or any alcohol) at all, simply because they could not afford to. In an age when the indigent and poor could make up as much as a third or more of the population (depending on the state of the harvest and other economic conditions), water was the only option for hydration because it was free. Despite the common belief that everyone drank wine, beer, and other alcoholic beverages at this time because the water supplies were polluted and fermented beverages were safer, a big slice of the European population was simply not in a financial position to replace water with alcohol.

THE DOUBLE STANDARD OF DRINKING

All the evidence supports the conclusion that men were far more likely than women to drink wine and other alcoholic beverages and that men found drinking by women to be problematic and threatening. Here we need to recognize that studies of historical drinking patterns generally adopt a male perspective. Women's drinking might not have been at all problematic from the point of view of women, but it was almost always men who established the social norms, who wrote the social commentaries, who passed the laws regarding alcohol consumption, and whose voice dominates the history of alcohol. As we shall see, women also had voices when it came to drinking, but they were far fewer than men's and they are far less audible in the historical record.

A woman who was seen drinking was generally believed by men to be in the process of losing her moral bearings. This need not be an incorrect assumption if the woman in question drank heartily, as we know that the course of intoxication at some point leads to impaired decisions and risky behaviour that can easily involve poor decisions about sexual activity. The same applied to men who drank, of course, but their careless sexual behaviour was of less concern. This is not to say that illicit sexual activity by men has historically been taken lightly, but that it has seldom been regarded as being as serious as women's.

The reason is the double standard of sexual morality which has been integral to attitudes, behaviour, and law for thousands of years. The double standard essentially permits men a degree and scope of sexual activity that is denied to women, and it is an intrinsic part of the patriarchal system that has permitted men to dominate and control women. It effectively gave men qualified property rights over women, and it was long justified in various ways. A common justification was that men needed to control the sexual activities of their unmarried daughters and wives so that they did not become pregnant. It was difficult to marry off a daughter with a child, and the primary fear of a wife's adultery was that it would be impossible to ascertain whether any child she bore was her husband's or another man's. Beyond pregnancy and the birth of a child from a pre-marital or adulterous relationship, there was the matter of reputation and honour. Among the propertied classes at least, an unmarried woman with a reputation for being sexually active enjoyed reduced chances of marriage. As for a wife who committed adultery that became public knowledge, she destroyed her husband's honour and made him a cuckold, someone to be ridiculed as being, at the very least, a man who could not control his wife or his household.

It seems that the anxiety over the implications of drinking led some men simply to forbid their wives to drink wine. In the sixteenth-century poem *Le monologue du bon vigneron* (*The Monologue of the Good Vigneron*), the 'good vigneron' declares that he drinks his own good wine but refuses to drink water, which is good only for using in soup and for his wife: 'I leave that [water] for my wife to drink ... Women, children, and many of the poor can spend their entire lives without wine and with only water.' There are many other accounts suggesting that women did not drink wine, drank very little wine, or in some cases drank water that their husbands gave a little colour to by adding a splash of red wine.

Denying a wife wine or restricting her to a small quantity makes sense within the male understanding of the effects of wine on women and the cultural anxiety about retaining the honour that a man was bound to lose if a woman he was responsible for transgressed sexual boundaries: if his daughter committed fornication or his wife committed adultery, or if either simply allowed themselves to be found in compromising circumstances. Honour was not a vague, abstract notion but a concrete concept and it had to be protected. It is worth noting, however, that by protecting their own honour, men put their wives' and daughters' lives at risk. Many of these accounts come from the sixteenth to eighteenth centuries, when there was heightened concern about the safety of European supplies of drinking water. Most physicians advised against drinking any water at all and recommended rehydrating with wine or beer. A man who denied his wife these safer options must have been aware that he was putting her health and even her life at risk.

This unbalanced power relationship between men and women lay at the heart of all cultures where wine was produced and consumed. It made gender not only as fundamental as any other social distinction, such as wealth, class, age, and ethnicity, but it was arguably even more fundamental, as disparities of gendered power existed within all these other categories. Wine and other alcoholic beverages are an important part of the picture because the effects of consuming alcohol introduced a dangerously unpredictable variable to social behaviour. Alcohol made men and women more sociable and more careless of social conventions, and it had the power to loosen both tongues and clothing.

As we have seen, the divergence in attitudes towards drinking by women and men can be traced back to the ancient world, where men drank freely but were anxious about women doing the same thing unless they were prostitutes or others for whom sexual activity was planned. Egypt presents ambiguous evidence. Wall drawings depict both men and women passing out and vomiting from drinking too much wine and beer, and there is no clear sense that drinking to this extent was considered morally more wrong when women were involved. The various strictures by Egyptian sages against excessive drinking were expressed in gender-neutral terms.

The double standard of drinking persisted into the Middle Ages and beyond, and it is still perceptible today. In the fourteenth century we find a man living in Paris writing instructions for his young wife on managing his household and herself. One thing she was enjoined to do was to avoid vices such as gluttony, and the example her husband gave of gluttony was a woman who had trouble getting up in the morning to go to church because she had a hangover. 'When she has with some difficulty risen, know you what be her hours? Her matins are: "Ha! what shall we drink? Is there nought left over from last night?" Then she says her lauds, thus: "Ha! we drank good wine yesterday evening." Afterwards she says her orisons, thus: "My head aches; I shall not be at ease until I have had a drink".'

There were in the Middle Ages some women and men who chose not to drink wine: holy people who adopted an ascetic lifestyle. Catherine of Siena, for example, abstained from wine (and bread) throughout her adult life, but it was a choice she made in order to prepare herself for a mystical union with Christ. She did not disapprove of wine in itself and one of the miracles attributed to her was the filling of her father's wine cask after he had given all his wine to the poor. Ascetic holy men also abstained from wine, but in general both men and women in religious orders drank wine or ale, whichever was the more readily available. Saint Benedict reluctantly allowed monks in his Benedictine order to drink about a third of a litre of wine a day, and they less reluctantly consumed it. That was the model for many religious orders. Women in religious orders also drank wine and ale, but it might not always have been as a right. In 1249 the Archbishop of Rouen ordered that the nuns in the convent of St Amand de Rouen should receive 'a measure of wine ... each according to her needs and in equal measure', which suggests that they had not been drinking wine to that point.

PUBLIC DRINKING SPACES

The distinction between men and women can be traced through all aspects of wine culture for almost a thousand years up to the 1800s, as A. Lynn Martin has shown in his book, *Alcohol, Sex, and Gender in Late Medieval and Early Modern Europe*. It began with simple access to alcohol, as women were generally barred from drinking in public drinking spaces such as taverns. The rules and practices varied from place to place: in Augsburg, in Germany, women could drink in taverns only if they were married and if their husbands were also in the tavern, drinking with them. In France their activities might have been restricted simply to going to taverns with their husbands but not drinking. Visiting France in the 1670s, the English philosopher John Locke noted of women that 'if they accompany their husbands or their kinsmen to the tavern, it is to wait on them respectfully, but not to share their refreshment'. The fact that Locke found this noteworthy might mean that he was surprised to see women in a tavern or surprised that women with their husbands were not drinking. Other women might enter a tavern for specific purposes, such as to sell goods to the patrons, to buy wine or beer to take home to drink, or to carry out commercial transactions.

But women did not go to taverns alone, and as casually as men, to drink and pass the time with friends and workmates. For the most part single or married women who entered a tavern alone were thought of as 'common' or 'dishonourable' and might be suspected of being sexually promiscuous or prostitutes. Of course, these suppositions assumed that the men in the tavern were receptive to such women, but the double standard of sexual morality shielded them from social opprobrium. Such was the stigma of a woman's entering a public drinking place that some women who came to a tavern to fetch their husbands home would stand outside a window or at the door and call for them, rather than place even a foot inside.

Women might well go to taverns to retrieve their husbands because men were known to drink away their wages instead of spending them on food and other necessities for their families. This was one of the main complaints against men's drinking in Early Modern Germany. One case, from Augsburg in 1600, is especially illustrative. Barbara Burkman complained to a court that her husband spent most of his money in taverns, leaving her and her child hungry, such that they survived only thanks to help from her parents. Burkman had even spent her entire dowry of 150 *gulden*, and his drinking had caused him to go so far into debt that he had pawned off their clothing and other goods. Worse, in the historian Ann Tlusty's summary of Barbara Burkman's statement to the court, 'he would come home from his pub-crawling, drunk and covered in filth like a pig and then curse and cause a scene, generally behaving like an unreasonable beast'. Husbands like Burkman were often ordered to stay out of taverns and to avoid social drinking of any kind, but there is plenty of evidence that these bans were widely ignored.

Like men, women who squandered family resources on drinking could find themselves before the courts, but there was a critical difference in these cases. Men had overall responsibility for their families' finances, and there was a problem only if they spent so much on drink that their families began to suffer. But a woman who spent money on drink was assumed to be taking it from resources that the family needed. They were sometimes accused of stealing money from their husbands if they spent anything on drink whereas they could, of course, spend money on other things. It was the object of their spending that defined it as theft, not the means of obtaining the money, the usual definition of theft.

WINE IN RITUALS

All this said, there were times when both men and women were expected to drink. Before marriages in Europe were formalized and were not considered valid unless celebrated by a priest, unions were often effected by an exchange of goods or by sharing a drink. Sipping wine from the same cup could, in fact, effectively cement a relationship, a custom that lasted well into the Middle Ages. One fifteenth-century example from Troyes, in the Loire region of France, involved Jean Binet and Henriette Legouge. Binet had asked Legouge to marry him, she had agreed and her father had given his consent. The account of the ceremony went: 'Then the father told his daughter to sit at the table beside Jean Binet, then he put some wine in a glass and told Binet to give it to his daughter to drink in the name of marriage ... That done, Henriette's uncle said to her "give it to Jean to drink in the name of marriage, as he gave it to you to drink." Henriette gave the drink to Binet ... He drank from her hand, then said, "I wish you to receive a kiss from me in the name of marriage," and then he kissed her.'

Ann Tlusty reports that wine remained an integral part of the marriage process in Early Modern Germany, where every contract was concluded with a drink. Engagements, whether legitimate or not, were sealed with a drink and celebrated at an inn afterwards. At weddings, toasts to the bride and groom were usual and there was drinking at the communal table. Even so, marriages were not binding until they were consummated, and wine played a role there, too. According to German practice, the couple would be led to their bed by the wedding guests who would then join them in a wedding toast, often with wine (*Ansing* wine) that had been blessed in church. Tlusty writes, 'In the *Ansing* wine, the spiritual aspect of the union merged with the economic and sexual. Wine shared in marriage represented the hope of a fruitful union, both in terms of productive labour and fertility. Not only on the level of symbolic intimacy, but in a practical sense, wine could enhance a couple's chance of producing children. According to early modern medical beliefs, alcohol, with its heating effect on the body, had the power to inflame passions and especially to increase virility in men.'

This property attributed to wine is nicely expressed in a 1538 letter written to Hans Jacob Fugger, a wealthy resident of Augsburg by his former teacher, Wigle van Aytta. Fugger was well known for preferring water to wine – a brave practice at a time when anxieties over the safety of drinking water were rising – but van Aytta's concern was not Fugger's health but his future prospects. She warned him, writes Tlusty, 'that his watery ways could only result in relationships that were pale, bloodless, and passionless, and, ultimately, a marriage doomed to remain childless'.

YOUTH AND MASCULINITY

Heavy drinking by young men to assert or demonstrate their maturity seems to have taken off during the Early Modern period, when it was associated with the growth of formal education. In England, for example, the number of young men being educated (in universities, grammar schools, or as lawyers) in the early 1600s was not exceeded until after the First World War. These boys and young men were from well-off families, and they drank beer and wine copiously. (It is worth noting that there was no minimum drinking age and that boys took on adult responsibilities in their early to mid-teens.) Drinking occurred not only in initiation rites, during drinking games, and on specific binging occasions, but daily. The universities at Oxford and Cambridge had a number of clubs that were largely dedicated to heavy drinking. Women, who were not admitted to British universities until the late 1800s, clearly could not participate in these drinking activities that were designed to reinforce camaraderie and solidarity among young men.

When it comes to drinking by young people in the Netherlands during the seventeenth century, Benjamin Roberts tellingly refers to excessive drinking as 'drinking like a man'. Young people in the Netherlands learned to drink from an early age and, as one would expect of a Calvinist society, they were told to drink moderately. Calvin, whose works inspired the Puritans, did not condemn drinking as such, and he accepted wine as a gift of God that was good to drink and one that had medicinal value. But he condemned social and excessive drinking and he established rules for the public drinking places frequented by men in Geneva in the 1540s: a Bible in every tavern and no treating or drinking to one's health, as well as a scale of penalties (fines and imprisonment) for drunkenness. These rules were applied in the Calvinist Netherlands, too. In the town of Emden in the second half of the 1500s drunkenness made up more than a quarter of all breaches of the social order that appeared before the courts. It is notable that among people arraigned for drunkenness, men outnumbered women by five to one.

'L'Yvrogne/The Drunk.' A drunk young man raises a glass in one hand while spilling wine from a bottle in the other. Etching (Germany, 1784) by F. Brichet after J.F. de Göz.

A hundred years later, Dutch youths seem to have continued in this tradition, something facilitated because the wealth of the Netherlands – which dominated long-distance sea trade in the seventeenth century – made imported alcohol more readily available to the country's expanding middle class. Visitors remarked on the extent of drinking, and the Dutch Republic became known for 'wine and Calvin', even though brandy and gin had become much more widely consumed by the mid-seventeenth century. Even so, wines from many countries – Germany, France, Spain, Italy, and Greece – were widely available, and although wine tended to be drunk mainly by the wealthy, it became increasingly affordable because prices scarcely changed between the late 1500s and mid-1600s. Wine and other alcohols became embedded in Dutch culture, and drinking accompanied everything from homecomings, farewells, and announcements of pregnancy, as well as the usual get-togethers at the time of births, marriages, and deaths. Benjamin Roberts writes that 'much like a church clock ringing in the hours of the day, drinking alcohol sounded in the significant phases of life'.

This need not have led to more frequent excess drinking, but it did, and it was Dutch males who proved far more problematic than females to the religious and secular authorities. Boys generally left home in their early teens, either to study or to be apprenticed, and although they were supervised in their new living arrangements and were subjected to sermons in church and many publications that warned against excessive drinking, they also had a new sense of freedom. One 1661 book warned young men that excessive drinking would make them bald, lead to numerous other physical ailments that plague old men, impoverish them, and make them social outcasts.

It was young men who were the object of these warnings; moralists simply ignored young women. Perhaps there was an understanding that young women would not drink to the point of drunkenness because a virtuous reputation was their most valuable asset. A woman who became intoxicated earned a reputation only marginally better than that of a prostitute. Indeed, the double standards of drinking and sexuality were so closely entwined that a woman who got drunk could be assumed to have been engaged in sexual activity as a result, just as a married woman who left her husband – for any reason, including violence – was assumed in law to have been adulterous. This assumption seems to have been persistent on the part of men: that women were always seeking sex and were constantly on the verge of having sex, making it an obligation of their fathers and husbands (and sometimes their brothers) to control them. The best way of achieving this, of course, was to prevent them from drinking. In this vein, the Spanish humanist Juan Luis Vives noted that there was a fine line between excessive drinking and premarital sex, and he advised young women to drink only water so as to remain chaste.

As this suggests, excessive drinking was seen as the fundamental sin for both men and women in that it invariably led to other sins. In the sixteenth century Sebastiaen Franck asked rhetorically which was worse, a drunkard, a gambler, or a womanizer. His answer was 'a drunkard', because a drunkard was also a gambler and a womanizer. After drinking wine or beer, Franck explained, a drunkard would want to gamble and then have sex. There is a non-rational quality here in that an intoxicated man was seen as acting not with reason but more as a wine-fuelled automaton moving from one sin to another. Benjamin Roberts makes the point that in this sense of losing self-control – something men were expected to possess, but women were not – drunkenness made men more like women than men. But paradoxically, although drunkenness gave men one of the attributes of women, it was seen as a sign of masculinity in seventeenth-century Netherlands, just like having facial hair, wearing certain clothes, smoking, being violent, and carrying a sword or a gun. The role models for young Dutch men were the hard-living, hard-drinking sailors of the Dutch East India Company, which was central to the booming economy of the Netherlands.

Dutch university students, all male at this time, were a particular category of heavy drinkers, and sometimes their preferences were catered to. The University of Leiden, anxious to attract students, exempted them from paying taxes on a basic allowance of alcohol: each student was allowed to buy 194 litres of wine and ten barrels of beer (1,500 litres), tax-free, each year. That amounted to half a litre of wine and four litres of beer a day, and if that were not enough, students could purchase more if they paid the tax. There were some restrictions, however: scholarship students were not permitted to drink on the university's playing fields. Professors also participated in the excess drinking. After a number of heavy drinking bouts, Everard Bronckhorst, a professor of law at the University of Leiden, noted in his diary (like Samuel Pepys) that he would never drink again. The constant drinking at university festivities and events, he wrote, was affecting his health.

Although much of the drunkenness of students was expressed in high spirits, it also concerned the authorities. Intoxicated students made a noise at night and did damage to property. More seriously they brawled, assaulted members of the public, and sometimes raped young women. These actions were generally written off by the university authorities as behaviour that was to be expected of young men. But it was, of course, excused as the behaviour to be expected of *wealthy* young men. The sexual assault of women from the working class or poor of the town was unimportant because the chastity so desirable in women from better-off families was not expected of the lower classes. If parents were concerned about their sons' riotous behaviour as students, it was not because of their victims but because of the dishonour that fell on the family. Students could be incarcerated at their parents' request, and between 1680 and 1805, a full 40 per cent of these requests were based on persistent drunkenness.

THE FAMILY

The association of males, drunkenness, and social problems persisted beyond the period of youth and entered marriage. About a fifth of the cases presented before the church council in Rotterdam and Delft involved marital fights and petitions for divorce due to a drunken husband. Heavy drinking and drunkenness were commonly mentioned in such cases in France, where divorce was legalized for the first time during the French Revolution, and again it was almost always men who were involved. Women associated the most terrible episodes of domestic violence with feast days, when their husbands came home drunk from a day in the tavern. One husband told a court that 'he admits having ill-treated his wife … that the abuse, harsh words, and threats he directed at her … often occurred when he was drunk'. One woman told a court that her husband 'gets drunk every day and uses his condition to ill-treat her', while another 'behaved this way especially when he was drunk, a state in which he unfortunately often found himself'. A number of women described being assaulted by husbands when they were 'seized by wine'. Domestic violence by men occurred throughout all classes in western society and it was often fuelled by drinking, as court and other records only too fully show.

Women also drank to the point of drunkenness but less often than men, and drunken women were rarely the instigators of violence, as the divorce courts of Revolutionary France suggest. In one Rouen case a husband's petition noted that 'she is always in a state of drunkenness, which does not allow the couple to live together as they should'. Another husband complained that his wife 'drank wine and got drunk to the point of losing her mind and abandoning herself to the greatest immorality she was capable of'. Throughout these court records, men's drunkenness was consistently associated with violence, while women's was associated with adultery and neglect of their domestic duties. One man complained that his wife's drinking made her neglect their children, including failing to comb their daughter's hair.

On the other hand, violence by intoxicated women is reported in sixteenth-century Germany. An Augsburg carpenter, Hans Gullman, alleged that his wife attacked him with a knife when she had been drinking, and Melchior Clausenburger told a court that his wife struck him far more often than he hit her, and that she often left him bleeding. In Constance, neighbours claimed that Friedle Sauter's wife was drunk on a daily basis and beat her husband 'so shamefully that he had to be bandaged'. Drinking might well have brought couples together, but alcohol could just as easily corrode the bonds of marriage.

It was from the middle of the nineteenth century that drinking to excess was perceived to be such a problem that it was made a ground for separation or divorce. Generally the issue was framed in law as 'drunkenness' or 'habitual drunkenness', but also as 'gross and confirmed habits of intoxication'. In New Zealand, drunkenness in itself was not a ground for divorce but it became one when combined with the husband's failure to support his family or the wife's failure to perform her domestic duties. In Scotland, drunkenness was specifically made equivalent to cruelty for the purpose of getting a separation. Clauses such as these were added to laws of separation and divorce in many American and Australian states, Germany, Scandinavia, and England.

ILLICIT SEXUALITY

Wine was a problem outside marriage as much as – or perhaps more than – in it. Like any alcoholic beverage, wine gradually intoxicates and has a cascading series of effects on drinkers, At a certain point it loosens inhibitions and leads drinkers to take risks that might take any form but certainly include taking sexual risks – such as having sex in a place, at a time, or with a person that they would not consider while sober. The problem with drinking is that this point is largely unpredictable, as it depends on who is drinking, their physical and emotional state, how much they drink in a certain period, and the alcoholic strength of the wine or other beverage. It is this unpredictability, together with a male belief that women were easily given to sexual infidelity or promiscuity, that made men anxious about women drinking.

These are generalizations, of course. For every married woman who committed adultery and for every unmarried woman who committed fornication, there was a man willing to have sex with her and who, it seems, was quite happy about women's supposed sexual tendencies. We cannot rule out love in these cases, of course, and in fact alcohol has long been implicated in sex and love. One connection between wine and love is the literary notion that men fall in love with women who feed them wine. There is some hint of wine being a love potion here, as in the lines by the sixteenth-century French poet Pierre de Ronsard:

> My lady drinks to me: then giving her cup to me,
> 'Drink', she says, 'this reminder where I have poured my heart':
> And then I press to my lips the vessel,
> Which, like a ferryman, passes her heart to mine.

There is a similar narrative in Giambattista Basile's *Pentameron*, where a king fell in love with a peasant's daughter who served him wine: 'She filled his cup so often and well that he drank as much love from her eyes as wine from her cup.' In this case the woman in question was a stranger, rather than de Ronsard's 'my lady', but stories like these are common in the chivalric genre of literature and speak to a romantic connection made by wine.

It is one thing to lock dewy eyes over a glass of wine, but at a more banal level wine simply lubricated the social processes that might lead to sex. A seventeenth-century English ballad described an encounter between Thomas and Mary at a fair:

> We'll drink before we part;
> Come, give us a bottle of wine ...
> And when they were full of Canary [wine],
> Their stomachs began to rise,
> Then Thomas began to court Mary,
> With hand upon one of her thighs.

It is likely that wine or another alcohol had a regular place in the rituals of courtship, whether that implied an interest in marriage or a more transient relationship. There is nothing remarkable in this, as sharing food and drink are common features of relationships at all stages, but it is possible that alcohol was employed to accelerate the process. There are plenty of literary references to men and women providing prospective partners with wine as a way of making them sexually more compliant. In one sixteenth-century French work, Jean Bodin's *Villain de Bailleul*, a peasant's wife serves capon, cake, and wine to a priest before, as Lynn Martin puts it, 'offering him dessert'.

Cases of female seduction are much less common in literature than instances where men use alcohol to persuade women to have sex. An episode in Boccaccio's *Decameron* has an Italian noble fall in love with the daughter of the Sultan of Babylon. She did not return his feelings, and so he gave her wine at a banquet. As a Muslim, she was unaccustomed to alcohol, and was easily intoxicated to the point that she took off her clothes as soon as the guests at the banquet left.

The use of wine, other alcohol, and other substances to render women agreeable to having sex or unaware of what is happening was for centuries referred to as seduction. It was not a literary device but a well-known strategy. In eighteenth-century France unmarried women who became pregnant were required to provide the police with information on the circumstances in which this happened. These statements were called *déclarations de grossesse* (declarations of pregnancy) and they detail episodes of sex freely entered into (often when a man promised to marry), sex under duress (such as when an employer threatened to fire a woman servant), and rape. These accounts are often detailed and in a number of them we see wine employed as a way of weakening a woman's opposition to having sex. Today, of course, using alcohol or any other drug to obtain sex is seen as undermining the ability of the other person to consent, making sexual intercourse in these circumstances tantamount to sexual assault.

Adultery was also associated with wine. In a sense, adultery at times when contraception was at best unreliable was a safer form of non-marital sex than fornication (sex involving two unmarried people). If a women got pregnant – and assuming she was continuing to have sex with her husband while having an affair – the pregnancy could be attributed to the husband. This was, of course, every well-off husband's fear, that he might raise and eventually pass on his property to a child that was not his. Before DNA testing, however, this would never be more than a suspicion unless the adulterous relationship became known or for some reason the child could not be the husband's. Adultery tends to be framed like this – as if it is women who commit adultery – but all studies suggest that men were more likely to be unfaithful – and they, needless to say, did not have to deal directly with a pregnancy that might result.

Wine appears in the records of adultery in many roles, as Lynn Martin shows. Some women claimed that they were adulterous because their husbands were habitually drunk. Some wives took advantage of their husband's drunkenness while others got their husbands blind drunk so that they could meet their accomplices. The possibilities provide material for drama and comedy. In *The Heptameron*, Marguerite de Navarre has the young wife of a farmer pursue an affair with a priest. When her husband comes home unexpectedly, she hides the priest and then gives her husband so much wine that he falls asleep, enabling the priest to escape.

Finally, there is prostitution. We have noted that women who entered taverns alone were often at risk of being thought of as prostitutes. This is an indication of the strength of the association of women and alcohol, although we must also consider that women were entering a resolutely male space. Police and other reporting agencies make it clear that prostitutes were sometimes present in public drinking places for the very good reason that they were likely to find clients there. Similarly, men looking for prostitutes knew that they had a good chance of finding one in a public drinking place. For the same reason, brothels were often situated near taverns. The link between drink and prostitutes is a common one in the historical record and in literature, as the fourteenth-century Italian poet Francesco di Vannozzo shows:

> The fume of the wine
> Goes straight to the head,
> And the body is filled with lust
> For human flesh with such great rage
> That until the next day
> They stay with the vile whores.

HEAVY DRINKING

If some men were plied with wine by their adulterous wives, others needed no inducement. Heavy drinking was an intrinsic part of male culture in many places, but nowhere more than in England. While broad patterns of drinking (frequency and volume) were generally differentiated by gender, there were of course men who chose not to drink (as distinct from those who could not afford to) and women who not only drank but did so to excess. Phil Withington has noted that in the English town of York in the early 1600s, just at the time when wine imports to England rose dramatically, drunkenness became a notable part of insults directed by and toward women. As an example, a 1637 court record shows that one Marjorie Wilson called Elizabeth Simpson 'a scurvy Queane and scurvy drunken Queane, and drunken companion'. References to drunkenness such as this cut into the usual string of sexual allegations, such as one Katherine Brooke's somewhat unimaginative tirade describing Elizabeth Wetton as 'a whore, arrand whore, scurvy whore, Queane, scold, common scold, drabbe [prostitute], filthy drabbe ... God's wound, thou art a whore and an arrand whore'.

Women's drinking really came to the fore in England early in the eighteenth century, not in respect of wine, but because women were believed to be drinking inordinate volumes of gin – a term that encompassed a wide range of distilled alcoholic beverages. Wanting to reduce imports of brandy from France, the British parliament had made it easier to make and sell gin, and the result was that in major towns, especially London, gin became widely available in 'dram shops' – bars that sold inexpensive shots of gin.

What is remarkable about this period, often known as the 'gin craze' – which was at its height from about 1720 to 1740 – is that concern was focused on women. Women ran the dram shops and women were said to be most of the customers, a dramatic break from the practice of women not drinking in public. Gin itself was feminized – it was called 'Madame Geneva' and 'mother's folly' – and the authorities and social commentators focused on the harm that women did to themselves and their families by drinking it. Front and centre of William Hogarth's famous print, *Gin Lane*, is a drunken women sitting on a flight of steps to breastfeed her child but allowing it to slip from her grasp and fall head-first to the street below, presumably to its death. Only slightly less sensational were lurid accounts of deformed babies born to gin-addicted mothers, and children deprived of food because their mothers spent all their money on gin.

English men also drank gin in this period, of course, and Hogarth's print shows men dead drunk and simply dead. Other men are shown pawning the tools of their trades – giving up their means of living and supporting their families, in short – to get money to buy gin. But the most insistent criticisms focused on women. Gin was alleged to make women forget what were considered their natural obligations, to care for their children and their families and, in the broader picture, to provide a growing population to sustain England's economy and global political power. Drinking alcohol subverted these roles. In this case it was gin, and distilled spirits were particularly problematic because of their relatively high level of alcohol. Still, drunkenness was drunkenness, whether it was achieved quickly by spirits or more sedately by wine or beer. The so-called gin craze (whose real scale remains unclear) was about women and gin, to be sure, but it was also about women and alcohol more broadly.

Later in the eighteenth century, when the production and consumption of gin had subsided, port imports to England rebounded after a period of crisis (see pp. 218–21), rising from 5.5 million litres in 1756 to 19 million in the 1770s and an amazing 44 million litres in 1799. It was this flood of port that made possible the achievements of the 'three-bottle men' recounted earlier in this chapter. But there was no suggestion of a 'port craze' analogous to the 'gin craze', and no outcry about the impending demise of the family and the onset of a national crisis. The guzzlers of port were well-off and powerful men, not working-class women. The distinction is telling of the way attitudes to drinking differed, depending on whether the drinkers were women or men – although class was also a factor here.

PORT AND MASCULINITY

If the aggregate volume of port imports to England was impressive, so were the amounts of port that some individual men went through. Between 1763 and 1767 the fourth Duke of Marlborough ordered 20,472 bottles of wine, just over half of which were port – more than 10,000 bottles in four years, although there is no suggestion that the Duke consumed them all single-handedly. In his households port easily eclipsed claret, the red wine so beloved in England in earlier times; claret represented only a tenth of the Duke's purchases. Actual consumption patterns are not recorded, but Charles Ludington, who has written an important article on the subject, notes: 'Nor is there much evidence of middling and elite women drinking port, except in small amounts and usually at dinner parties prior to their withdrawing for tea and conversation. Meanwhile, the men stayed at the table and drank to the point that conversation could be difficult.'

'Two three-bottle men, Wine and Physic. What I was. What I am. A hint to jolly dogs.' An emaciated man (on left) who took medicine began to take wine instead and became a more substantial man (on right) who found life enjoyable. Ink [eighteenth century?].

Beyond the trial of simple masculinity that drinking three bottles of port could be, port-supported masculinity was closely tied to class. But unlike tea and tobacco, which were first embraced by the English aristocracy before spreading through all levels of society, port began as a middle-class drink that was taken up by aristocrats. The reason for this trickle-up effect was very much related to ideas about gender because in the second half of the eighteenth century claret began to be associated with effeminacy in a more general middle-class critique of the morals of the English upper classes. Their later adoption of port, and the trials of masculinity measured by the number of bottles they could drink, was part of an attempt by the English elites to protect themselves from portrayals as weak, ineffectual, and unmanly. Samuel Johnson's point (quoted at the beginning of this chapter) that claret was the drink for boys and port the drink for men was not just a clever throwaway line. It summed up the point that port was a manly drink and claret was not. He contrasted men to boys, but he might as well have contrasted men to women.

The middle-class attack on upper-class ineffectiveness was part of a broad political challenge to the establishment and formulating it in gendered terms was extremely effective. The various English military setbacks of the mid-1700s – such as the army's defeat by the French in the Ohio River Valley and the failure of Admiral Byng to relieve the British garrison in Minorca – were attributed to a lack of manly martial skills within the officer class of the army and navy. The officer ranks were, of course, dominated by men from England's upper classes. In 1757 the Reverend John Brown, of Newcastle, wrote that the strength of a nation depended on the character of its leaders and that the causes of the current shortcomings were the 'luxurious and effeminate Manners in the higher Ranks'.

Luxury and effeminacy were closely tied in this political challenge, with the upper classes portrayed as gorging themselves on the luxury goods only they could afford, and becoming feminized in the process. (The critique was directed at males, of course, because women played no formal role in the exercise of state power at the time.) This was where wine came in, because the wines favoured by the English elites were claret, champagne, and burgundy. All came from France, and France was regarded by the English middle classes as the most effeminate nation in Europe. Imports of French luxuries, then, were seen as sapping England's manly strength, with dire consequences for its place in the international order, despite the British gains over France in the Seven Years' War.

A 1757 print by L.P. Boitard, entitled 'The Imports of Great Britain from France', showed French cooks, dancers, artisans, and others disembarking from their ship in London. They include an effeminate man with a huge muff and a hairdresser with a long queue and a pair of curling tongs. Many of the English men and women at the front of the crowd are dressed in the elaborate finery associated with the French nobility. Meanwhile the ship's cargo, already unloaded and lying on the dock, includes cheeses spilling out of upended barrels, and opened boxes of bottles that contain men's pomade, perfume, and other products. But the most prominent items are three large barrels that are clearly marked with the words claret, burgundy, and champagne. The main elements of the middle-class social and political critique are present in the print – France, luxury, and effeminacy – and it was clear to its audience precisely who the English consumers of these corrupting goods and services were. The elites, with their bright clothing and coiffed hair, holding their glasses of claret in their silk-gloved hands, were under attack.

There appears to have been no effective response to these criticisms except for the elites to give up what was effeminate and rally to what was masculine – effectively conceding the argument to the middle classes. We cannot fix with any precision the period during which upper class Englishmen adopted port, but the shift was well under way during the 1770s. It was in 1779, at a dinner party hosted by the painter Sir Joshua Reynolds, that Samuel Johnson expressed his disdain for claret. Johnson himself was not drinking alcohol at the time and was persuaded to sip a little claret so that he could remind himself what it tasted like. He did so and declared that it was 'poor stuff!' – and that those who drank it were boys, not men. Evidence of port's being adopted by the upper classes lies in more and more appearing in the most prestigious auctions at Christie's. In 1775 Sir Edward Barry, a celebrated physician, declared that 'port wines are now universally preferred to the French claret.' The numbers backed up this claim: between 1777 and 1791, Portugal accounted for three-quarters of the wine imported into England (the great bulk of which was port) while French producers shipped between 3 and 4 per cent.

The onset of the French Revolutionary wars in 1793 made French wine even less available in England, but the shift from claret to port had already taken place. Charles Ludington writes: 'to drink port was to drink a glass of English manliness, which was precisely what middle-ranking critics said the ruling elite lacked. And without true manliness ... the elite ... were no longer politically legitimate. After all, to be a "woman" or a "boy" was to be politically disqualified.' This might seem a complicated and subtle explanation of the upper-class shift from claret to port, especially at a time when England was in conflict with France and drinking claret might seem unpatriotic. But the two countries had been at war for ages, on and off, and claret had retained its strong appeal even when trade was cut off (see pp. 195–6). At the same time that the English elites shifted from feminine claret to masculine port, their clothing styles evolved from being brightly coloured and featuring silk and lace to darker coloured, less ornate suits made from English wool. In art and architecture, simpler neo-classical styles replaced more ornate styles. Claret and port were part of a general movement from the mid-eighteenth century toward a culture that was considered masculine. Some modern wine writers still apply gendered values to some wines, calling them either feminine or masculine (see pp. 141–6). But at no time has this paradigm had a greater implication than in the later 1700s, when it led to a sea change in the drinking habits of England's ruling classes.

TEMPERANCE AND PROHIBITION

In a sense the culmination of centuries of the double standard of drinking were the anti-alcohol movements of the 1800s and early 1900s. In broad terms, the temperance and prohibition campaigns of the period set women and men against one another, in that the organizations involved had a largely female membership while the targets of their activities were drinking men.

Several historical trends led to these movements in the nineteenth century. The period was one of rapid social change throughout much of Europe and North America. The population grew rapidly in many countries, economies industrialized, and cities swelled with immigrants from the countryside looking for work. In these disruptive conditions middle-class commentators believed that social norms were breaking down. Cities seemed to promote all kinds of social pathologies such as violence, crime, prostitution, family breakdown, insanity, and suicide, and the new science of statistics churned out series of figures that seemed to show that disruptive and decadent behaviour of all kind was on the increase. Repeating an argument that had been made for centuries, many commentators blamed alcohol for what appeared to be the breakdown of society generally. Although issues such as prostitution and crime were important in themselves, many church and political leaders concluded that reducing or eliminating alcohol consumption would solve the other problems.

At the same time, large public works projects began to deliver fresh drinkable water to many large cities in Europe and North America, sometimes in response to water-borne epidemics, such as the widespread outbreaks of cholera in the 1830s. Regular supplies of clean drinking water replaced the water that urban populations had drawn from polluted wells and rivers, and it was a boon to the poor, who had no choice but to drink water. But it undercut the argument that because water was too dangerous to drink, people should drink wine and beer instead. In fact, the argument could be turned on its head: that instead of drinking wine and beer, which as alcoholic drinks were known to be physically and socially dangerous, people should turn exclusively to the supplies of safe, clean, potable water.

These developments provided the preconditions for anti-alcohol movements (as we can call the temperance and prohibition campaigns) but another trend shaped the form of the movements, and that was a belief that women, by their nature, had a special interest in moral reform, starting with restrictions on alcohol. The nineteenth century saw the emergence of a cult of domesticity that planted women squarely within home and family and portrayed them as essentially moral and nurturing. Men, on the other hand, were engaged in the wider world, and working-class men in particular were crass and given to immorality.

Most of the influential temperance and prohibitionist movements were women's movements such as the Woman's Christian Temperance Union, which began in the United States but soon had branches in many countries. Women were to the fore for the very reason that it was their responsibility to protect the family and social morality, and 'drink' (as alcohol came to be known) represented the greatest threat. The story of these movements need not be retold here, but it is notable that women, who had historically been discouraged from drinking alcohol, endorsed anti-alcohol positions more than men did; men, as the majority of drinkers, were the target of the temperance organizations. Although there were many men who supported anti-alcohol movements and women who did not, there was a clear gender divide that reflected the longer history of men, women, and alcohol.

Wine, we might note, was seldom mentioned in the anti-alcohol campaigns in the United States because it was drunk by very few people. The main targets were spirits and beer and the saloons where men drank. In Europe's main wine-producing countries, France, Italy, and Spain, the anti-alcohol movements made virtually no headway, partly because the movements were dominated by Protestants (see pp. 88–9), and partly because their medical professions and governments saw wine as a solution to alcohol problems rather than part of the problem.

Throughout the twentieth century the historic relationships of women and men to wine began to erode, largely as a result of changes in gender relations in society more generally. Women continued to drink less wine than men and a greater proportion of women than men in every country abstained totally from alcohol. But women who did drink alcohol were more likely to drink wine than to drink beer or spirits, which were seen as men's drinks. Women were also said to prefer sweeter wines and to be drawn to rosé wines. Somewhat sweet pink wines, such as White Zinfandel, were drunk primarily by women.

The emergence of a more defined wine culture since the 1980s has seen these historic gendered patterns break down even more rapidly. Women are as fully engaged in wine education as men, and in many countries more wine is purchased by women than men. Women are well and increasingly represented in all aspects of the wine industry, as winemakers, viticulturists, scientists, and marketers. Many of the most prominent wine writers are women, and women make up half the judges in many of the leading wine competitions. Even gendered wine has changed. Where rosé wine used to be thought of and ghettoized as a 'woman's wine', it has now entered the mainstream. More and more producers are making rosé wines, and almost a third of wine sold in French supermarkets is rosé.

There are still vestiges of the longer-term history of women, men, and wine. The use of alcohol, as well as other drugs, to render women incapable of consenting to sex is still a problem. The associations of wine with romance, love, and sex are still with us. And some men still worry that women who drink will become sexually careless, without equivalent concern for men being sexually promiscuous. The double standard might not be what it was, but it is what it is. There is however, little expectation these days that women should not drink wine.

3

WINE AND RELIGION

In 1999 a disagreement over wine disrupted a planned state visit to France by the president of Iran. An integral part of any state visit is a state dinner, and the French planned to serve wine because, for them, a state dinner without their iconic wines was unthinkable. But for the Iranian government, which held to a strict interpretation of the Muslim ban on alcohol, a dinner with wine was equally unthinkable. Not only would the president of Iran not drink wine, but he could not countenance even sitting at a table where wine was served. Apart from the irony that the earliest evidence of wine in western Asia comes from the frontiers of Iran, the difference of views highlighted the divergent positions of wine in Islam and Christianity. From its beginning, mainstream Christianity embraced wine as no religion before it had done, and this religious position was one of the foundations of the identification of France with wine. Islam, in contrast, rejected the centuries-old wine cultures in many of the regions where it took root, and banned the production and consumption of wine and any other alcoholic beverages. As for the French–Iranian state dinner, neither side would give way, and the state visit was downgraded to an official visit, which did not require a formal dinner. The crisis over wine was averted.

WINE AND RELIGION IN THE ANCIENT WORLD

If Islam and Christianity, two of the main global religions, forged specific but divergent relationships with wine, many regional religions did so much earlier. At one level it is not difficult to explain the presence of wine gods in many cultures because they were polytheistic, with many gods associated with a wide range of products and commodities. The ancient Egyptians, for example, had scores of gods associated not only with wine and beer, but also with grain and agriculture more generally, not to mention with the sun and the sky, milk and breastfeeding, and the dead.

In a sense, then, gods of wine did not stand out any more than other gods, and there is perhaps less need to explain the religious or supernatural connotations of wine than a number of historians have suggested. In fact, some of the explanations put forward to explain the religious associations of wine are less than convincing. It has been suggested, for example, that when the grape vine comes back to life after its winter dormancy – when the apparently dead trunk and canes suddenly sprout leaves and berries – observers likened it to a resurrection. But the grape vine is hardly unique in experiencing this transformation: other deciduous trees, shrubs, and vines go through the same annual cycle without being attributed any supernatural character.

But it is fair enough to argue that some aspects of wine must have appeared supernatural. One was fermentation itself. If grapes were pressed in a container and the juice left exposed to ambient yeasts, observers would see an inert pool of liquid gradually begin to roil and bubble. If they felt it, they would find that it was warm, even though there was no external source of heating, such as a fire. And if they tasted the liquid before and after fermentation, they would find that it had lost all or most of its sweetness, as the sugar was converted to alcohol. These transformations, all verifiable by the senses, could not but have seemed other-worldly, as there was no banal explanation for them.

The experience of drinking the fermented juice produced another wonder: intoxication. Anyone consuming the finished wine must have noticed its effects on themselves and on anyone else near them who was also drinking wine. It began with a feeling of light-headedness that intensified as more wine was consumed, and a sense of uncertainty, confusion and physical instability set in. Fellow drinkers, even though their actions and speech could be gauged with decreasing accuracy, became less intelligible in speech and unsteady on their feet. Perhaps the members of the drinking group became uncharacteristically philosophical, argumentative, fatigued, amorous, or aggressive, or all the above. Clearly wine, however it was thought of, was responsible for changes in behaviour. To one degree or another, depending on how much was consumed, it occupied and took control of people's minds and bodies. How could such a beverage, made in a magical way, not be supernatural? There are, then, both banal explanations for wine gods – that polytheistic religions had gods for everything, including wine – and explanations based on the peculiar properties of fermentation and the effects of drinking wine.

Beer, of course, possessed the same properties of alcoholic fermentation and intoxication, although the typically higher alcohol level of wine brought on intoxication more rapidly. But there was another critical difference between beer and wine: scarcity value. Beer was made from grain that could be harvested and stored over a long period of time, enabling people to make bread and brew beer throughout the year. Frequent brewing in small batches was necessary until hops were widely used because unhopped beer (ale) lasted only a short time, meaning that it had to be made frequently in small volumes. It could, however, be made all year, unlike wine which could be made only once, when the grapes were ripe. Made annually and in relatively small volumes, wine was much scarcer than beer, and that translated into higher prices and the monopolization of wine by the wealthier and more powerful strata of ancient societies where beer was the most commonly consumed beverage.

We can see these various points at work in the way the religions of the ancient world related to wine. Most had wine gods, some female and some male. In Sumer the goddess of the vine was Gestin, while in Syria the demi-god Danel was assisted by his daughter when cultivating the vines. Some Egyptian gods associated with wine were female but they were replaced, over time, by male deities. The most important was Osiris, the god of nature, death, and rebirth, who was also god of the vine. It was Osiris who presided over the festivities at the time of the annual flooding of the Nile, which was essential for the survival of agriculture, including viticulture, in much of Egypt.

Egyptian temple offering of wine, flowers, cakes, and bread. Wall relief in the temple of Kom Ombo in Southern Upper Egypt, 1570–1070 BCE.

Wine was often used in libations, the pouring of a liquid (beer and oil were also often used) in the name of a god, generally as prayers were said. In Mesopotamia wine was present on the tables of food and drink offered to the gods. In Egypt, where vineyards were owned and wine was consumed only by the religious and secular elites, the planting of vines was a spiritual obligation. Addressing the great god Amon-Re, Ramses III declared, 'I planted for thee wine gardens on the Southern Oasis, and Northern Oasis likewise, without numbers.' He claimed to have presented almost 60,000 jars of wine to Amon-Re. Egypt presents a complicated set of images linking wine to the supernatural. Some texts depict wine as the personification of Re, the sun god; others refer to red wine as the right eye of the god Horus, and white wine as his left eye. Wine was also – this is a common theme –

associated with blood. Shesmu, the Egyptian god of the wine press, is sometimes shown as a slaughterer.

Among the plethora of wine gods in the ancient world, one stands out: the god known as Dionysus in Greece and Bacchus in Rome. Both gods emerged from cultures where wine was virtually the only alcoholic drink – beer was not consumed in either region, and mead (fermented water and honey) was a minor beverage – and both assumed a higher profile in their wine-centred cultures than other wine gods did in their predominantly beer-drinking societies.

In the Greek context, Dionysus was the god of the grape harvest and wine, and also of ritual madness and fertility. Although there are several accounts of his origins, he was distinctive among Greek gods for being said by some to have been born of a male god and a mortal woman, although some explanations of his origins have him as the child of two gods. In the first explanation his father was Zeus, the king of the gods, and his mother Semele, the daughter of the king of Thebes, with Dionysus the result of an adulterous relationship because Zeus was married. In a complicated narrative, the pregnant Semele was burned to death but Zeus plucked Dionysus from her womb and sewed him into his thigh, from where he was eventually born. Dionysus was later expelled from his home on Crete and fled to Egypt, where he learned the art of making wine before eventually returning to Crete, taking with him knowledge of viticulture and winemaking. The story parallels the transfer of the knowledge of viticulture and winemaking from Egypt to Crete and then to the Greek mainland.

Although referred to as a male, Dionysus is often shown as a sensuous, beardless youth who is somewhat androgynous. He is frequently depicted in scenes imbued with frenzied sexuality, often attended by female followers (maenads) and bearded satyrs with erect penises. In images of processions, Dionysus is often borne in a chariot pulled by exotic animals such as lions and tigers. Quite clearly he was more than a simple wine god but represented the disorderliness that can result from drinking wine. He was, in a sense, a counterpoint to the symposia, the formalized occasions in which upper-class Greek males got together to drink wine, discuss philosophy and politics, and listen to music and poetry. Undoubtedly many symposia were little more than drinking parties punctuated by sex, but in principle the participants were expected to remain this side of drunkenness.

The cult of Bacchus, the Roman wine god, was adapted from Dionysus when the Greeks colonized southern Italy about 200 BC. He replaced Liber Pater (the Free Father) who was a god of wine with a state-sanctioned cult. According to the Roman historian Livy, the Bacchic cult that superseded Liber Pater was much more disorderly and threatening. Men and women devotees gathered together as often as five times a month, got drunk on wine, and enjoyed evenings of unrestrained sexual activity that became known as bacchanalia. According to Livy, these occasions offended Rome's moral codes and there were fears that the bacchanalia might be breeding grounds for political opposition and sedition. For that reason, the cult was suppressed and thousands of Bacchus's followers were executed. Livy's sensational account has been questioned, but the Roman senate did regulate gatherings of Bacchus's followers; they needed prior permission to meet, and participants at any gathering were limited to three women and two men – enough for group sex, but not on the scale of the legendary bacchanalia.

What made Dionysus and Bacchus stand out is that both existed within cultures where wine was the most important drink, but even more because they were associated not simply with wine in itself but with specific and proscribed modes of consuming wine. Although wine was officially viewed as a civilized and civilizing beverage, it had the power to disrupt civilized behaviour. It was widely associated with disorder, sexuality, and fertility because even low levels of intoxication reduced social inhibitions and led to behaviour that was potentially disruptive. These were common cultural associations that were expressed in warnings against excessive drinking and in the tightly prescribed rules for the Greek symposium and its Roman equivalent, the convivium. Dionysus and Bacchus were, in a sense, the bad boys among the wine gods, and they represented the danger that wine implicitly posed. They transgressed rules about drinking, rules about sex, and – in their androgynous portrayals – rules about gender. They attracted the attention of their host populations (and the attention of historians) and they were far more active than the rather banal wine gods of other cultures who did little more than watch over the vines and the harvest.

WINE IN JUDAISM AND CHRISTIANITY

Wine was also important to Judaism, a minor religion in the ancient world that was centred on the eastern shore of the Mediterranean Sea. The main Jewish religious text, the Torah, is replete with references to the grape vine and wine. It was later incorporated into the Christian Bible as the Old Testament, and therefore became important for understanding the place of wine in Christianity, but the Jews had their own special relationship with wine. There were more references to the vine in the Torah than to any other plant, and it was highly valued by the Jews because it produced wine. The status of the vine was so high that it was implicated in key episodes in Jewish history. One of Noah's first acts, after the Great Flood subsided and the ark came to rest, was to plant a vineyard. Then, after the Jews, led by Moses, had escaped from their enslavement in Egypt, scouts were sent ahead to look for the land that God had promised them. They came back successful, describing a land of milk and honey, indicative of a home that would be fertile and sweet. But the evidence they brought was not milk and honey or a cow and a bee, but a bunch of grapes that was so big and heavy that the scouts had to share its weight by carrying it on a pole across their shoulders.

So important was wine to the Jews that throughout the Torah it represents the gifts that their god had promised them. Whenever prophets threaten the Jews that they will be punished for being sinful, they threaten to withhold the fruits of the vine: 'wail, you vinedressers … the vine has withered' and 'you will … press the grape but never drink wine from it'. Similarly, the Torah warns of the consequences of abusing the divine gift by getting drunk. Noah not only planted grape vines and made wine, but he drank a lot of it, became inebriated, stripped off his clothes, and fell asleep. When his sons found him, one of them saw his father naked (some scholars read this as incest) and was later struck dead. Again, when Lot's wife was turned to a pillar of salt, his daughters conceived a plan to continue the family line by plying their father with wine so that he would have sexual intercourse with them and impregnate them without realizing they were his daughters. In both cases, wine was linked to horrifying incestuous behaviour. At the same time as the Torah warned against excessive wine drinking, it recognized the pleasure that wine brought. Wine was given by God, after all, and it had to be a good thing in itself. What made it problematic was the way it was sometimes abused.

Lot, fed wine until he became drunk, rests in the arms of one daughter while the other pours him more wine. 1630 engraving by W. Kent after D. Zampieri, il Domenichimo.

The importance of wine in Judaism carried over almost seamlessly to Christianity which, almost from the very beginning, established a tight relationship with wine. The first miracle by Jesus recorded in the New Testament is the turning of water into wine at the wedding at Cana. This was straightforward as miracles go, but also culturally complex. At some point during the wedding celebrations, the wine ran out, suggesting that the organizers had underestimated the number of guests or that the guests had consumed more wine than expected. Mary, Jesus's mother, suggested that he should make more wine, a request that is odd in itself, as it seems a trivial use of miraculous powers. Jesus obliged, summoning some jars of water used for washing and transforming them into wine without, apparently, making any gestures or speaking any words. It must have been white wine because the appearance of the water did not change and those present did not realize there was now wine in the jars until Jesus invited them to taste it. Not only did Jesus make wine from dishwater but it was declared to be better than any that had been served that day. The custom was to serve the best wine first, while the drinkers were less intoxicated and their palates were more discriminating, and then to serve the poorer-quality wine. Not knowing the divine source of the wine, the steward at the wedding praised the groom: 'People generally serve the best wine first, and keep the cheaper sort until the guests have had plenty to drink; but you have kept the best wine until now.' The wine made from water was, then, not just *vin ordinaire*, but Premier Cru quality, as befitted the first miracle.

Wine is the most commonly cited beverage in the New Testament, as in the Old. It was recommended as a medicine, as when Timothy advised drinking some wine 'for thy stomach's sake'. It was associated with joyful occasions, such as the wedding at Cana, when the excessive consumption implied by the shortage of wine was overlooked. For examples of the misuse of wine, however, Christians had to look back to the Old Testament, where there were such intoxicated sexual transgressors as Noah and Lot. In this sense, the New Testament seems to be more positive than the Old toward wine. The authors of the New Testament seem anxious to make a clear distinction between wine before the Crucifixion, the old world when people had not been redeemed by the death of Christ, and the newly regenerated Christian world. This is a different Old World, New World wine distinction from the one we are used to today.

The overwhelmingly positive view of wine that Christians promoted is vividly illustrated by the representation of wine – presumably red wine was more convincing than white – as the blood of Christ. This was most clearly stated in the doctrine of transubstantiation which taught that during the Eucharist, when the faithful sipped wine, the essence of the wine was transformed into the blood of Christ even though it maintained the outward appearance of wine – just as the bread at the Eucharist was transformed into the flesh of Christ, while keeping the outward form of bread. Something close to this process was captured in a genre of Medieval religious paintings known as 'Christ in the Wine Press'. These images show Christ, bleeding from the wounds suffered before and during the Crucifixion, treading grapes in a vat. The blood flowing from wounds in his head, side, and hands (and, presumably, from his feet) runs into the vat where it mixes with the grape juice. The liquid running from the press into barrels for fermentation is thus a blend of grape must and Christ's blood, which reinforces their essential identity.

The transformation of wine into Christ's blood that is essential to the Christian Eucharist was predated by the humoral system, the paradigm for understanding the human body for two millennia, until the eighteenth century (see pp. 8–14). In this system, wine and blood had the same value (both were considered warm and moist) and wine reinforced the influence of blood in the human body. Many Greek, Roman, and Medieval physicians believed that when wine was consumed, it was converted to blood, and to this extent the doctrine of transubstantiation – the transformation of blood into wine – might not have been such a strange idea to Christians until quite recently. It is not clear whether the colour or hue of the wine was important. It seems easier to believe that fairly dark red wine was blood than that light red and whites were, simply on the basis of similarity of colour. Nevertheless, the wine used in communion in the Middle Ages was diluted red wine. Diluted white wine, it was thought, would too easily be confused with water.

It is far from fanciful to think that Christ, the god with wine flowing through his body, was often thought of as a wine god. That must certainly have been the case when Christian missionaries started to proselytize among the beer-drinking populations of Europe, such as the Celts of ancient France. They had their beer gods, but they lacked a wine god because wine was virtually unknown to them. The Romans spread viticulture throughout beer-drinking Europe, and no doubt introduced Bacchus as they went, but the Christian missions were either hard on their heels or, in some cases, in advance of them. Because of the importance of wine to their religion, Christians planted vineyards wherever they could – it later became an obligation for Christian institutions to plant grape vines – and they introduced wine both as a beverage and as an element of religious ritual. The simultaneous arrival of Christians and viticulture, and the belief that the blood of Christ was in some sense wine, must surely have made him a wine god in the eyes of many of the newly converted. There is a compelling fifth-century AD mosaic from Cyprus that shows a child, his head lit by a halo, sitting on an adult's lap and surrounded by worshippers. At first glance it is a classic example of the 'Adoration of the Magi' genre, with Jesus on Mary's lap. But the child is, in fact, Dionysus, the Greek god of wine, sitting on the lap of Eros. The transfer of iconography speaks to the association of wine and divinity in the Greco-Roman and Christian traditions.

'A monkish vision.' A monk asleep in his chair dreams of being offered food and wine by young women. Etching (1797) by Cruikshank after George M. Woodward.

Wine and Christianity were so closely associated in the early period of the religion, and the stress on spreading not only the Word but viticulture was so strong, that there have been suggestions that converts showed their allegiance to the new faith by drinking wine instead of beer. But there is no evidence of this. Indeed, the dominant rule for monks, whom we might see as having been, in principle at least, the most pious Christians, advised against drinking any wine at all. Saint Benedict, whose rules for his religious order (the Benedictines) became a model for many other orders, noted that 'wine is no drink for monks; but since nowadays monks cannot be persuaded of this, let us at least agree upon this, that we drink temperately and not to satiety ... we believe that a *hermina* [about a third of a litre] of wine a day is sufficient for each. But upon those whom God bestows the gift of abstinence, they should know they have a special reward.' Monks who were ill were permitted wine over and above this ration, but it was then a medicine, not a discretionary beverage. Benedict did not mention beer because beer was not consumed in Italy, but when monasteries were established in beer-drinking regions such as France, monks were permitted to drink beer as well as wine.

In the first Christian millennium, thanks first to the Romans and then to the Christian Church, viticulture had spread throughout much of Europe, including regions that are only now coming back into production thanks to climate change. By 1000 AD, grapes were grown and wine was made from Portugal in the west to Poland in the east, and from England in the north to Sicily in the south. But at this very time, another faith that was to become a global religion, Islam, adopted a diametrically different position on wine and alcohol more generally.

WINE AND ISLAM

The Middle Eastern regions where Islam arose in the fifth century had vibrant wine cultures, although growing conditions for grape vines were so limiting that most of the population drank water or beer. That was also true of most of the Mediterranean shore of Africa where Islam extended its authority in the seventh century. In the very earliest period of Islam, drinking wine made from grapes, dates, pomegranates, and other produce was permitted, but the Prophet Muhammad quickly decided that the effects of drinking were socially disruptive and incompatible with the life of a faithful Muslim. There are various accounts of this decision. One is that Muhammad went to a wedding where the guests were celebrating with wine, leading him to think that wine was a good thing because it facilitated happiness and friendship. But on returning to the wedding later, he discovered that the guests had drunk wine to the point of intoxication and had begun to brawl. The scene of damage and injury led Muhammad to conclude that humans could not be trusted with wine, even though it was good in itself.

Unlike Christians and most other religious and secular authorities, which permitted drinking but punished drunkenness, Muhammad took the position that was later adopted by Prohibitionists in the nineteenth and twentieth centuries: that even if only a minority of people abused alcohol, the dangers it posed to religion and social order were so great that it was better to ban the consumption of intoxicating drinks altogether. Unlike later forms of Prohibition, however, Islam's was comprehensive and total. It did not allow exceptions for religious or medicinal purposes (as Prohibition in the United States did), and it forbade not only the production and sale of alcohol, but also its consumption. The Islamic policy toward wine and other intoxicating beverages represents the world's first, most rigorous, and longest-lasting prohibition policy.

Historically, the Islamic world was no more monolithic in terms of alcohol than it is today, when some Muslim countries ban alcohol completely and others allow for some access to wine and other alcohols. As Islam spread from its original territory to the Mediterranean area, across North Africa and incorporating Sicily, Crete, and Spain (and even, briefly, parts of south-west France) local authorities adopted a range of positions on alcohol within the broad Muslim doctrine of disapproval. Some Muslim rulers made wine production illegal by law but tolerated it in practice and even gave it recognition by taxing it. Arabic sources suggest that vineyards were widespread in southern Spain, especially in Andalusia, and in the Coimbra area of Portugal. Islamic horticulture was so advanced that the number of varieties of grapes increased, and some Muslim texts on agriculture included instructions on taking care of fermentation vats to be used for wine production.

In Spain a minority interpretation of the ban on alcohol allowed wine to continue to be drunk there. It was argued that the drink referred to in the Qur'an was only wine made from grapes and that wine made from dates was therefore excluded from the prohibition. But, went the argument, if date wine was permitted, so was grape wine, as long as it was no stronger than date wine. Wine made from dates is typically lower in alcohol than wine made from grapes because the sugar content of dates is lower, so this was an argument for the acceptability of grape wine as long as it was relatively low in alcohol. It is not clear whether this could be achieved by making wine in the usual way and then diluting it before drinking it, or whether the fermentation would have to be stopped to control the alcohol level. Either way, the argument for low-alcohol wine did not respond to the Muslim objection that, even if drinking wine did not lead to drunkenness and immorality (which would take longer with low-alcohol wine), it distracted pious Muslims from their religious duties.

There is clear evidence that Muslims in Spain did drink wine, although we have no idea of its alcoholic strength, and it is thought that Muslims generally drank less than Christians. Muslims drank at occasions reminiscent of the Greek symposia, with men gathering after the evening meal to relax on cushions, drink wine, and talk. Wine was served by boys and there was entertainment of singing and dancing by women. The male participants were expected to spend all night talking, drinking, and dozing. The same sort of occasion seems to have been common among Jews in Muslim Spain, too, and between the tenth and twelfth centuries such gatherings gave rise to a genre of poetry that praised wine for its ability to banish cares and bring joy and happiness to the drinker.

But some Muslim rulers implemented the ban of alcohol. In the tenth century the caliph Ozman ordered the destruction of two thirds of the vineyards of Valencia, perhaps leaving one third for the production of table grapes to be eaten as fresh fruit. Yet if there were some setbacks to Spanish viticulture under Muslim rule, they were reversed as Muslims were slowly driven from the Iberian peninsula. There were many contracts for new vineyards in Aragon between 1150 and 1180 and they can only mean that wine was being exported from the region. By the middle of the 1200s, Spanish producers were shipping large volumes of wine to England, indicating a rapid recovery of the country's vineyards.

It is not unusual for practices to vary on the geographical fringes of a religious empire from the orthodoxy at its centre – in the sixteenth century Christian practices in Iceland differed markedly from doctrine in Rome – but it is possible that wine continued to be made and consumed even in the heartland of Islam. Vineyards did not disappear, but were turned to producing grapes for eating, and although these grapes might not have made excellent wine, their juice could certainly have been fermented. Poetry might not be the best evidence of a continuing wine culture under Islam, but the rich genre of wine poetry in the Arab world that had preceded Islam persisted after the rise of the new faith. One early ninth-century poet, Abu Nuwas, seemed to defy the prohibition on wine as he wrote, 'You have made me fear God, your Lord ... If you will not drink with me for fear of [God's] punishment then I will drink alone.'

In the twelfth and thirteenth centuries a group of Persian poets, including the well-known Omar Khayyam, made wine and love prominent themes in their works. Khayyam's *Ruba'iyat*, a long work in praise of wine, contains sentiments such as 'I cannot live without the sparkling vintage/Cannot bear the body's burden without wine.' This might be interpreted as a plaintive cry in an arid, wine-less world, but elsewhere in the poem Khayyam suggests that illegal drinking (and illicit sexual relationships) was common:

> They say lovers and drunkards go to hell,
> A controversial dictum not easy to accept:
> If the lover and the drunkard go to hell,
> Tomorrow Paradise will be empty.

It is possible that the wine poetry that flourished half a millennium after the coming of Islam drew on a distant cultural memory. But it is also possible, or more likely, that it reflected the continuing production and consumption of wine in the Muslim world. The ban on wine was, after all, effectively a rigorous policy of prohibition, and experience of that policy in other places in the twentieth century shows how difficult it is to enforce completely.

WINE IN CHRISTIAN CHURCHES

As imperfectly imposed and observed as it was, the wine doctrine of Islam was a stark contrast with Christianity, which embraced wine and allowed the consumption of beer and other alcoholic beverages. Drinking wine and beer in moderation was not only acceptable, but the faithful could be excused for thinking that drinking wine was a good thing. Only excessive drinking was problematic, as shown by the way that drunkenness was treated in the penitentials, manuals written from the sixth century onward to guide priests who had to deal with Christians who had committed sins. Almost all the penitentials prescribed penances to be performed when people drank to excess; whether or not they committed other sinful acts while drunk, being drunk was in itself a sinful state. An early eighth-century penitential ascribed to the Venerable Bede set out a penance when a Christian had drunk to the point that 'the tongue babbles and the eyes are wild and there is dizziness and distention of the stomach and pain follows'. This sounds like the result of a particularly serious bout of drinking. The offender had to perform a penance of abstaining from wine and meat for three days if a layman, seven days if a priest, two weeks if a monk, three weeks if a deacon, four weeks if a presbyter, and five weeks if a bishop. In other words, offenders whose clerical rank created higher expectations of virtuous behaviour were punished more severely.

Another penitential, this one from the monastery of Silos in Spain, made further distinctions. A cleric who got drunk was to do penance for twenty days, but if he vomited as a result he did penance for forty days, and if he compounded the offence by vomiting up the bread from the Eucharist, the penance was extended to sixty days. The penances for a lay person in these circumstances were less severe, and were set at ten, twenty, and forty days, respectively.

For the most part the small sip of wine that Christians took at communion was clearly not implicated in concerns about intoxication. Not only was it only a sip, but communion wine was usually diluted with water. Initially the priest and the lay participants received both bread and wine, the form that is known as 'communion under both kinds', but in the twelfth and thirteenth centuries the wine was gradually withdrawn from the laity and in 1415 the Council of Constance ruled that communion under both kinds was a heresy. This decision was partly a response to a heretical doctrine that declared that both the bread and the wine were absolutely necessary for salvation. But it also reflected growing concern, expressed by Thomas Aquinas and others, that the communion wine would be spilled as the chalice was passed from person to person. This was when the practice began of the priest placing the bread or wafer on the tongue of the communicant, so as to prevent any crumbs falling to the floor. The sanctity of the communion bread and wine was paramount and any abuse of it was equally deplored. As we have seen, one penitential took a very grave view of drinking the communion wine to the point of vomiting both it and the bread.

Removing communion wine from the laity also reduced the volume of wine needed for this purpose, and reflected the practical problems of supplying wine to remote parishes that were not in wine-producing regions. Confining communion wine to the priest meant that only minute volumes of wine were needed, but even this sometimes became impossible when the Church's activities expanded far outside Europe, as they did from the 1500s onwards. In the seventeenth century, missionaries evangelizing among native peoples in parts of Canada cut off from the main centres of European settlement often found themselves without wine. In 1623 the Franciscan missionary Nicolas Viel noted from an area (now in Ontario) near Lake Huron that when the wine which he had brought from Quebec City in a little barrel that held 12 quarts [about 23 litres] turned bad, 'we made some of wild grapes which was very good'. But making wine from native grapes was not always possible and one missionary reported later in the century that he had been unable to celebrate mass for nine months because of the lack of wine.

Where grapes grew well – or well enough – monasteries became early centres for winemaking. Elsewhere they became known for brewing and later, from the 1100s, for distilling. A small amount of the wine they produced was dedicated to religious purposes, but the bulk was for consumption – by the monks on a daily basis, at more elaborate meals on feast days, and by guests and travellers who stayed at the monastery. Finally, some of the wine was sold on the open market to provide income for the religious house. So closely have monks and monasteries been associated with wine that they have been credited with saving the vineyards of western Europe from the beer-guzzling tribes that invaded the region from central and Eastern Europe in the so-called 'Barbarian Invasions' and with many of the innovations in viticulture and winemaking in the Middle Ages.

Yet although the Church – in the form of parishes, bishoprics, and religious houses – owned many vineyards, many others were owned by secular proprietors. It is impossible to calculate the respective numbers of vineyards and planted areas that each owned, but the apparent preponderance of Church-owned vineyards very likely results from the better record-keeping habits of the Church. The clergy, whether priests or monks, were generally more literate than the lay population, and their records were kept more carefully and effectively than those of private landowners. In fact we often know of vineyards owned by secular proprietors only when they were donated to the Church in exchange for prayers to be said for the family giving the vineyards. For example, the monastery of St. Nazarius of Lauresham, near Heidelberg, was given vineyards by two lay owners when it was founded in 764, and within a century it had been given another hundred vineyards in nearby Dienheim alone. Many exchanges of this sort took place during the Crusades, in the twelfth and thirteenth centuries, when families wanted prayers said for Crusaders who might die in foreign lands.

There is no doubt that the Church owned vast tracts of land planted in vines. In the ninth century, the monastery at Saint-Germain-des-Prés, near Paris, owned a total of 20,000 hectares of land, 300 to 400 of them vineyards. But it was the Burgundy-based Cistercian order, with its mother house at Cîteaux, that amassed such extensive areas of vineyard in many regions and states – it had an empire of 400 houses within fifty years of being founded – that it appeared to be the Constellation Brands of its day. In the twelfth century, almost every house belonging to the order received donations of vineyards. The core of its holdings were in Burgundy, where by the 1300s the Cistercians owned hundreds of hectares of vines in what are now some of the most prestigious communes, including Pommard, Nuits, and Corton. By 1336 the Cistercians owned 50 hectares of vines in Vougeot alone, then the largest single area of vines in Burgundy. When the Cistercians founded Kloster Eberbach in the Rhine Valley, it soon accumulated nearly 700 hectares of vineyards, the largest known vineyard estate in Europe.

Yet we still do not know whether most vines in Europe were owned, or whether most wine was made, by the Church. If eleventh-century England is anything to go by, most vineyards were in secular hands: the Domesday Book, an agricultural census of England carried out in 1086, showed that there were forty-two vineyards, only twelve (29 per cent) of them owned by the Church. Clearly the ratio of secular- to Church-owned vineyards was fluid, changing as new vineyards were planted and changed hands. Moreover, we do not know the size of each vineyard, and it could be that the group owning more vineyards owned less land area planted in vines. The main point is that we should be careful not to overstate the participation of the Church in viticulture and wine production.

Not only is the Church often assumed to have been the major owner of vineyards in the long Medieval period from about 800 to 1500, it has also been credited with many of the innovations in viticulture and winemaking of the time. It is true that monks seem to have been fastidious in their attention to agriculture, and they might well have given particular attention to viticulture, given the emphasis on the vine and wine in Christian doctrine and ritual – although we should remember that monks consumed far more wine as a daily beverage than at communion. Monks kept careful records of their activities, and we can see them using egg whites and isinglass (fish bladder) for fining wines, and making vinegar from poor wine and oil from grape seeds. Practices such as these might well have been recorded by monks, but we have no idea whether the monks were innovating or adopting practices that were already in common usage. Nor is it clear that monks innovated in recognizing terroir in their vineyards as they noticed that the wine from one parcel of vines was consistently different from the wine made from different but nearby vines.

We must, then, take care not to overstate the role of the Church in wine production and in viticultural and winemaking innovation. Yet there is no doubt that for the first millennium and a half of its existence the Church promoted the production and consumption of wine and contributed to its becoming a daily beverage for many Europeans – especially in wine-producing regions where wine was cheaper because prices did not include the costs of transportation. In other regions, especially in northern Europe, beer remained the alcoholic drink of the mass of the population and wine was consumed by the better-off. But in the later Middle Ages the Church came under attack by reformers within it, many arguing that the ecclesiastical authorities were lax in enforcing the laws regarding drinking, sexual activity, and blasphemy. Too many clergy and lay people, they argued, were getting drunk, committing fornication and adultery – drink and sex were often associated in the minds of social critics – and the Church was enabling them by turning a blind eye to offenders.

Although there is no way of quantifying the extent of drunkenness in the Middle Ages, there are plenty of reports of clergy drinking to the point of drunkenness. The bishop of Tours was reported to be 'so often befuddled with wine that it would take four men to carry him from the table', while the bishop of Soissons was said to have been 'out of his mind … for nearly four years, through drinking to excess'. He even had to be locked up whenever there was a royal visit to the city for fear that he would embarrass everyone. Gregory of Tours complained that monks spent more time in taverns, drinking, than in their cells, praying. If a disproportionate number of drunk clerics than lay people turn up in the records, it probably means that their higher profile made their offences more reprehensible and noteworthy. Protestant commentators were particularly harsh in their attacks on clergy who abused alcohol because the clergy were expected to set a standard of behaviour for the Christian community, the exact point made in pentitentials that punished clerical drunkenness more severely than lay.

Drink, then, was one of the important issues taken up by the Protestant Reformers, notably Martin Luther and Jean Calvin, when they criticized the Church. Like later critics of drinking, they argued that, by loosening the bonds of self-discipline, excessive drinking led people into sinful acts they would not have committed while sober. Calvin, in particular, took excessive drinking very seriously, although he was not at all averse to drinking in itself – he drank wine and approved a priest providing it 'for the weaker brethren, and those who without it cannot attain bodily health'. But he was concerned about public drinking, as previously noted. This was almost always a matter of men drinking in taverns, often during church services, generally accompanied by excessive drinking, swearing, and blaspheming, and sometimes by gambling. Calvin placed French-language Bibles in Geneva's taverns, a precursor to the distribution of Bibles in hotel rooms by Gideons International in the twentieth century. This blurred what had been a stark distinction between tavern and church and forced men to drink, swear, and blaspheme in the presence of the holy word. Going even further, Calvin banned widely accepted tavern practices such as treating others to drinks and drinking to someone's health. As for drunkenness, the Geneva ordinances punished a first offence by a fine of three sous, a second by five sous, and a third offence by a fine of ten sous and a term of imprisonment.

Policies such as these gave the impression that Protestantism, at least in its Calvinist form (the form dominant in Scotland, the Netherlands, and Switzerland, and that inspired the English Puritans), was hostile to wine. But the fundamental thrust of Calvin's and other Protestants' doctrines was essentially the same as those of what now became known as the Church of Rome or the Catholic Church: that drinking wine and other alcoholic beverages was not problematic until it was excessive. The Protestants seemed to present a more positive position when they restored wine to the laity at communion. Calvin wrote that the Church had 'stolen or snatched wine from the greater part of God's people … [and] given a special property to a few shaven and anointed men'. In response the (Catholic) Council of Trent, which codified Catholic doctrine following the Reformation, reaffirmed that wine was strictly forbidden to the laity at communion, and that it was to be taken on behalf of the congregation by the officiating priest.

As Calvin was reining in excessive wine consumption in Geneva, Spanish missionaries were expanding viticulture from Europe to the New World. Starting in New Spain (Mexico) in the 1520s, the Spanish conquistadores occupied much of Central and South America and introduced viticulture as they moved south. The speed was remarkable and vineyards were successfully planted in Chile and Argentina within three decades of the initial but unsuccessful attempts to grow vines in the area of what is now Mexico City. As they had been in much of Europe in the early Christian era, missionaries were responsible for spreading wine production throughout Latin America, but on this occasion they accompanied the Spanish armies. With a sure eye for location, the Jesuit and Franciscan missions planted their vines in locations now recognized as some of the best in South America.

The motivation for producing wine in Latin America was partly religious: the monks needed wine for communion at the missions they established, and importing wine from Spain was hazardous. In the sixteenth century wine was generally unstable and what did complete the voyage across the Atlantic, then being shipped over land and by water to destinations on the Pacific coast, was often in poor shape when it reached its destination. In principle, wine did not have to be of good quality to be used in communion and very little was needed because only the clergy sipped it. But the overwhelming purpose of wine was for daily consumption by the Spanish settlers, whether military, clerical, or civilian. Spain was a wine-drinking country and settlers wanted regular supplies of potable wine so that they could replicate their home diets as much as possible. Despite attempts by Spanish wine producers to prevent wine production in the Americas, the Church sponsored what became the beginning of several major wine industries.

In Europe itself there were few developments that affected the relationship between wine and religion during most of the Early Modern period, about 1500 to 1800. The Catholic Church and its institutions, such as bishoprics, parishes, and religious houses, continued to own vineyards. As far as we can tell, they expanded their holding of this kind, thanks to continued donations on the part of secular owners. In 1635, for example, the wine-producing parish of Volnay, near Beaune (now one of the most prestigious wine communes in Burgundy), was the recipient of six *ouvrées* of Pinot Noir vines in three locations and two *ouvrées* of Gamay, a total of about a third of a hectare. In 1679, Claude Baptheault gave the same parish two and a half hectares of vines. The gifts continued in the following century. In 1749 one Jaquette Grozelier, 'bed-ridden and ill but healthy in mind and judgment', gave the parish one and a half *ouvrées* of vines 'for the repose of her soul and the souls of her parents'. Later in the same year, François Poulleaux gave the parish a vineyard of three and a half *ouvrées*. These and other gifts were generally small, but they added up and made a significant contribution to the income of the parish of Volnay.

The records of abbé F. Delachere, the priest who served Volnay for half a century in the middle of the eighteenth century (1726–77), show that religion impinged on wine in various ways. Even though the eighteenth century is often thought of as a period when secular ideas began to dominate religion (this is the period when *philosophes* such as Voltaire and Diderot were writing) it is clear that Christianity still had a hold on the population, especially in times of hardship. The middle of the 1700s saw a run of poor harvests thanks to hail and storms that ruined vineyards, fields of grain, and orchards of fruit trees. The villagers of Volnay were threatened with disaster when their crops were poor or failed entirely: they lived from year to year, had no reserves and no savings, and nor was there any social welfare save what the Church could offer by way of charity. What appears to us as a poor wine vintage was to them a sentence to indigence, hunger, and sometimes death.

In the worst times the vignerons undoubtedly prayed individually, but they also turned to the priest to say public prayers. Delachere and his fellow priests must often have prayed at mass for good harvests, but at critical periods more public and sustained invocations were needed. Sometimes they led public prayers for the crops after hailstorms, but periods of drought more often provoked the clergy to action. On 1 August 1746, during a long, dry summer, Delachere performed public prayers for rain and two days later a storm brought relief to the districts around the villages of Volnay, Pommard, Beaune, and Savigny – but it also delivered heavy rain and damaging hail to several villages near Beaune. At times of critical drought the relic of Saint Reverien (a piece of his skull), which was kept in a church near Nuits, was carried in a procession to a church in Beaune as prayers for rain were recited by the participants. This was clearly to be done only in the most extreme circumstances, and a request to display the relic was denied one year because the drought was not thought to be serious enough. But the relic was brought out in 1771 when vines were dying for lack of water.

The vineyard area owned by the Church in France and elsewhere might have expanded during the 1700s, but during the French Revolution all the lands and property of the Church were seized and put up for auction. The Revolutionary government that came to power in 1789 had assumed the massive state debt accumulated by France's kings, and they saw in the Church's vast properties a resource that would help pay it off. It was part of a general reorganization of the Church that involved reducing the number of clergy in the upper ranks and dissolving religious houses. The impact on vineyards varied from region to region, but there were few parts of France where the Church did not own vines. The transfer of ownership was especially dramatic in Burgundy, where the Cistercians alone owned vast tracts of land planted in vines and where parishes, colleges, and other Church establishments also owned vineyards.

Most of Burgundy's Church-owned vineyards and other wine-related properties (such as buildings, cellars, and wine presses) were auctioned off in 1791 and 1792, many to local vignerons, others to buyers from Paris and elsewhere. They fetched prices well above the valuations. For example, one lot consisting of buildings, cellars, wine presses, vineyards, and other land, with a total valuation of 69,850 *livres*, sold for 150,000. The buyer was a royal notary from the town of Arnay. Another lot, this one 30 *ouvrées* of vines (slightly more than a hectare) in Meursault, belonging to a church in Beaune and valued at 7,048 *livres*, was bought by a vigneron of Meursault for 10,600 *livres*.

In this way, the Church in France (and elsewhere in Europe where the Revolutionaries extended their policies) lost the vineyards that some might well have owned for more than a thousand years. We might note that these actions by the French state were not unprecedented. Religious houses had been dissolved in various parts of Europe in the eighteenth century – by the Emperor Joseph II in the Habsburg Empire, for example – and their associated vineyards were disposed of by the state. The French Revolution was, however, an important and widespread rupture in the continuity of vineyard ownership by the Church. From then on there was no question whether more vineyards were in ecclesiastical or secular hands.

The next important phase in the history of wine and religion coincided with the rise of anti-alcohol movements in much of the western world. They were broadly divided into Temperance movements, which (initially, at least) argued for moderate drinking, and Prohibitionist movements, which campaigned for a total ban on the production and sale of all alcoholic beverages. Most of these organizations were composed of women (they saw women enter the political sphere in unprecedented numbers) and most had religious associations. The best known, the Woman's Christian Temperance Union, had a membership drawn mainly from Protestant denominations. Catholic women were put off by the organization's frequent criticisms of recent Irish immigrants as being hopelessly addicted to alcohol, while Jewish women found the word Christian a deterrent to membership.

Catholics and Jews formed their own temperance associations, but they were by no means as large or significant as the Protestants', and it is notable that not only was the Catholic clergy less engaged with temperance activities, but also that these movements were largely ineffective in countries with predominantly Catholic populations.

There were no significant anti-alcohol movements in France, Italy, and Spain, but there were in the United States, Canada, and Scandinavia. In the United States, where Prohibition became more important than Temperance, pressure from these movements led state after state to enact Prohibition laws before National Prohibition was finally introduced in 1920 after an amendment to the Constitution. During the First World War, Canadian provinces adopted a variety of laws that restricted alcohol production and sales; in Ontario, only wine could be sold, but in minimum volumes and only directly from the winery. The Scandinavian states adopted Prohibition for varying periods.

It is not clear why there was such a stark distinction between Protestants and Catholics when it came to pressing for policies to restrict or ban the production and sale of alcohol, but it is tempting to look back several centuries to the earliest comprehensive regulations, which happened to be in Protestant communities. They included Geneva under Calvin in the 1500s; Protestant cities such as Augsburg, in Germany, where rigorous regulations were applied to distilled spirits in the 1500s; and the New England colonies, where the Puritan authorities strictly regulated drinking during the 1600s – going so far as to limit the time a patron could spend in a tavern to thirty minutes. Even though there was no fundamental difference between Catholic and Protestant doctrines of drinking – both allowed moderate drinking but forbade drinking to excess – the Protestant authorities were historically more prepared to adopt and apply concrete policies that not only restricted consumption, but disrupted existing cultures of drinking. It is possible that this was the difference exhibited in their divergent levels of enthusiasm for temperance and Prohibition in the 1800s.

One of the reasons for positive attitudes towards drinking wine and beer throughout much of the Early Modern period was a general anxiety about the safety of water in Europe, an anxiety that spread to North American cities in the 1800s. It was accepted that beer and wine should be consumed as they were safer means of hydration. By the nineteenth century, however, there was a broader range of non-alcoholic beverages to choose from: the price of tea and coffee had fallen to the point that they had become beverages of mass consumption. Even more important, large-scale public works had begun to deliver regular supplies of fresh, potable water to the major cities and towns of Europe and North America. Water could now safely be consumed, and along with tea, coffee, and other non-alcoholic beverages, there was enough choice to make alcoholic beverages unnecessary.

In very broad terms many Protestants, who seem to have tolerated alcohol as a necessary evil rather than have approved of it positively, were now able to argue that wine, beer, and distilled spirits were merely discretionary and therefore unnecessary, and that the obviously harmful effects that flowed from their consumption demanded Prohibition. Catholics did not reach the same conclusion. In this sense it seems that it took the arrival of mass-consumption non-alcoholic drinks to clearly demarcate the divergent alcohol doctrines of Catholics and Protestants. There was, of course, a diversity of positions within each broad denomination. Some Protestants resisted stringent controls on alcohol and some Catholic clergy campaigned for them, but the broad picture seems clear enough.

The reasons that religious anti-alcohol movements were hostile to alcohol were not necessarily based in any religious doctrine. Drinking was widely seen as a gateway activity, behaviour that led to sexual promiscuity, crime, gambling, poverty, the neglect of children, marriage breakdown, suicide, and insanity. These were forms of social behaviour that also worried secular commentators in the nineteenth century, partly because the new industrial cities concentrated people and made socially unacceptable behaviour more easily observable. Moreover, the development of statistics enabled authorities to begin to quantify such things as suicides, crimes, admissions to asylums, and the extent of poverty. The statistics were not always reliable, and they were often misused, but they reinforced an impression among the middle and upper classes that society was going downhill at a rapid pace.

Drinking – the word took on the restricted meaning of drinking alcohol in the nineteenth century – was seen as the fundamental cause of all the other problems. Alcohol loosened inhibitions and led people to take risks and do things that they would not have done when they were sober. The view became widespread that if it were possible to curb drinking, or better still to stop it altogether, then the other problems that afflicted society would disappear. This is why there was so much emphasis on temperance and prohibition. They attracted much more attention than the other issues because drinking was viewed as the fundamental problem.

Churches took up the anti-alcohol cause because of their historic involvement in moral issues. Before civil courts took over, ecclesiastical courts had jurisdiction over moral and religious issues. They judged cases involving sexual immorality, drunkenness, and general immorality as well as more focused religious issues such as blasphemy. Although they no longer had jurisdiction over such cases, the churches claimed to be guardians of morality, making their intervention in 'the drink question' understandable in historical terms. The churches also had a vested interest in the stability of marriages and families, in so far as many people identifying as Christians in the nineteenth century (it varied by place and class) married in church and had their children baptised.

The anti-alcohol movement targeted alcoholic beverages broadly, even though there was general agreement that distilled beverages (rum and whiskey in the United States) did most harm. Still, where prohibition was implemented, wine was included almost everywhere, and the position that wine was dangerous posed a dilemma for some Christians: if wine was sinful, how could Jesus have turned water into wine? Why was wine referred to positively as well as negatively in the Bible? And how could wine, one of Satan's works, represent the blood of Christ?

The solution was the 'two-wine theory' that a number of Christian Prohibitionists promoted in the early 1800s. According to this theory, the references to wine in the Bible referred to two beverages, rather than one: when wine was referred to in a positive way, it was grape juice, but when it was referred to in a negative way, it was fermented grape juice, or what we usually understand as wine. This meant, for example, that when Jesus turned water into wine at the wedding at Cana, he turned it into grape juice – which some might think a rather less impressive miracle. This interpretation makes little sense when read in broader context, as it has the steward at the wedding saying that it was usual to serve the better quality grape juice at the beginning of a celebration, rather than at the end – although it is possible to argue, of course, that palates can be tired by sugar as much as by alcohol. Another putative reference to grape juice in the Bible was Timothy's recommendation of it as an aid to digestion. As for fermented grape juice, which contains alcohol, it was only too easy to point to cases in the Bible where consuming it had led to dire consequences. The examples of Noah and Lot were frequently cited.

The two-wine explanation of the positive and negative references to wine led a number of churches to replace wine with grape juice for the purposes of communion. The process of pasteurization allowed grape juice to be produced without risk of fermentation, and producers of grape juice began to advertise 'unfermented wine' (an oxymoron) for use in communion. Despite aggressive advertising campaigns, few churches gave up wine for grape juice, and those that did were all Protestant. It is estimated that about 7 per cent of New York Episcopalian (essentially Anglican) congregations had replaced wine with grape juice by the middle of the 1800s. But the Methodist Episcopal Church, a supporter of temperance, did not endorse grape juice until 1880. A campaign was mounted in Great Britain to have the Anglican Church replace wine with grape juice, but it was unsuccessful. Even some clergy who were sympathetic to the anti-alcohol cause seem to have been reluctant to abandon the tradition of serving wine at communion. For the Catholic clergy it was a different issue, of course, because only the priest sipped the wine.

Some church leaders embraced grape juice not only for the purposes of communion, but for everyday drinking, a non-alcoholic version of the centuries-old endorsement by churches of wine as a daily beverage. Frederic R. Lees, a Methodist anti-alcohol activist, wrote in a commentary on Deuteronomy 32:14 (which refers to drinking 'the blood of the grape') that 'Among the blessings of the good land that the Israelites were "to go up and possess" was the blood of the grape, which in its unfermented, uncorrupted state is proved, by chemical analysis, to constitute one of the most perfect of alimentary substances – to be really food and drink in one.'

There were, moreover, some churches where the issue of substituting grape juice for wine was moot because they did not provide wine at communion in any case. In the later nineteenth century a number of new churches were established that reflected the prevailing views about alcohol and forbade their members to drink. Denominations such as the Church of Jesus Christ of the Latter Day Saints (Mormons), the Church of Christ, Scientist, and the Salvation Army all eschewed alcohol and did not provide wine as part of their rituals. Mormons, who understand transubstantiation in symbolic rather than literal terms, use water instead of wine in their weekly communion; the Church of Christ, Scientist, has a communion without any bread or wine, while the Salvation Army has no communion ritual at all.

During the twentieth century there have been few major developments in the relationship of wine to religion, but one important change was a shift in the Catholic Church's position on wine in communion. In the 1960s the Second Vatican Council abandoned the doctrine that celebrating communion under two kinds was heretical. It allowed for cases where the laity might receive the wine, after a hiatus of about 700 years. These cases included people who were newly baptised or newly confirmed, the bride and bridegroom at a wedding, and the relatives and friends of a newly ordained priest. The range of permitted lay people and occasions expanded and by 1978 bishops in the United States allowed communion under both kinds at all masses, as long as the priest was satisfied that it could be done 'in an orderly and reverent manner'. In communions in the United States and elsewhere, wine is being restored to the status it had had in the early Church.

This issue aside, religion plays a relatively minor part in modern wine cultures. As far as we can tell, there is little difference between Protestants and Catholics in patterns of wine consumption, and certainly less than can be plotted among different ethnic, generational, and income groups. If the Vatican City regularly posts the highest per capita wine consumption rate in the world, it might have something to do with the Church's historically positive attitude toward wine. But it is very likely more a reflection of the fact that Vatican City is disproportionately populated by older men, the key wine-drinking demographic almost everywhere.

4

WINE AND LANDSCAPE

In 1584 the French philosopher and essayist Michel de Montaigne was travelling with a party of companions near Mulhouse, in Alsace. He noted in his diary that one day 'in the morning we came across a fine, broad plain, flanked on its left side by slopes covered with vines that were beautiful and very well cultivated and so extensive that the Gascons [people from the Bordeaux region] who were there said they had never seen the equal'. The vineyards he was referring to were in what is now the Haut-Rhin region, home to most of Alsace's Grand Cru vineyards. But what struck Montaigne and his companions was not the quality of the wine (which they had not tasted) but the sheer extent of the vineyards that covered the slopes. It impressed even his travelling companions from Bordeaux, where the area planted in vines had increased dramatically in the previous centuries – largely to meet foreign demand for clairet, the light red wine that was then Bordeaux's signature wine, and which became popular in England as 'claret'.

Unlike Montaigne and his company, who were so impressed by vine-covered slopes, anyone who visits many of the world's wine regions today will very likely soon become blasé at the sight of vineyards covering hundreds of hectares and stretching far into the distance. These are the landscapes of wine regions as diverse as Champagne in France, La Mancha in Spain, the Barossa Valley in Australia, and the Central Valley in Chile. In these and many other regions, viticulture has become the dominant and even the sole form of agriculture as it has progressively taken over land that had been used for other agricultural purposes. In Paso Robles, in central California, much of the land now in vines was formerly dedicated to farming beef cattle, while in many parts of New Zealand sheep and dairy cattle have been shunted aside to make room for grapes. (In New Zealand it is not only sheep that vastly outnumber people; vines now easily outnumber sheep.) In yet other cases, vineyards have been extended to areas that had not before been cultivated. Some grow where the land is too steep for other forms of cultivation, as in the Mosel Valley, where slopes can be as steep as 70 degrees; some vines are planted at altitudes that are too high for other crops, as they are in the foothills of the Andes in Argentina; other vineyards have been planted in areas that were previously forest or scrubland, such as the vineyards in plots cleared from garrigue in Languedoc; yet other vineyards, such as many in Bordeaux's Médoc district, are located on previously marshy areas that were drained specifically for viticulture.

While these developments were and are based on calculations by landowners that producing wine would be a more profitable way of using their land, it is likely that not everyone was happy about the disruption to the landscape that planting vines led to. People who are not interested in wine were probably not thrilled to see vines displace other forms of agriculture or encroach on forests, woodland, or marshes that were home to game and other wildlife. In his witty and perceptive book on Germany, *Germania*, Simon Winder notes that German wine producers 'battle constantly against a cold, rough climate and short summer', but he continues 'Germany does have some fabulous wine areas. The train trip from Koblenz to Trier down the Mosel Valley is a hymn to grapes, with every tiny jut or near-vertical slope stuffed with vines. For non-drinkers it might seem a rather depressing monoculture – the Mosel must have looked very pretty before wine wrecked it – not unlike driving through an oil-palm or rubber plantation. But for those, like me, in favour, it is a grapey Angkor Wat.'

Whether or not it has been universally welcomed, the result is that, over time, vines have occupied an increasing part of the land surface in many parts of the world, although the world's total viticultural area peaked in about 2003 and has declined somewhat since. Even so, vineyards occupy only a small part of the earth's cultivated surface. The world's total vineyard area is about 7.5 million hectares, which is a small but significant decline from the almost 8 million hectares recorded in 2003. These 7.5 million hectares represent about twice the area of land dedicated to growing tea (3.7 million hectares) but are somewhat less than the 10.5 million hectares devoted to growing coffee beans.

Despite the recent decline in world vineyard area (which is almost certain to be slowly reversed in the coming decades) there are many more hectares of vines today than at almost any time in history – despite the fact that some national vineyard areas have shrunk dramatically, including those of Europe's two biggest wine producers. The vineyard area of Italy declined by half between 1970 and 2015, going from 1.3 million to 680,000 hectares. In France there has been a staggering decline in vineyard area in the last 150 years, from 2.5 million hectares in the 1870s to about 780,000 hectares today, a decline of about two-thirds. The area occupied by vines in France continues to decline steadily, year after year. In contrast Spain, which is Europe's other major wine producer, has seen its vineyard area stabilize since 2011, after some significant shrinkage in the preceding four years (2008 to 2011).

The steady overall contraction of Europe's vineyard area since 2000 largely accounts for the decline in the area under vines worldwide because of the importance of European wine to world production. Although some wine regions outside Europe have expanded, they have not yet done so enough to counteract the decline of Europe's vineyards. The most important driver of growth is China, which now has almost 850,000 hectares of vines, making it second only to Spain (with a little over a million hectares) in terms of the size of its vineyard area. Between 2012 and 2016, China's vineyard area grew by a fifth, by far the fastest rate of increase anywhere. If China's vineyard area continues to expand as it has in the last decade or so, it will begin to compensate for losses in Europe. It is quite easy to foresee China becoming the world's biggest producer of wine, as vineyards extend their presence across the regions suitable for viticulture.

It is a dramatic understatement to say that the extent and the dynamic state of the world's vineyards today is far removed from the early status of grape vines. Growing wild, as members of the genus *Vitis*, grape vines were part of the landscapes of much of Asia and North America for millions of years. But only in the last few thousand years, when they have been domesticated and cultivated, have they in any way stood out from other flora. Instead, for most of their history, grape vines were integrated into their biodiverse environments. The approximately sixty species in the genus *Vitis* grow in various ways and in diverse contexts. Some grow up trees, seeking the sunlight needed to ripen their fruit, while others trail along the ground; some flourish in forests, others thrive along riverbanks.

One species, *Vitis vinifera sylvestris* – the forest-dwelling, tree-climbing species that now produces the great bulk of the world's wine today and includes varieties such as Chardonnay, Riesling, Merlot, and Pinot Noir – stands out, because it is the main species to have been domesticated and widely planted for wine production. A few other species are used for raisins and currants, and for products such as grape juice and jelly. But grape varieties other than *Vitis vinifera* are also used for wine, even though in very small volumes. Some varieties of the *Vitis labrusca* species, such as Catawba and Niagara, are used to make wine in some regions of the United States, as is Scuppernong, a variety of the *Vitis rotundifolia* species. Non-*vinifera* varieties have also been employed to create hybrids when they possess desirable characteristics such as cold-hardiness or resistance to phylloxera. At the same time, dozens of species of *Vitis* that are not used for wine or any other produce continue to grow wild in North America and Asia, largely ignored by humans.

When people began to use grapes to make wine, they undoubtedly at first picked the grapes from the vines as they grew wild without any human intervention. Very likely they initially picked the same grapes to eat fresh and – although this is all speculation – the first wine was made by accident when grapes intended for eating were crushed under their own weight and the juice fermented. At this early point, whether grapes were for eating or making wine, the species and variety must have been unimportant; people picked any grapes that were to hand. What eventually became important was the suitability of the grapes to make wine, no matter what the volume or quality, and the reasonable proximity of the vines to human settlements. An archaeologist who helped excavate the oldest known winemaking facility, dating back 8,000 years and located in the South Caucasus region of Georgia, speculated that the grapes that were processed in it had been growing wild on the nearby hillsides and were harvested and brought to the community to be fermented.

EARLY VINEYARDS

With the development of settled communities in the Neolithic period and the spread of cultivation and agriculture, some species and varieties of grapes were clearly found to be more suitable than others for winemaking – perhaps because they had a better flesh-to-seeds ratio or smaller seeds, or simply made better-flavoured wine. These varieties were transplanted into designated plots – the earliest vineyards – and over time, as varieties were even more carefully selected and bred, they became the grape varieties used to make wine today. Many of these varieties, such as Chardonnay, Pinot Grigio, Merlot, and Cabernet Sauvignon, are familiar to wine drinkers, but most are not. The standard reference work, *Wine Grapes* by Jancis Robinson, Julia Harding, and José Vouillamoz, lists more than 1,300 varieties used to make wine throughout the world. It includes not only the couple of dozen varieties familiar to most wine drinkers, but also such little-known varieties as Gamaret, Maligia, Prunesta, and Shevka.

A critical underpinning of the success of *Vitis vinifera* was the evolution of the wild species, *Vitis vinifera sylvestris*, from being dioecious to hermaphroditic. Dioecious vines have male flowers on one plant and female flowers on another, so that pollination is needed for fruit to form. Hermaphroditic vines have flowers that are both male and female. They thus produce fruit spontaneously, which makes them far more reliable as producers and enables them to be used commercially. How and at what point in the process of domestication this change took place, we do not know, but it was after vines were taken from their indigenous habitat in forests and woods, and transplanted in the biodiverse gardens that were the earliest vineyards.

Needless to say, we have no information on the size of these vineyards, how the vines in them were spaced and organized (in rows or randomly), and how they grew – whether they trailed along the ground, grew up the trunks of trees, or were trained up dedicated stakes driven into the ground to stand in for trees. Among early depictions of vines, a relief from the royal palace at Nineveh (about 650 BC) shows King Ashurbanipal and his queen drinking wine from shallow cups, while seated under a bower of grape vines. This suggests that vines were trained in a way that is similar to a pergola system where the grapes hang down from a trellis supported by vertical posts. This method of training vines provides some protection from birds (the bunches of grapes are hidden from birds as they fly over the vineyard) and it also enables farmers to grow some shade-tolerant crops under the pergola.

Even earlier Egyptian representations of viticulture and winemaking, dating from about 1450 BC, also depict vines trained the same way. The vines are shown growing vertically from the trunk, running overhead, and then down the other side. With the vines planted side by side in a straight line, the arbour effectively became a tunnel of vines. These Egyptian paintings show big bunches of grapes hanging from the sides and roof of the tunnel, with a few stray, untrained canes hanging down to give these idealized images a touch of verisimilitude. The grape harvesters are shown in the middle of the arbour, picking grapes from the sides and roof. Sometimes the trellis is high enough that the harvesters are able to stand upright, but sometimes the roof of vines is so low that the pickers have to crouch.

Despite the suggestion that vines were planted in straight lines and on trellises in Egypt, we have little information on the patterns of planting in most other parts of the ancient world. Were vines planted in rows or were they planted randomly, like trees in a forest? Spaces between rows are needed when animals and machinery are used in vineyards, but not when grapes were harvested by hand or when animals were simply let loose to graze at will among vines. We might expect patterns of planting to show some consistency as knowledge and techniques of viticulture were transferred from region to region. If the Egyptian vineyards looked the way they are depicted in wall paintings, we might assume that the Egyptians learn to train vines in an arbour from the regions to the east (such as Mesopotamia) where wine was produced earlier, and that the Egyptians in turn passed this technique on to vineyard owners in Crete and the Greek mainland.

MEDIEVAL AND EARLY MODERN VINEYARDS

To judge by images of vineyards, there seems to have been no standard consistent system of planting vines during the Middle Ages. An illuminated illustration from the Khamseh of Nizami, now in Iran, dating from the sixteenth century, clearly shows vines growing on an overhead trellis system. The vertical stakes that support the trellis have forked tops in which the cross-beams are secured, and the vines are trained along the roof of the trellis. But an illumination from the *Très Riches Heures du Duc de Berry*, dating from the early 1400s and showing the grape harvest in northern France in September, equally clearly depicts bush vines (without any external support, such as stakes or trellis) growing randomly. A third image, from a book on distilling published in 1500, shows several techniques of training vines. There are vines growing on flat-topped and inverted U-shaped trellises, vines trained up trees, and vines growing up stakes that are evenly spaced in rows. But vines growing randomly are not shown.

In the Early Modern period, from about 1500 to 1800, we continue to find various patterns of planting. A manual on viticulture written in the 1620s by a native of Languedoc to guide English settlers in Virginia recommended planting vines equally spaced in rows. It suggested laying a length of rope along the ground to make sure the rows were straight. The vines were to be planted directly into the soil, but the author also suggested training them up trees or poles stuck in the ground. Training vines up trees growing in woods and forests would have led to a random pattern of planting. While touring France in the late eighteenth century, the English agronomist Arthur Young noted several patterns of planting vines. In general, he noted 'The vines are planted promiscuously, three or four feet or two and a half from each other' and were 'tied to the props [stakes] with small straw bands'. But near Toulouse he also saw vines being trained up trees: 'Here, for the first time, see rows of maples, with vines, trained in festoons, from tree to tree; they are conducted by a rope of bramble, vine cutting, or willow. They give many grapes, but bad wine.' The account books of Burgundy vignerons in the eighteenth century show purchases of stakes and ties, indicative of the method used there at the time.

Despite scattered evidence that vines were in some places trained up trees or planted in rows, the overall weight of evidence suggests that throughout most of Europe until the late nineteenth and early twentieth centuries, the straight rows of vines that are the rule today were rare. Instead, vines were generally planted randomly in vineyards, largely because instead of being planted individually, vines were propagated by a method known as *provignage*. This involves taking a cane from an existing vine, stretching it out and burying the end of it. The part of the cane that is buried grows roots and becomes a new vine, after which the piece of cane linking it to its parent can be cut – although that is not necessary.

As far as planting patterns are concerned, vines in such vineyards were spaced as far apart as the regenerating cane would extend. In principle it is possible to position vines in what would probably be ragged rows, but it would have been easier to bury canes wherever they did not interfere with existing vines. There was, after all, no reason at that time to plant vines in straight rows. Randomly planted they might have been, but French vineyards were well looked after, as Arthur Young noted in the late 1700s: 'their vineyards are gardens; the turnips of Norfolk, the carrots of Suffolk, the beans of Kent, and the cabbages of an English gentleman are not so clean as the vines of France.'

THE EXTENT OF VINEYARDS

We have spotty and incomplete information on the extent of vineyards over time, whether it is of the size of individual vineyards or the area planted in vines in specific districts, regions, or later in entire countries. But it is clear that there was no smooth, linear increase in the area of land planted in vines. Rather, because vineyards were the basis of a wine business – whether at the smaller scale of an individual vigneron's household, the substantial holdings of a monastery, or at a big-production corporate level – financial and economic calculations underlay decisions to increase or decrease the area planted in vines. Decisions to extend the size of vineyards might result from a shortage of wine, increased demand, rising prices, or all three, while a fall in demand and prices might result in decisions to allow vineyards to fall into decay or to pull out the vines and replant the land with more profitable crops.

In some cases we can only guess at motivations. During the last millennium BC, the Assyrians embarked on a massive vine-planting programme. In what Patrick McGovern refers to as the 'Assyrian Domesday Book' they recorded tens of thousands of grape vines in the upper Balikh Valley. More were planted, some up hillsides as high as 1500 metres – rather like many high-altitude vineyards in Argentina today – in the eastern regions of the kingdom north-east of Nineveh. But the Assyrians also destroyed vineyards. When they crossed into what is now Azerbaijan in about 700 BC, they noted the extensive vineyards at the fortresses of Urartu. Practising a scorched-earth policy, the Assyrian armies 'came down like the wolf on the fold', as Lord Byron put it, but their aim was not to kill sheep but to destroy the vineyards of their enemy – while at the same time helping themselves to the wine stored in the buried ceramic jars (*kvevris*) in which it had been made.

Vines fill the landscape in a harvest scene,
probably from the sixteenth century. Engraving (no date).

As for the initial spread of vineyards in Greece and Italy, it was almost certainly a response to demand, probably from the elites who had become accustomed to drinking imported wine from places such as Crete and Egypt. When vineyards were planted in Greece (at first close to centres of population) the supply of wine increased, and it in turn stimulated additional demand. In both Greece and Italy, wine was by far the most common alcoholic beverage – in fact, it was for all intents and purposes the only alcoholic beverage, because beer was not produced and mead was made in very small volumes. As virtually the sole alcoholic drink in Greece, wine was such an important product – with cereal and olive oil, it was one of the three most-traded commodities in the Mediterranean region – that vineyards soon spread beyond the mainland to the islands of the Aegean Sea. As for the Romans, wine became fundamental to their diet, and they planted vineyards throughout their European empire in the first couple of centuries AD.

The expansion of vineyards in Europe seems to have stalled when the Roman Empire broke up and much of western Europe was dominated by the migrant populations from eastern Europe (the so-called 'Barbarian invasions') but there was another surge of vine planting at the end of the first millennium AD. There is some evidence that around the year 1000 the climate warmed in a number of regions, enabling grapes to ripen on a regular basis in areas where viticulture had been marginal or impossible. Just as important, Europe's population increased, and clusters of large towns (with relatively prosperous wine-drinking middle classes engaged in business and the professions) developed in northern Italy and northern Europe.

All these conditions encouraged the expansion of vineyards in order to provide wine for the new and growing markets. Some regions, such as Tuscany in north-central Italy, supplied wine to nearby population centres that included Florence, Venice, Genoa, and Milan. Others, such as vineyards in Germany's Rhine and Mosel Valleys and in northern and western France, shipped their wines to London, Ghent, Brussels, Bruges, and other markets in northern Europe as well as in the Baltic area. As Paris grew, so did the area in surrounding regions that was planted with vines.

The number of vineyards along the Rhine and Mosel Rivers seems to have increased appreciably at about this time. One study shows that along the Rhine River between Bonn and Bingen and along the Mosel River between Koblenz and Trier, about seventy vineyards were mentioned in documents before 900 AD but another sixty-five were first mentioned between 901 and 1050. In other words, it could well be that as many vineyards were planted in the 150 years after 900 as in the preceding 700 or 800 years.

Bordeaux's vineyards also expanded at this time. In the early 1100s, viticulture was largely confined to the gravel soils around the town itself, but as the wine trade with England grew, vines extended as far as 4 or 5 kilometres from the town walls, until they encountered the small communities of Bordeaux's hinterland. Here vines were planted with other crops and generally took up no more than a fifth of the land. In some areas – north of the town of Bordeaux and on the Right Bank of the Garonne – marshes were drained so that vines could be planted. Some of the region's vineyards were surrounded by hedges or marked off by ditches, but most were not. Bordeaux's viticultural landscape throughout the Medieval and Early Modern periods must have had an open and rural appearance quite different from that of today.

But the growth of vineyards was neither steady nor constant. Throughout much of Europe in the late 1300s, the Black Death killed a third or more of the population, reducing demand for wine (and all goods and services) as well as cutting into the labour supply needed to tend the vines. Many vineyards were simply abandoned and effectively disappeared, but as population and markets began to grow again, there was another surge of vine planting, part of a general recovery of agriculture. It was at this time, at the end of the 1400s, that the Florentine humanist and agronomist Michelangiolo Tanaglia encouraged the expansion of vineyards in his verse treatise *De Agricultura*:

Now is the time, in my opinion,
On the open hills to never tire,
Of planting vines, of the best kind,
Or of attending the plant of Bacchus.

ATTEMPTS TO PREVENT THE EXPANSION OF VINEYARDS

The expansion of vineyards as a response to growing demand was no doubt welcomed by people who had grown accustomed to drinking wine. But at some historical moments the rapid spread of vineyards was a cause for concern and there were attempts to rein it in. One of the earliest examples was an edict issued by the Roman emperor Domitian in 92 AD that forbade the planting of any more vines in Italy and ordered the grubbing up of half the vines already planted in Rome's non-Italian territories. It is not clear whether the edict was motivated by a belief that vines were taking over land that was needed for cereal production or a desire to protect Italian wine producers from competition. In the end the edict was widely ignored and it was repealed about two centuries later, in 282 AD.

Even though it doesn't provide us with any statistics on vineyard area, Domitian's ban alerts us to perceptions of the spread of viticulture in the first century AD, when Romans were extending wine production throughout Europe. In the years before the edict, vineyards were planted in nearly all France's major modern wine regions, including Languedoc, Bordeaux, Burgundy, and the Rhône Valley, as well as in parts of what are now Germany, Austria, and Poland.

It is possible that Domitian's edict was a result of lobbying by wine producers on the Italian peninsula who wanted to sell their wine throughout Europe and sought to reduce competition. If that was so, it was echoed by one issued by King Philip II of Spain almost exactly 1,500 years later, when Spanish producers opposed the planting of vast vineyards in Spain's South American colonies. We have no reliable information on the number of hectares of vines planted as the Spanish armies swept south from Mexico from 1520, but within three decades they had established substantial vineyards in what are now Peru, Chile, and Argentina. An indication of the extent of vineyards is that in 1567 a Spanish official called for the planting of 1,000 to 1,500 more vines in an existing vineyard near Lake Titicaca, in southern Peru.

Some estimates suggest that river valleys in Peru proved so good for vines that by the 1560s, barely twenty years after the first vines were planted, the region's vineyards amounted to thousands of hectares. More is known of specific settlements. In 1596 a farm in the Escapagua settlement consisted of 22 hectares of land, of which 4 hectares were planted with 10,000 vines. As a general rule it seems that about 10 per cent of cultivated land was given over to vineyards.

The impetus for viticulture in South America was not only the markets resulting from the spread of Spanish settlements on the Pacific coast and inland but also the indigenous labour force in the lucrative silver mines. Foreshadowing the supply of cheap spirits to blacks in South Africa's gold mines in the late 1800s and 1900s, much of the wine made in Peru was distilled into brandy for the workers in the silver mines that enriched Spain in the sixteenth century. In the eighteenth century the town of Moquegua, in southern Peru, was distilling almost 7 million litres of wine into brandy each year. In addition to brandy, Peru also produced pisco, but there is an on-going debate whether pisco was first made in Peru or across the border in the northern valleys of Chile.

The success of regional wine industries throughout South America was dismaying to Spanish wine producers, who had rebuilt their wine industry in the 1500s after the expulsion of the Muslim authorities. Spanish vineyard owners had hoped to expand their market by supplying wine to their compatriots who settled in the New World and who needed the wine to replicate the daily diet they had enjoyed in Spain. Producers petitioned King Philip II and in 1595 he issued an edict forbidding further vine planting in Spain's colonies, except by monasteries. As in the case of Emperor Domitian's edict, Philip's was widely ignored, not least because locally produced wine was far less expensive than wine imported from Spain. Bringing Spanish wine so far was difficult and expensive, involving shipping barrels across the ocean, then transporting them overland to the Pacific before getting them down the Pacific coast to their destinations. Much of the wine arrived in poor condition and that (together with the higher prices that included the cost of transportation) led landowners, especially in Chile and Argentina, to continue the planting that became the basis of two of the world's most important wine industries.

In the 1700s, attempts were made to restrain the expansion of vineyards in France, although in quite different circumstances. The winter of 1709 was devastating to the country's vineyards (and other crops), with temperatures falling to -16°C in Montpellier and -24°C in Bordeaux. Contemporary accounts (some believable, others not) tell of ink freezing solid in inkwells, frozen birds falling from the sky, and water freezing as it was poured from pitcher to cup. The cold temperatures killed many vines, and those that survived were severely damaged. Much of the wine that was in cellars awaiting sale, only two or three months after fermentation, froze and expanded, splitting the barrels it was stored in. The upshot was a shortage of wine from the 1709 vintage throughout much of France and short crops in the following years because of the damage to vines. A priest in Angers, in the important Loire region, wrote that two-thirds of the vines in Anjou had been killed by the cold.

Strictly speaking, all that French wine producers needed to do was to replace the dead and damaged vines to bring production back to where it had been before the devastating winter. But what they actually did was expand the area planted in vineyards dramatically. It was probably in response to the immediate shortage of wine and the high prices that merchants would pay for whatever wine was available. There seems to have been no sense that in a few years, when the new vines in existing vineyards and the new vineyards began to produce wine, prices might plummet under the impact of a wine surplus. As we shall see, their decision was the right one over the longer term, but it initially ran into problems. In 1724 the royal representative in Bordeaux wrote, more in alarm than approval, 'for ten leagues [about 40 kilometres] around [the city of] Bordeaux you see nothing but vines. The same mania has taken hold in the rest of the region.' The same happened elsewhere in France. In Béarn, a tiny province in the foothills of the Pyrenees, peasants protested in 1725 at the planting of vineyards on parts of the higher land that had been used for other crops. The authorities agreed with them and in 1727 prohibited the planting of grape vines on land suitable for cereals. For good measure, they ordered the ripping out of any vineyards planted after 1714.

There was general alarm throughout France at the vineyard planting 'mania'. The overriding concern was that vineyards were encroaching on arable lands, and that for all wine might be an essential part of the daily diet for those who could afford it, France still had to produce an adequate supply of bread, which was the staple diet of the mass of the French population. Anxiety about a shortage of grain was based not only on the altruistic wish to see people adequately fed, but on the need to maintain public order: the poor of France, who lived on the verge of indigence and hunger, had a rich tradition of rioting when cereal or bread was in short supply or became expensive. Grain and bread riots were a feature of the French social landscape in times of hardship, but no one resorted to direct action of this sort when there was a shortage of wine or the price of wine suddenly rose. It was better to have a shortage of wine than one of bread.

As a result of the flurry of vine planting following the terrible winter of 1709, the various Parlements (royal courts) throughout France, which had responsibility for the wellbeing of their regions, began to react. In 1722 the Parlement of Metz, in Lorraine (which was then a more significant wine region than it is now) ordered the ripping out of vines planted since 1700 in areas where vines had not been planted before. In Bordeaux a 1724 edict ordered the ripping out of all vines planted since 1709 and forbade any new plantings. In 1731 the Parlement of Besançon ordered recent plantings grubbed up. Finally, in the same year, the royal government forbade any vine planting anywhere within the kingdom without the express permission of the king.

Landowners who wanted to profit from high wine prices pushed back against these various edicts. One was the political philosopher Montesquieu, who owned vineyards in the Entre-Deux-Mers and Graves districts of Bordeaux and who in 1725 had bought land in Pessac, near the Haut-Brion estate, to plant more vineyards. He opposed the bans on planting on the ground that they interfered with the natural right of owners to use their property as they wished. In the end, however, these bans went largely ignored, and when a survey showed that vineyard land had expanded without causing a grain shortage, the royal prohibition on planting was repealed in 1758. As it happened, the population of France, which had been largely stationary for a century or more, began to grow rapidly from the 1730s, thus increasing the demand for wine and other products. Although this growth in France's population could not have been predicted in 1709 (and was not even acknowledged by economists until about 1770) the expansion of the country's vineyards in the first half of the eighteenth century proved to be beneficial to French wine drinkers.

By the time the French Revolution began in 1789, many regions of France were well planted in vines. The English agronomist Arthur Young toured the country three times (in 1787, 1788, and 1789) and commented on agriculture in general and viticulture in particular. He noted that it was virtually impossible to calculate the area of land under vines and wine production, not least because of the 'infinite variety of

French measures of land and liquids' – until measures were standardized during the French Revolution, each province (and many towns and districts) used its own. Young thought the best contemporary estimates of total French vineyard area were about 1.6 million arpents (about 320,000 hectares) but for some reason he himself was 'inclined to calculate the vineyards of France at five millions of acres' – equivalent to a little more than two million hectares.

It is impossible to get any reliable sense of the extent of vineyards in France (or elsewhere, for that matter) at this time. Young also provided impressions such as this of Champagne: 'At Epernay, etc. in Champagne, two-thirds of all the country around, about Aye, Cumiere, Piery, Disy, Hautvilliers, etc. [is] under vines: and here all the famous Champagne wines are made.' In the Loire Valley, near the Château de Chambord, Young remarked that 'the quantity of vines is very great; they have them very flourishing on a flat poor blowing sand. How well satisfied would my friend Le Blanc be if his poorest sands at Cavenham gave him 100 dozen of good wine per acre per annum!'

Young described vines as inhabiting every sort of landscape: 'I found them on the noble and fertile plain of the Garonne; on the richest lands in the vale which extends from Narbonne to Nîmes; in the vales of Dauphiné and the Loire; and, in a word, indiscriminately on every sort of land in all the wine provinces, but I found them also on such rocky and bad soils as I have described, and in so great quantities as to show how well adapted they are to such soils and situations.' He also noted that he saw 'in every part of France … new vineyards already planted, or begun to be planted, on corn lands'. It was very likely this impression of the ubiquity of vineyards that led him to such a high estimate of the extent of vineyards in France.

Although the area of land devoted to viticulture in Europe and elsewhere expanded from the Middle Ages onwards, the trajectory of growth was anything but smooth. At times vineyard area declined precipitously as a result of such factors as sudden population decline, devastating climatic events, or disastrous vine diseases. At other times the area devoted to vines expanded rapidly. But whether increase and decline were steady or sudden, they often reflected the broader context of changes in the size of population and in the economy, which either favoured or discouraged investment in viticulture and wine production.

THE CHARACTER OF VINEYARDS

To this point we have been discussing the landscape of viticulture in broad terms, rather than in terms of individual parcels of vines. For the most part we have little information on the size of vineyards in this sense – except for vineyards in Europe owned by the Church. The ecclesiastical authorities often recorded the size of their vineyards, and whenever vineyards were donated to the Church or to religious houses, the transfer of ownership noted the location and size of the land concerned. For example, donations to parishes in Burgundy from the sixteenth to the eighteenth centuries specified the name of the donor, the location of the vineyard, and its size expressed in *ouvrées* (there were about 23 *ouvrées* to the hectare).

But only since the nineteenth century have statistics on vineyard size and viticultural areas been systematically kept, particularly as authorities have wanted to keep track of wine production and wine quality. Where yields are regulated as hectolitres of wine per hectare of vineyard, as they are throughout much of Europe today, it is necessary to keep track of both the volume of wine produced and the area of the vineyards from which the grapes were sourced.

One important transformation of the vineyard landscape in many regions has been the shift from vines sharing space with other crops to viticulture becoming the sole form of agriculture. The image of grape vines growing among other crops can be traced back thousands of years. In ancient Egypt, for example, vines were commonly grown in walled gardens among other plants and trees that undoubtedly played host to indigenous yeasts. One private garden belonging to a high official of Saqqara in about 2550 BC was described as an estate '200 cubits long and 200 cubits wide … very plentiful trees and vines were set out, a great quantity of wine was made there'. The 40,000 square cubits would have given this garden an area of about a hectare, but we do not know what proportion of it was planted in vines. Unless we can be sure that it was mostly vines, it seems safer to call it a garden (with mixed crops) than to refer to it as a vineyard.

The practice of planting vines alongside or among other crops appears to have lasted a long time in some regions, particularly on land farmed by small-scale producers who cultivated several crops as a hedge against any one of them failing in any year. In Burgundy we learn of the planting of other crops with vines in the late eighteenth century from an odd source: the criminal courts. In 1791 Antoine Laborey, a vigneron who lived in Dijon, was convicted of stealing produce that was growing in different *climats* (vineyards) at the northern end of the Côte de Nuits. Several witnesses said they saw Laborey stealing asparagus from the Saint Jacqueret *climat* (possibly the Saint Jacques *climat* in Marsannay-la-Côte, which is not too far from Dijon) and peaches from another. One witness, also a vigneron, said that he had been in his own vineyard tending his cherry trees, when he saw Laborey stealing the asparagus. Asparagus, peaches, and cherries, then, shared space with grape vines in some of Burgundy's vineyards, and it is reasonable to think there were other crops, too.

As for how long growing vines as part of polyculture continued, it clearly persisted in France to the late 1800s and came to light during the attempts to eradicate phylloxera in the 1880s and 1890s. Among the available treatments was spraying vines with chemicals, including carbon disulphide, which was highly toxic and flammable. The problem was that many small-scale vignerons, especially in the south of France, continued to grow vines and other crops together, and although chemical treatments killed phylloxera and saved their vines, they also killed the other crops. For this reason, many of these vignerons rejected the treatments and said they would rather take their chances with phylloxera.

These and other examples suggest that planting vines together with other crops continued in some places to the twentieth century, although we have no way of knowing how extensive the practice was at any given time. It probably became less common among larger producers who found viticulture and wine production profitable, but changed more slowly in the vineyards of small producers who farmed on a subsistence basis and needed a range of produce or other crops as a back-up in case the grape harvest failed. The priest of Volnay, in Burgundy, noted that in a number of years in the 1700s hail damaged not only the vines but also other crops, such as cereals and fruit. Although he did not specify the relative location of the crops, it is likely that the fruit trees, at least, shared land with the vines.

In recent years there has been some movement back to planting other crops with grape vines because biodiversity promotes a healthier environment for the vines. This is a common feature in vineyards farmed biodynamically, but it is increasingly found everywhere. Often biodiversity involves growing groundcover to provide nutrients and to help deal with vineyard pests, but in some cases other crops are integrated into vineyards. For example, at Rocca delle Macìe, in the Chianti Classico region of Tuscany, several varieties of olive trees share the land with vines. Southbrook Vineyards, in Ontario's Niagara Peninsula, uses its land to raise sheep as well as grapes.

Over the long haul vines and vineyards have had a major impact on landscapes in many parts of the world. They have transformed landscapes and at this point in their history, when the area under vineyards is relatively stable, it is difficult to imagine what it was like when vines seemed to be taking over. It is hard for us to imagine the steep slopes of the Mosel Valley without vines or what the Douro River Valley looked like before terraces were built on the schist slopes to facilitate the planting of vines. In other areas, where vines have disappeared, as in the regions around Paris that helped supply the capital with wine for centuries until the early 1800s, it is hard to imagine vineyards flourishing. For all that they are part of agriculture and imposed on landscapes, vineyards in many regions have become naturalized. They have become part of the landscape.

PUTTING LANDSCAPE INTO WINE

If wine has had an impact on landscape, landscape is sometimes believed to reciprocate: not only does the landscape accommodate vines, but the landscape, the environment in which vines grow, is sometimes said to be expressed in the wines made from those grapes. These wines, their marketers are fond of saying, have a 'sense of place'. That, at least, is one interpretation of the notion of terroir, the idea that there are particular links between environment and wine. Terroir is the subject of a great deal of misunderstanding and confusion and it is a subject of vigorous and sometimes heated debate in the world of wine. What terroir is and what its significance might be are subjects that bear directly on the relationship of wine to landscape.

In one sense, the notion of terroir is more banal than complicated or controversial: that the environmental conditions in which grapes grow influence the quality and character of the grapes. By environmental conditions we mean principally the character and structure of the top strata of the soil (whether it is, for example, predominantly sand, loam, clay, or stony) and its substructure (such as limestone, basalt, and granite); temperature, rainfall, and sunshine hours and their daily and annual distribution; and the slope and exposure to the sun of the terrain the vines are planted on.

All those add up to the growing conditions of the vine, the landscape on which it is located. While a landscape might be thought of as composed exclusively of topographic and physical features – hills, valleys, plains, rivers, lakes, and the like – climate (expressed as weather) clearly also has a role, as any representation of a landscape demonstrates. Photographs, paintings, and other depictions of landscapes must always show weather conditions (rain, sunshine, stormy clouds) and changing the weather changes perceptions of the landscape – to the point that they are inseparable.

Soil character and structure remain essentially the same from year to year. It is true that there are constant changes as rain and wind cause erosion of the topmost layers, that wind may deposit new material, and that vineyard machinery compacts the ground, but these effects are generally gradual, allowing us to think of the soil as essentially constant over time. In contrast the weather varies each year and gives vintage variation to the wine. But weather patterns usually vary within limited ranges so that it is possible to generalize about the climatic conditions of any wine-producing district or region.

Understood in this strictly physical sense, the notion of terroir is uncontroversial because all plants and their produce perform differently in different growing conditions. Oranges grow in Florida and in the north of New Zealand's North Island, but they are markedly different, as are peaches grown in the Niagara region of Ontario, in Canada, from those grown in the south of France. But although oranges and peaches are generally labelled by provenance for retailing purposes, they are never said to reflect their terroir. To do so would be redundant, because terroir in its purely environmental sense means nothing more than the conditions the orange and peach trees were grown in and in which the fruit ripened. More to the point, the same is true of grapes grown to be eaten fresh: they might be labelled as coming from Chile, California, or Spain, but they are never explicitly thought of as being grown in a specific terroir, as their wine-producing counterparts often are.

The geographical provenance of wine is almost always shown on the label and it has become a key variable which consumers use to select one wine over another. But whereas that is all the information that might be given for other products, wines are often described in terms of the broad climatic conditions in which the vines grew. Wines with high acidity might come from cool-climate regions while others with intense fruit flavours or high alcohol might be made from grapes that grew in a warm climate. Even in these broad terms, of course, we must allow for abnormal vintages (an unusually warm growing season in a cool-climate region and vice versa), for viticultural practices such as early or late harvesting, and for winemaking practices such as drying grapes before pressing, chaptalization, and acidification.

Where the notion of terroir starts to become complicated is the attribution of specific qualities not to grapes that are defined by their environmental conditions, but to the wine made from the grapes. Viticulture is a branch of agriculture and therefore a human activity, but although myriad human decisions and actions lie behind a bunch of grapes ready to be pressed and vinified (where to plant, what to plant, how to space, when to harvest, and so on) it is still possible to see the character and quality of grapes as reflecting their growing conditions. Making wine from the grapes is a human activity where a winemaker can intervene as little as possible (as the makers of 'natural wine' do) or more intrusively.

The question is how much of the influence of the terroir, defined as the environment, can be detected after the wine is made. Wines that are called 'terroir-driven' are said to show where they came from, and the argument is often made that conventional winemaking obliterates the effects of terroir by the many techniques open to winemakers, including adding acid, sugar, and tannins, micro-oxygenation, controlled-temperature fermentation, and barrel ageing. Promoters of terroir argue that wine should reflect its growing conditions, and because the growing conditions of every location are unique – no two sites have the same combination of aspect, soil structure, precipitation, sunshine, and so on – every place where vines grow has a unique terroir. In this sense, by embodying its growing environment, a wine embodies the place where it originated.

When the argument is made that some wines – wines sometimes said to be 'terroir-driven' – have a sense of place, particular emphasis is given to the soil structure of the vineyard. It has become a commonplace to relate the character of some individual wines to the soils in which they grow. Wines with 'minerality' (a disputed term in itself) are often said to derive it from limestone or basalt, or from specific minerals or other properties in the soil. Referring to the Chablis wine region, the wine-searcher.com website states: '**Kimmeridgian soil** … contains greater levels of mineral-rich clay, as well as the essential marine fossils which are responsible for its significant lime content. **Kimmeridgian soil**s are the source of the trademark minerality in premier and grand cru wines from Chablis.' Wines from grapes that grow in heavier clay soils are sometimes said to have more body for that reason, and wines from the steeply sloped, slate-strewn vineyards of the Mosel Valley are often said to have a 'slatey' character.

Wines from vineyards growing in volcanic landscapes have come in for particular attention, perhaps because volcanoes, with their destructive and deadly potential, grab our attention more than merely steep hillsides and gentle south-facing slopes. Volcanoes have special resonance in Western culture, as do islands, where many volcanoes are located. Wines from volcanic regions as varied as Mount Etna on Sicily, the Canary Islands, and Santorini have sometimes been described as 'fiery', 'smoky', smelling of 'volcanic ash', and tasting of 'the fury of the earth'. The authoritative book on these wines, John Szabo's *Volcanic Wines* is subtitled 'Salt, Grit, and Power', implying that wines from vineyards in volcanic soils possess these qualities in common. Szabo argues that volcanic wines might be a discrete category of wines in that they have distinct qualities derived from relatively high levels of mineral salts and potassium in volcanic soils. He says there is no scientific evidence that volcanic wines have peculiar organoleptic properties, but that many tasters (including him) believe they do.

SOIL AND LANDSCAPE

As these examples show, soil has become privileged within the notion of terroir. Although the word generally refers to the whole environment in which vines grow, climate is rarely thought to be determinative of the essential character of wine. Climate is unstable and fickle, and is expressed as weather patterns that are never the same from one year to another. The soil is permanent and provides the foundation of the vineyard century after century – as we are reminded, from time to time, by advertisements for French wines that can trace their vineyards back hundreds of years.

Beyond the basic flavours and quality of their wine, back labels on wine bottles are as likely to inform consumers of the type of soil in the vineyard as anything else about the wine – although information on the generational depth of family-owned vineyards is also common. The label of a Pinot Noir from Ontario's Prince Edward County refers to the 'rocky, sparse, windswept soils where our estate vineyard is planted'. The label of a Syrah–Grenache blend from AOC Languedoc Grès de Montpellier notes that the 'terroir is characterized by round pebble gravels and sea sprays favouring the culture of the vine'. (This label also describes the wine as 'round'.) Even when texts such as these make no explicit link between soil and wine, it is implied. If the soil had no bearing on the wine, there would be no more point in describing it than telling a consumer the breed of the winemaker's dog.

However, the idea that soil can influence wine flavour and texture (at all or at perceptible levels) has been challenged by scientists such as Alex Maltman and Mark A. Matthews. Maltman describes what he calls the 'passive-descriptive approach' to explaining wine: 'You describe the geology and wine from place A (preferably with lots of nice maps, pictures, and big words) and then the geology from place B where, oh!, the wines are different! You then take it as read that it is the geology that is responsible for the differences, ignoring everything else and making no attempt to explain what it is the geology is supposed to be doing. It's so misleading, at so many levels.' Matthews's position is clear from the title of his book, *Terroir and Other Myths of Winegrowing*, although he devotes a much more complex and nuanced discussion to the subject in the text.

Reactions in the wine world to the arguments of scientists like Maltman and Matthews have varied, with some wine writers embracing their findings and others rejecting them. The English wine writer Andrew Jefford wrote an important column in *Decanter* in 2013 that called for a more careful description of the relationship between soil and wine: 'Maltman's painstakingly argued critique has certainly made me aware of the difficulties inherent in drawing any direct inference about aroma and flavour from vineyard soil and geology. I'm happy about using 'mineral', 'stone' or 'earth' in a strictly metaphorical sense, of course, to allude to a certain sensorial repertoire we associate with worked earth or rocks, just as we use cat's pee, cream or cassis in similar metaphorical sense ... The problem with wielding these metaphors, though, is that if I describe a wine whose vine is growing in slate as "slatey", the metaphor is quickly gobbled up by the literal image, and the trusting reader assumes a direct line of transmission.'

Other wine writers have been less favourable to critiques of the idea of terroir. When Matthews published his book on terroir in 2015, with its very title asserting that terroir was a myth, some wine writers reacted strongly. Writing in *The World of Fine Wine*, the English wine writer and scientist Jamie Goode dismissed the idea that terroir was a myth as an 'absurdity'. But later in the same review he offered a much more nuanced judgment that 'given a halfway sensible, conventional definition of terroir, I can't see many scientists accepting that it's a complete myth'.

Meanwhile in *Wine Spectator* the American wine writer Matt Kramer denounced Matthews and other terroir-sceptical scientists for their 'scientism' and argued that scientists don't understand wine: 'One of the features of Professor Matthews' book – and virtually all of the others of its sort penned by his fellow academic wine scientists – is that it never reports actually *tasting* wines, let alone trying to correlate tasting experience with academic knowledge. Nowhere ... does the author refer to a tasting experience. Such a thing is too subjective and thus inherently suspect.'

Kramer summarized Matthews as saying: 'Bottom line: There are no data proving that soil informs wine. Therefore it's a shuck. *Terroir* is a fake. Distinctions among wines are mere public relations for which the ambiguous word *terroir* is conveniently invoked. *Terroir* is a myth promulgated by romanticists such as wine writers and cynical marketing sorts seeking to distinguish their wines from those of the competition.' Kramer's response was: 'All I can say is this: Taste some wine. Is a good Chablis really the same as any other Chardonnay grown in a comparably cool climate, never mind whether the soil is chalk or clay or sand? Really? Does Cabernet Sauvignon grown in Stags Leap District taste the same as that grown on Howell Mountain?

Of course it doesn't. Anyone can taste the difference if presented with two well-made examples. Or ten such examples for that matter. Of course there are reasons: climate, microclimate, elevation, sunlight intensity, wine, rain and yes, soil. Believers in the existence of *terroir* are the first to mention all of these and more. Such differences are collectively called *terroir*. What's so hard to accept about that? What's so difficult in accepting such a notion as both real and legitimate?'

TERROIR IN HISTORY

If terroir is controversial today, it is perhaps because it has a very murky lineage and its limits and implications have never been clearly defined. How far does terroir go back in the history of wine? As with much of the history of wine, there is a great deal of lore that proves to be on shaky ground. It is often said that during the Middle Ages monks discovered terroir when they noticed that vines from one vineyard consistently produced wine that tasted different from wine made from grapes grown in a nearby vineyard. The terroir of each vineyard, it was said, accounted for the difference, even though the closest wines in each vineyard might be separated by only a metre or two. Monks are sometimes said to have chewed the dirt of their vineyards so as to understand its qualities.

Chewing dirt to understand its character was not unknown in earlier times, and there is one winery in the southern Rhône today where visitors are invited to taste samples of dirt from different parts of the vineyard along with wines from vines grown there, in order to appreciate the role that soil plays in wine character and quality. But the narratives of monks and terroir have virtually no documentary basis and they raise more questions than can be answered. For one thing, they suppose that monks made separate wines from different parcels of vines, no matter what their size – a very inefficient use of presses and vats. From what we know it is more likely that grapes from many parcels were pressed and fermented together (just as different grape varieties were) thus obliterating any differences there might have been among them.

Thomas Parker has set out the long-term history of the idea of terroir in his book, *Tasting French Terroir*, and one thing that emerges clearly is that for centuries the notion of terroir was applied as much to human character, art, food, and language, as to wine. Moreover, terroir was generally considered a negative thing, not something to be sought out and treasured. In general, until the eighteenth century, any evidence of terroir (*goût de terroir*) was a corruption and anyone looking for quality – whether it was in human character, art, food, language, or wine – was advised to search for purity and perfection that were not tainted and ruined by terroir.

Montaigne, whose observations on vineyards in Alsace opened this chapter, was to the fore in arguing that terroir determined the character of humans: 'the very form of our being – not only our colour, build, complexion, and behaviour, but our mental faculties as well – depends upon our native air, climate and terroir'. He goes on to liken humans to plants and animals in the way they relate to terroir: 'then men must vary as flora and fauna do: whether they are more warlike, just, equable, clever or dull, depends on where they were born. Here they are addicted to wine; there to robbery and lechery; here they are inclined towards superstition; there to belief; here to freedom; there to slavery ... all depending on inclinations arising from their physical environment. Change their location and, like trees, they take on a new character.'

By the physical environment and terroir, Montaigne and other writers in this vein meant essentially what is understood by terroir in the modern environmental sense: the soil and climate of a given area. But if humans were not rooted in the soil like plants, but lived on the surface of the earth, how did the soil have any influence? The active force here was the vapours that were understood to rise from the earth and imbue humans with the properties that were derived from the soils beneath the earth's surface.

Language, too, was seen as a product of terroir. A seventeenth-century text states that terroir imprints itself on speech: 'Each language seems to be influenced by the nature of the terroir where those who speak it live: such that the Gascon and the Provençal have a lively and amusing *jargon*, whereas the Norman and the Picard possess something of a rude drawl.' 'Jargon', we should note, is a corrupted language, so even though the people of Gascony (the Bordeaux region) might speak in a lively and amusing way, their language was still second rate. In contrast, the region around Paris was free of terroir, and the language of Paris (which eventually became the French language) was not corrupted.

In so far as wine reflected its terroir, it was within this general understanding of the idea. Over time the application of terroir has contracted, and we no longer attribute regional accents, dialects, and languages to terroir. Nor do we invoke terroir when we ascribe emotional, intellectual, and personality traits to people of a particular region, country, or ethnicity. By the mid-twentieth century, in fact, the notion of terroir was applied only to French wine. It has since been extended to wines from other regions, and in more recent years has been applied to more and more commodities, including beverages such as coffee, tea, beer, water, and milk.

Wine fits into the longer-term and more general history of terroir. For much of it, terroir, or the *goût de terroir* (broadly, the evidence of terroir in an entity that can be perceived by the senses, but the flavour of wine in this case), was considered a negative attribute in wine. This became clear in a seventeenth-century battle between Champagne and Burgundy over the respective character and quality of their wines. The partisans of Champagne described their increasingly important sparkling wines as lively and effervescent, far removed from earthly and earthy influences, while they stressed the heaviness of the wines of Burgundy. One physician from the medical faculty of Reims, in Champagne, declared that wine from Burgundy gave off a terrible odour: 'A burnt exhalation that injures the organ and which smells of the reddish, mineral dirt of the land.'

On the other hand, there were positive assessments of the effects of terroir on wine. The *Encyclopédie*, the massive compilation of knowledge in eighteenth-century France, stated that not only do wines smell and taste of their terroir, but they ought to. Rather than praise wines that were pure and free of terroir, the *Encyclopédie* gave value to wines that had a sense of place. Instead of searching for wines that were pure and perfect in some disembodied, objective sense, people were encouraged to look for wines that were true to their provenance. Whereas *goût de terroir* had previously been thought of as a negative property, late eighteenth-century writers made a distinction between two sorts: natural *goût de terroir*, which was a good thing in wine, and artificial *goût de terroir*, which was a defect. The first resulted from minerals and metals in vineyard soil that were taken up by the vine and appeared in the wine as delicate aromas and specific flavours, such as raspberry and truffles. Artificial *goût de terroir*, in contrast, resulted from such sources as trees growing close to the vines, the wrong kind of fertilizer, and smoke from nearby kilns, stoves, or fires.

The positive sense of this natural *goût de terroir* is very close to the way terroir is used by some writers today, although the means by which the properties of the soil are transmitted to the grapes and the wine were conceived differently two centuries ago. In both cases, however, there is a clear sense that the land imprints itself on wine, as surely as soil was thought to imprint itself on the character of the people who lived there and the way they spoke. It is important to note, too, that within the total environment that is implicated in the idea of terroir, the soil was – and still is – given a privileged status. The soil is the constant that determines the essential character of the wine. In contrast, the climatic facets of the environment are variable and explain the annual variations in the wine from a given terroir.

MODERN TERROIR

The influence of terroir on wine was pursued through the nineteenth century when it was integrated into the new scientific approaches to wine and food. Jean Antoine Chaptal, who wrote an influential book on viticulture and winemaking at the very beginning of the century, discussed the impact of soil and climate on the character and quality of wines. He did, on the other hand, suggest that winemakers could and should neutralize the effects of terroir when necessary – when poor weather produced inferior wines, for example. Meanwhile the science of gastronomy that emerged in France gave further force to the impact of terroir on foods more generally.

Terroir in these discussions was interpreted in the sense of environment – soil and climate – but following the First World War terroir was reinterpreted in a way that incorporated some of the cultural elements it had included in the sixteenth and seventeenth centuries. This reinterpretation took place in a precise context: Burgundy. This was no accident because Burgundy had long been seen as the region where terroir was most easily detected in wine. As we have seen, Early Modern writers singled out the wines of Burgundy as being particularly influenced (or tainted) by terroir and the region is still widely regarded in that way. Burgundy's viticultural area is divided into hundreds of small vineyards, known as *climats*. Each is said to represent an individual and distinctive terroir, such that Grands Crus and Premiers Crus are named for their *climats*. Moreover, the signature red grape variety of Burgundy, Pinot Noir, is often said to be the variety that most sensitively expresses terroir. In addition, until the French Revolution, vineyard ownership in Burgundy was dominated by the Church – mainly in the form of the Cistercian order, based at the Abbaye de Cîteaux – and the common narrative of the monks and terroir reinforced the identification of terroir with Burgundy.

The Burgundian take on terroir that was created in the interwar period rested on particular notions of both soil and society. Although soil was referred to as soil – the novelist Colette, a Burgundian herself, wrote that 'the secrets of the soil are expressed through the grape' – what was meant was soil as a metaphor: something that embodied history and communicated tradition and meaning to the vines that grew in it and to the people who worked it. This was closer to the earlier cultural meaning of soil, the kind that imprinted character on people and languages, than to the modern sense that includes limestone, granite, and clay and the geological structure of vineyards.

The cultural force of terroir was buttressed as links were made between Burgundy's folkways and the physical environment – the landscape – of the region. Burgundy was portrayed as rustic and traditional, a contrast with the modern France that was emerging in the 1920s and 1930s. France was becoming a country that was more urban than rural (the balance shifted in the early 1930s) and increasingly industrial. Artisans were losing ground to workers on assembly lines, and even in agriculture, concentration of ownership was turning owner-farmers into employees of absentee proprietors. In France, as elsewhere, society and economy were in transition, and the effect of restating the importance of terroir was to make the point that Burgundy was resisting these changes and clinging to a world that too many regions had already lost.

At the heart of the Burgundian image was the noble vigneron, a man (he was always portrayed as a man) who was as deeply rooted to the land as his vines and who was as much a part of the landscape as his vineyards. There was no separation of 'man' and 'nature' here: man was part of nature and Burgundians were intrinsic elements of their physical environment. There is more than an echo here of the notion that terroir determined the character of the people who lived there. It was argued that even the work that vignerons did in their vineyards was essentially natural, too. It might have been different from the effects of the sun and rain, but it was no less natural. Vignerons were at the core of a timeless peasant culture that was imagined and given life in festivities, fairs, feasts, and dances, all rituals that celebrated folkways that, it was said, could be traced back to time immemorial. It was an exercise in calculated nostalgia and the invention of traditions.

A key figure in linking the notion of terroir to the landscape and broadening it to include vignerons and their culture was Gaston Roupnel, a historian who spent much of his life in Burgundy. Roupnel wrote extensively about the Burgundian countryside and the relationship between the Burgundian people and their natural milieu. He argued that wine emanated from this relationship: wine, he wrote, 'is a world larger than us. Because it contains the spirit of the past and is sustained by that which preceded it, its destiny is determined in proportion to its distant origins ... It transcends time and the brief passage of human life.'

For Roupnel the dimensions of soil, landscape, countryside, labour, the vigneron, and tradition and time made up a single, integrated explanation of the wines of Burgundy. But we must note that it was not a transferable explanation: it applied only to Burgundy. Although in principle it was a template that could be reworked to enable other regions to interpret their wines, Roupnel's point was that wine was at the centre of Burgundy's essence and that could be said of few, if any, other French regions. It might be true of Champagne, but the Champenois had never embraced the notion of terroir since they were declared terroir-free in the 1600s, and terroir remains a weak concept in a region where wines are generally blends, in any case. Nor has Bordeaux ever claimed more than a weak form of terroir. Its wines, even the Crus Classés, are drawn from larger areas, and in some cases more than one area, as is true for lower classifications of burgundy.

Making terroir so specifically Burgundian hobbled the use of the notion for many years. It was relatively insignificant in the drawing up of French appellations between the wars, for example. Appellation boundaries were generally the political boundaries of *départements* or communes, and soil structure and topographical features were rarely employed as criteria except in so far as a river might mark a boundary. When terroir did come into wider usage in the 1980s and 1990s, the roles of humans, tradition, and time were still there. James Wilson, an American scientist whose book *Terroir: The Role of Geology, Climate, and Culture in the Making of French Wines* is full of geological maps and cross-cut diagrams of rock strata, argued that 'beyond the measurable ecosystem, there is an additional dimension – the spiritual aspect that recognizes the joys, the heartbreaks, the pride, the sweat, and the frustrations of [the vineyard's] history'.

The historical component of terroir in the Burgundian sense made it difficult for many New World wine regions to adopt it. Even though some could count their history as wine producers back hundreds of years – Chile and Argentina to the early 1500s, South Africa to the mid-1600s – terroir applied to specific vineyards. The upshot was that New World producers initially rejected the idea of terroir as simply a means the French were using to signal the distinctiveness (and superiority) of their wines. By the end of the twentieth century, however, they had embraced the idea of terroir – but in the restricted form of the physical environment of the vineyard, without any consideration of history, traditions, or the winemaker/vigneron.

Topological and climatic considerations – the essence of New World notions of terroir – are the criteria for defining appellations in most of the New World. American Viticultural Areas (AVAs), for example, must be distinctive in climate, geology, soils, and physical features such as elevation. Anyone petitioning to establish an AVA must show how these features affect viticulture within the area, and how viticulture outside the area is different. American appellations are more explicitly based on the idea of terroir than their French counterparts.

From the perspectives of history and geography, the idea of terroir can be seen to be very unstable and in this sense it nicely encapsulates the broad relationship of wine to landscape. Over the long term, vineyards have occupied varying shares of the agricultural landscape, expanding at some times, contracting at others. There is no clear pattern over time or space. Similarly the idea of terroir, which places not just wine but wine character and quality in the landscape, has expanded and contracted. Wine, we can see, has a much more complex relationship with landscape than the simple matter of planting vines.

5

WINE AND WORDS

'We have travelled from Harry Waugh's tentative, modest, exploratory appraisals, to far-from-modest judgments of a pretended absolute. From stumbling translation from French, to ludicrous lists of random fruit. We have fumbled with (usually half-baked) chemistry, some of us sniffy and hissy, claiming various pimples of moral high ground, as the skill of tasting, and writing about it, has blossomed from earnest bud to exotic flower.'

As the famous English wine writer Hugh Johnson notes here, using a metaphor that reflects his love of gardening, wine writing has a long lineage and has taken many forms. It goes back longer than Johnson's incisive survey, for wine has been written about for thousands of years. There are scattered passages on wine in early manuscripts from Mesopotamia and Ancient Egypt and many extensive works on viticulture, winemaking, wine regions, and specific wines written by Greek and Roman authors. Between about 500 and 1500 AD relatively little on wine was written (or survives), but the invention of the printing press gave writing about wine a boost and there was a solid corpus of wine literature in the Early Modern period (about 1500 to 1800), much of it on viticulture and wine production. The nineteenth century saw the emergence of what we might recognize as modern wine writing, with numerous books on winemaking, wine regions, styles of wines, and specific wines. These genres made up wine writing for most of the twentieth century.

It is impossible to express in quantitative terms how much was written on wine in any given period – how many words, lines, pages, or works. Even so, our own time is undoubtedly without precedent for the number of words devoted daily, monthly, and annually to wine.

Not only are thousands of books and popular and scholarly articles on wine published each year, but wine is the subject of newspaper columns, dedicated print periodicals, websites, blogs, and social media streams. Beyond the written word are scores of wine courses, delivered orally, for amateur wine lovers and wine professionals. The topics covered by this vast wine literature range from viticulture and winemaking to wine-tasting techniques and food and wine pairing. Hundreds of thousands of reviews of individual wines are published every year. These words are variously pitched to scientists, people in the myriad aspects of the wine business, serious wine lovers and wine collectors, and occasional wine drinkers. They are written in dozens of languages. Anyone regularly engaged with wine must feel that they are awash in words on wine. How did we get here and how have these words changed over time?

A genre of wine writing that appears to have had one of the longest histories is simply describing wines – setting out the flavour, character, style, and quality of particular categories of wine or individual wines. The wine writers of Greece and Rome drew attention to specific wines, and in order to distinguish them they described their individual characteristics, just as many wine writers today write tasting notes that describe the wines they taste. But the content and style of these descriptions have changed dramatically over time, as have the purposes for which the descriptions were written. Indeed, it is a fair question whether we are here looking at a history of a single genre or the history of several genres.

Before we look at Greek wine descriptions, we should note some from Egypt. One set is to be found on some of the three dozen ceramic jars of wine left in the tomb of King Tutankhamun in 1323 BC. (The king was nineteen when he died, just at the minimum legal drinking age in many Western countries.) Twenty-six of the jars bore seals that identified the estate the wine came from, the year of the vintage, and the name of the winemaker. One example read 'Year 5. Wine of the House-of-Tutankhamun Ruler-of-the-Southern-On ... [in] the Western River. By the Chief Winemaker Khaa.' These are probably the first wine labels.

The seals on some of the jars provided additional information that was descriptive of the style or quality of the wine itself, just as many wine back labels do today. For example, four jars were labelled 'sweet' and one was labelled 'wine of good quality'. The seals on jars of wine found in other locations carry descriptions such as 'good', 'very good wine', 'wine for merrymaking', 'wine for taxes', and 'wine for offerings'.

Clearly it took an insider – a contemporary winemaker, administrator, or regular wine drinker – to decode these terse labels. Even such banal terms as 'good' and 'very good' have no meaning when they have no context. Wine suitable for merrymaking – which sounds like an ancient party wine – might well have been of mediocre but passable quality, good enough for quaffing in volume and tasting less and less mediocre as the party went on. Wall drawings of Egyptian social occasions show participants vomiting and being carried away unconscious as a result of drinking to excess.

But what should we make of wine said to be good for paying taxes or for use in offerings? If the taxes were paid simply in the volume of wine, without regard to quality, it made sense for tax payers to remit poor-quality wine and keep better wine for their own use. Yet when wine was poured as a libation or employed in another way in a religious ritual, it might well have been thought that good-quality wine was more likely than mediocre wine to be effective in gaining divine intercession.

These Egyptian descriptions, then, comprised two broad types. They described quality in some cases and the purposes of the wine in others, but the purposes themselves might well have been code for quality to contemporaries. Quite possibly, too, the vintage of the wine (indicated as the year of Tutankhamun's reign) meant something in terms of quality, just as vintages can today. Labelling with seals was clearly done so as to enable the owners of the wine to select the right jar of wine for the right occasion: a mediocre wine for a boisterous party where the volume of wine was more important than its quality; better quality wine, perhaps, when entertaining fewer and more discriminating guests. The descriptions were minimal but enough to enable the owners of the wine to distinguish among them. We might note that there were no references to the colour of the wine. Wall paintings of wine production in Egypt consistently show wine as dark but chemical analysis of the residue in some of the jars in Tutankhamun's tomb shows that some wine was white and some made from dark-skinned grapes. Either the colour of wine was not important or there are clues to it on the seals that we are missing.

The first substantial corpus of wine descriptions is to be found in Ancient Greece and Rome and they vary greatly in style, content, and precision. When reading them we have to bear in mind that 'wine' in the ancient world was not as stable a concept as it is today, when it refers to fermented grape juice with relatively few additives (such as the influence of oak barrels and tartaric acid) that affect flavour and texture. Two or three thousand years ago, wine was seldom consumed without being first diluted with fresh water after the addition of other substances that might include sea water, honey, lead, roots, resin, ashes, and various herbs and spices. When we read of a Greek or Roman wine being sweet, then, it is not clear whether we are dealing with a wine with a high perceptible level of residual sugar or a wine to which honey had been added. To this extent, the descriptions written by classical writers might not tell us very much about the flavour and style of wine in its unadulterated form, the form that is discussed by wine writers today.

One writer who wrote extensively about wine was Pliny the Elder, who devoted most of Book 5 of his *Natural History* to the subject. In one chapter he does make it clear that he is discussing one wine in its unadulterated form: the famous Opimian wine, made in 'the year of the City 633', during the consulship of Opimius. That year, he wrote, 'the weather was remarkable for its sereneness, and the ripening of the grape … was fully effected by the sun'. This wine was 200 years old as Pliny wrote, and he described it as having 'the consistency of honey, with a rough taste' such that it needed to be mixed with water: 'For such, in fact, is the nature of wines that, when extremely old, it is impossible to drink them in a pure state, and they require to be mixed with water, as long keeping renders them intolerably bitter.' Water, then, was needed not only to dilute the viscosity of the wine, but also to make it more palatable. This is a warning either not to leave wines two centuries before drinking them or not to have high expectations of 200-year-old wines.

In their descriptions of wines Greek and Roman writers not only used flavour and texture descriptors that we might recognize – sweet, viscous ('the consistency of honey'), thin, bitter, and so on – but also described their medicinal properties. The wines from Surrentinum, in the Bay of Naples, Pliny wrote, 'are especially recommended to invalids for their thinness and their wholesomeness', although he noted that Tiberius Caesar had alleged that physicians had dignified Surrentinum wine even though it was really nothing more than 'generous vinegar'. This description, which combines qualities of the wine (thinness) and its medical value (wholesomeness), shows how the two approaches could be combined seamlessly. The point of these descriptions was not only to guide consumers to the wines because of their sensory properties or their intrinsic quality, but to show how appropriate they were in bodily terms. The medicinal value of wine must be understood within the humoral system, the dominant paradigm for explaining the human body and its functions that gave all foods and beverages – including wine – a role in maintaining health and curing illness (see pages 8–14).

Pliny the Elder moved easily between these two approaches throughout his writings on contemporary wines. He noted that the Egyptians made a wine from the Thasian grape that is 'remarkable for its sweetness and its laxative qualities'. Elsewhere in his *Natural History* he wrote that some wines 'are more agreeable to the palate than others'. But rather than going on to discuss the sensory qualities of these wines, as we might expect and hope, he turned immediately to their medicinal properties: 'Livia Augusta, who lived to her eighty-second year, attributed her longevity to the wine of Pucinum [on the Istrian Peninsula in Croatia], as she never drank any other … There is not a wine that is deemed superior to this for medicinal purposes.' He went on to write that the Emperor Augustus and the emperors who followed him preferred Setinum wine, 'having learnt from actual experience that there is no danger of indigestion and flatulence' as a result of drinking it.

This is not information that we would necessarily find useful or desirable in a wine label or in a wine review. Modern wine descriptions that give alcohol content and measurements of free sulphur might be helpful to consumers wanting to reduce their alcohol intake or who have genuine allergies to sulphites. But we would not expect to buy a Barossa Shiraz because it was an aid to digestion or a Rioja because it warded off flatulence. We tend to assume that as far as our health is concerned, and bearing in mind differences in alcohol, sugar, and free sulphur levels, one wine is very much like another.

The colour of wine (which is disappearing from modern wine descriptions) was of marginal interest to classical writers. Pliny noted that wine came in four colours: white, blood-coloured, black, and brown. We might think of them as white, red, dark red, and the brown of older wines – the dark amber of many old whites and the brick-hued browns that red wines take on as they age.

In a chapter of his *Natural History* headed 'Fifty kinds of generous wines', Pliny ranked the various wines available in Rome, providing a classification before classifications became popular. He drew particular attention to Falernian wine from Campania: 'There is now no wine known that ranks higher than the Falernian.' But how does he describe it? It is the only one 'that takes fire on the application of a flame' – which speaks to an alarmingly high level of alcohol for any wine – and that it comes in three styles: 'the rough, the sweet, and the thin'. Clearly, something is lost in translation. He points out, too, that the grapes that make Falernian and other highly reputed wine do not have 'by any means an agreeable flavour'. In the end, we are left without any real sense why Falernian was unparalleled as a wine, unless the competition was truly awful.

Pliny actually placed Falernian in the second tier of wines, making it an early 'super-second growth'. His first tier included Setinum from the hills of Setia, about 70 kilometres south of Rome (the wine that warded off indigestion and flatulence), and Caecubum ('which enjoyed the reputation of being the most generous of all the wines') from vines grown in marshy swamps near the coast of Latium. Caecuban wine was praised by many Greek and Roman writers as one of the best. By all accounts it was a white wine that turned 'the colour of fire' as it aged. Athenaeus wrote that it was a powerful wine when young and needed many years to mature, while Dioscorides described it as sweet. Horace placed Caecuban wine above the revered Falernian wine and indicated its status by pointing out that it was poured at important state occasions, such as celebrations of military victories. Unfortunately, only legends remained of Caecuban wine when Pliny wrote. He noted that the vineyards had been neglected through 'the carelessness of the cultivator' and that they were finally destroyed by the Emperor Nero when he began a project to build a canal.

The third tier of Pliny's classification included the wines from the region around Alba, the centre of the modern Piedmont wine region. They were 'remarkable for their sweetness' although they were sometimes, though rarely, rough. They were placed at the same level as wines from several other regions, but we are given little information to justify their status. One, a wine from Segni, southeast of Rome, 'is by far too rough to be used as wine, but is very useful as an astringent, and is consequently reckoned among the medicines for that purpose'.

Pliny mentioned two wines from Gaul, now France. Massilia (Marseille) produced two kinds of wine, 'one of which is richer and thicker than the other, and is used for seasoning other wines, being generally known as *succosum* [juicy]'. As for the wine from the region around modern Narbonne, Pliny was scathing: 'the growers of that country have absolutely established manufactories for the purpose of adulteration, where they give a dark hue to their wines by the agency of smoke; I only wish I could say, too, that they not employ various herbs and noxious drugs for the same purpose; indeed these dealers are even known to use aloes for the purpose of heightening the flavour and improving the colour of their wines.'

This is an odd criticism, given the common practice among the Greeks and Romans of flavouring wines with herbs and myriad other additives, but perhaps Pliny's complaint was that these 'dealers' were releasing their adulterated wines as if they were wine in its pure, unadulterated form, ready to receive additives. That would explain his complaints that the producers were using substances to deepen the colour of the wines.

Pliny followed his list of the fifty 'most generous wines' with notes on some of 'thirty-eight varieties of foreign wines'. They included a number from the Aegean islands, including the wine of Lesbos which 'has naturally a taste of sea water' – that is, it tasted of sea water without any being added to it. Perhaps it had the salinity that some modern tasters detect in wines from vineyards growing near the sea. As for the wine from Mount Tmolus, in Anatolia, it was held in high regard not because of its quality but because of its 'peculiar sweetness'. It was so sweet that it was mixed with other wines 'for the purpose of modifying their harsh flavour, by imparting to them a portion of its own sweetness'. Not only that, but once mixed with this wine, the other wines immediately tasted much older than they had before.

Pliny also discussed specific styles of wine. If the wine of Lesbos had a naturally salty flavour, other wines were artificially salted by the addition of sea water, and Pliny discussed salted wines as a separate category. He wrote that the people of Cos added large volumes of sea water to their wine – a practice they had learned from a thief who used to add sea water to wine after he had stolen some from a vat, so as bring the level back to a point where it would not arouse suspicions. Other wines were made to be sweet, some made by boiling must to a third or half its volume and then being further sweetened with honey. Fermentation in such cases would have been slow and would have ended leaving a high level of residual sugar, perhaps in the style of Icewine or Tokaji, if not that sweet.

If Greek and Roman writers described these wines in terms of their colour, weight, and texture, it was often to reinforce the medical properties being attributed to the wine. There is a vast difference between these descriptions and modern wine reviews where the writer tries to describe the wine in a way that the reader can imagine what the wine smells, tastes, and feels like by appealing to commonly recognized fruit and other commodities.

In his wide-ranging *Geography* written in the early part of the first century AD, Strabo's comments on wine were generally written in broad strokes, without much specificity. He wrote off the wines of one region in Egypt this way: 'The whole of this country produces no wine of a good quality, and the earthen jars contain more sea water than wine, which is called Libyan [although wine was often diluted with sea water, wine was usually the major part]; this and beer are the principal beverage of the common people of Alexandria. Antiphrae in particular was a subject of ridicule on account of its bad wine.' As wine notes they are not particularly useful except as a warning to stay away from wines from these regions.

Medical benefits remained important properties of wine from the ancient world until the eighteenth century. Over this long period the humoral system was the principal paradigm of the human body and wine played an important role in it. The humoral system is described in detail above (pp. 8–14) but in brief it taught that the human body and individual temperament were governed by four humours or liquids: blood, yellow bile, black bile, and phlegm. Each of the humours was located on axes of cold–hot and moist–dry. These humours should ideally be balanced in every body, and a body with an imbalance was defined as ill. Because the humoral system was the way physicians understood the body, illness, and therapy for some two thousand years, food and drink were viewed from medical as much as gastronomic perspectives over a long period, even into the nineteenth century. If the classical writers focused on the effects of wine on the body, later commentators added further layers, including discussion of the flavours and textures of wines in their own right. But the medicinal and therapeutic properties of wine were never far from the thoughts of wine writers in earlier times.

In the eighteenth and nineteenth centuries we see the beginning of attempts to describe wine by evoking similarities to other substances. It might well be that some ancient wines were described as honey-sweet, salty, and sooty, but part of the reason must have been that they tasted that way because of what had been added to them: honey, sea water, and ashes, in these cases. That is quite different from a modern wine writer describing the flavours of a wine as citrus, nectarine, and green apple. There is no suggestion that the wine has been flavoured by these fruits, although some consumers understand the descriptions that way. Rather, these words are used by wine writers to communicate the sense that a flavour in the wine reminded them of those fruit: assuming readers are familiar with the flavours, they are able to imagine a wine that has those flavours. That, at least, is the theory and explanation for the current widespread use of fruit descriptors in wine reviewing.

A few fruit descriptors began to creep into wine writing in the nineteenth century, when raspberry and violets were used to describe the flavours of some wines. But the emphasis was squarely on describing the colour, style, weight, and texture of wines, rather than their flavours. Cyrus Redding described a white wine from the Hermitage district of the northern Rhône Valley this way: 'Its colour should be straw-yellow; its odour is like that of no other known wine. It is of a rich taste, between that of the dry and the luscious wines.' The wines of nearby Condrieu, he wrote, 'are of a luscious taste, and have a smell and aroma remarkably agreeable. They keep a long while, and become of an amber colour by age.' As for the wines made around Avignon and Carpentras, 'the former have considerable spirit, little colour, and will keep a great while. The latter will not keep so long, having less body, and are in general obliged to be sold annually before the hot weather sets in.' These are austere wine descriptions, and throughout his book Redding focused on style, colour, and ageing potential. Flavour was unimportant in recommending or criticizing a wine.

There was some interest in defining the terms that were used by wine writers, and in his book on the cheap wines from several countries, Robert Druitt set out some of 'the large and exquisite set of phrases which the French have devised for the description of the qualities of wine'. He included basic terms such as 'Taste, *saveur* or *goût*' ('the effect on the nerves of taste on the palate'), *arôme* ('the effect on the throat'), and *bouquet* ('the effect on the nose'). As for specific properties, Druitt noted: 'A wine is said to be *corsé*, or to have *corps* (body, stoutness, or substance) when its constituent parts, intimately combined, seem to make one complete whole'; *dureté* in wine 'means a deficiency in unctuosity which marks the roughness of various saline and astringent particles'; *finesse* 'is a delicacy of taste, an absence of all that shocks the palate'; *velouté, soyeux, moëlleux* 'are terms to indicate the soft, silky, velvety, marrowy character of full-bodied wines that are neither sweet nor dry'; '*franchise de goût* signifies the absence of everything earthy'; '*franchise de goût de terroir,* that indescribable something which Cape [South African] wines used to taste of, – and the absence of all other taste indicating decay or disease in the grape or the wine, or mouldiness in the cask.' All these terms relate to the qualities of texture and weight, and there is no mention of flavours.

Druitt's descriptions of wines were less terse than Redding's but rarely expansive. Sometimes, however, he let himself go, as he did with wines from Volnay. Talking to the readers of his book, which focused on 'cheap wines', and was therefore presumably addressed to people of modest means who could not afford the great wines of Europe, he wrote:

'I advise the student [of wine] to invest four or five shillings in a bottle of good Volnay. Take care that the wine be not chilled nor the wine glass cold (58° Fah.), and drink it in the middle of dinner with roast meat, or, better still, with hare or other game. One bottle is quite enough for four persons. Then say what you think of it. Is it sweet, or sour, or hot, or strong? No, it is perfume. It is not a liquid *plus* perfume, but is itself a liquid perfume, one and indivisible. The perfume or bouquet is the first thing tasted and the last. It hangs on the tongue and palate, and leaves a permanently agreeable impression … If the taste be any guide to its nature and alliances, it ranks with the class of substances of which valerian, civet, and castor are examples.'

Druitt likens the flavour here to some ingredients common in perfume because of his insistence that Volnay is 'liquid perfume'. They are not to be thought of as in the wine in any literal sense, but they are a guide to the alliances – the likeness – of the flavour, which is the way in which fruit, berries, and other produce are used as descriptors for wine in modern wine notes. Druitt also occasionally mentions the medicinal properties of specific wines: 'In neglecting Burgundy wine, we ignore a most powerful remedy for poverty of the blood and an ill-nourished state of the nervous system.' As for Bordeaux, they 'like other fine light wines, make pure healthy blood, and at the same time favour the action of the excretory organs; they are good in the anaemia and chlorosis of growing girls'.

Nineteenth-century writing on wine was formal and mannered, but in the first half of the twentieth the approach to wine was dominated by a style that often incorporated literary allusions. The aim was not only to inform readers about wine but to do so in ways that elevated the wine in question. One writer was André Simon, who wrote a hundred books on wine and described a 1926 Chablis as having 'the grace of a silver willow'. It made the point, even if the reader had never seen a silver willow. The literary style – some might call it flowery – infused advertising, too. A 1955 publication by the English wine agents, Berry Bros & Rudd, read: 'Claret has well deserved this place in our national life, for it is not only the most perfectly balanced and subtly flavoured of the world's wines, but also – to quote André Simon – "the most natural and the most wholesome". If Burgundy is the King of red wines, then Claret is surely the Queen – and many would make her Queen Regnant.'

Fruit descriptors, now the dominant form of describing wines, were rare in this style of wine writing, and the full-fledged use of these and other terms dates back about half a century to the 1960s. One of the early influential exponents of the style was the American wine critic Robert Parker, who also gave the wine world the 100-point scoring system. Using fruit and other terms to describe wine gave emphasis to the aromas and flavour of wine more than ever before. Until that point, description had focused on style, rather than flavour. But while the style of wine could be described in a short note, aromas and flavours presented a broad canvas capable of accommodating a wide spectrum of descriptors drawn from the worlds of fruit, herbs, spices, and other sources of inspiration. Popular terms included 'barnyard' and 'forest floor', while some writers gave rein to phrases such as 'a hard-ridden horse' and 'sweaty horse'.

In 1990 Ann Noble, a sensory chemist at the University of California at Davis, the premier wine education institution in the United States, devised the Wine Aroma Wheel to give order to the riot of descriptors. The inner ring of the wheel broke aromas into several broad groups such as Tree Fruit, Citrus Fruit, Berry, Nutty, and Earthy. Each of these is divided into more precise aromas, so that Citrus is divided into Grapefruit and Lemon, while Berry is divided into Blackberry, Raspberry, Strawberry, and Blackcurrant (Cassis). To use the Aroma Wheel you sniff a glass of wine and look at the broad categories on the Wheel to decide whether the dominant aroma is Citrus, Berry, or another. Having settled on the broad category, you work your way down until you find a precise aroma that best describes the aromas you detect in the wine. It can be used over and over for the same wine if it has complex aromatics, and you can use the Wheel in the same way to describe flavours.

The Aroma Wheel was followed by a number of similar aids, including a Mouthfeel Wheel (to help a user decide if a wine had the soft texture of satin, silk, or chamois) and various Wine and Food Pairing Wheels. Whether wine writers used the Aroma Wheel or not, many embraced the wide range of fruit and other descriptors, and began to list them without any apparent regard for order of strength. It is not clear whether a wine described as having flavours of lemon, green apple, and gooseberry tasted predominantly, unmistakably, of lemon, with subtle notes of the other fruit, or whether these flavours were balanced within the wine's flavour profile.

Examples of notes include this one for a California Viognier: 'Fragrant nose of super-ripe apricots and stewed pears leads to off-dry apricot, lilac, orange blossom, nectarine and tangerine flavours with a whisper of spice on the finish.' A Nero d'Avola from Sicily 'starts with a sweet caramel apple aroma then zips along with flavours of dark toffee, sweet tobacco, red apple, ripe plum, and black pepper'. Finally, a port 'starts with intense cherry-almond and anise aromas that give way to flavours of cherry, sweet tobacco, almonds, anise, blackberry, coffee, cream, milk chocolate, and vanilla'.

Fruit and other descriptors multiplied, making each wine note a catalogue of fruit worthy of a salad or one of Carmen Miranda's hats (the Portuguese-born Brazilian singer was famous for wearing hats adorned with tropical fruit). These and similar descriptors have gradually pushed out other features that had been present in wine reviews; there is now far less attention to colour, for example. Wine writers used to be precise as to whether a wine was scarlet, ruby, garnet, cherry, carmine, cardinal, or crimson, but colour is now scarcely mentioned at all. 'Legs' and 'tears' have also virtually disappeared. These words refer to rings of clear liquid that form near the top of a glass of wine after it has been swirled, from which droplets continuously form and drain back into the wine. Legs used to be considered a mark of quality, but now that they are thought to be unrelated, they have disappeared. Finally, and appropriately, 'finish' is seldom referred to in wine notes. Finish is the length of time the flavour of a wine stays in a taster's mouth after the wine has been swallowed. The longer it remained, the longer the finish, and the better the wine was thought to be.

There has, then, been a long history of wine descriptions, and there are more styles than discussed here. What is clear is that it is an evolving genre and tends to reflect broader attitudes towards wine. Reference to a wine's putative medicinal properties made sense when wine was thought to be therapeutic, but it would be odd to see now – although a producer might well point out that a certain wine had an above-average level of resveratrol, the compound implicated in the French Paradox. Wine writers both respond to and shape what their readers want in their notes on wine, and it seems that wine writers and consumers today, especially in North America, are more interested in flavour at the expense of the other attributes of a wine. Thus wine writers continue in the relatively new mode of listing as many flavours as they can squeeze out of a tasting glass.

NUMBER WORDS

Numbers also play a role as words. It is now far more common than not to see reviews or notes on wines with scores, sometimes out of a hundred, sometimes out of twenty, and at other times expressed as stars or, in the case of the Italian food and wine magazine, *Gambero Rosso*, as a score out of three glasses (*tre bicchieri*). Giving a score out of three is quite different from giving a score out of a hundred. The latter allows for much more finesse and apparent precision in scoring, although most wine reviewers using the 100-point system score within a 10-point range from the mid-80s to the mid-90s.

The intuitive line between an acceptable (passing) wine and an unacceptable (failing) wine is 50, as it is in the academic marking scheme that most people are familiar with. But as the 100-point system has evolved, the cut-off point is in the low-80s, leaving more than 80 per cent of the scale unused. School or university essays and examinations that fail are scored below 50, whether the score is 40 per cent or 20 per cent. Failing wines, however, are seldom commented on by wine writers, leaving a question of why there are a hundred points to be allocated. The same is true of more limited scales: only about 15 to 20 is used on 20-point scales, and scores below three stars are rare on five-star scales.

Despite the latitude implicit in the 100-point system, some writers also use half points, giving a wine 89.5 when they think it is just not up to 90, which is widely seen as the beginning of 'excellence' on the scale. Some years ago a Canadian wine columnist facetiously proposed a 1000-point scale ('ten times better than a hundred points') to give even more scope for judging. For a week he marked wines out of a thousand, giving them scores such as 887 and 912.

Scoring wines out of a hundred points has been adopted by many wine writers, wine media, and wine competitions. The system was devised by the American wine critic Robert Parker, who also coined the term 'wine critic' in place of the 'wine writer' that had been used until then. The well-known British wine writer Hugh Johnson recalls the time a publisher showed him a wine review by Robert Parker that used the 100-point scoring system. 'It said the vintage of the wine and then there was another figure. It would say "1975" and then it would say "90", and I said, "What does that mean?" He said, "That's a score." I said, "What does a score mean? Wines don't get scores." He said, "Oh, that's the whole point of this. Robert Parker gives it scores, as if it was passing a school exam or something." And I said, "Well it doesn't make any sense to me." But it was the beginning of one of the most powerful influences that's ever hit the world of wine.'

It was true that until then wines had not been scored, at least not in numerical terms. In a way, wines had long been implicitly scored by being assessed in verbal terms. Wines were sometimes described using words that explicitly referred to quality – using words such as excellent, very good, good, and mediocre. Other words used to describe wines, such as balanced, unbalanced, sour, flabby, and integrated, suggest quality or aspects of quality. To anyone familiar with the meaning of the words as they apply to wine, a balanced and integrated wine is better than one that is unbalanced and flabby.

GENDERED WINE

A particular category of descriptors derives from the anthropomorphizing of wine by some wine writers. Wines are said to have a number of human characteristics, including body and character, and an extension or implication of this is that they also possess traits associated with genders. At its simplest form this is expressed by referring to wines as either 'feminine' or 'masculine'. These are descriptors that seem to have emerged in the early twentieth century and even though they were never very common, they occurred regularly. It seems that their usage has waned somewhat, but they still occur occasionally.

The persistence of their use is suggested by the fact that *Wine Enthusiast* magazine included 'feminine' in a list of the 'top wine terms'. To explain the term, it wrote: 'Don't automatically bristle at this gendered wine term. According to Ross Wheatley, director of food and beverage at Lucy Restaurant and Bar in Yountville, California, this term is not only "easy to relate to," it also perfectly describes wines that tend to be lower in alcohol and tannins. "Imagine a wine that has similar characteristics to a woman and her best qualities," says Wheatley. "A wine that is light, refined and delicate might be called feminine; the polar opposite of those so-called masculine qualities in wine – strong, muscular, larger and bigger".'

'Masculine' was not included in *Wine Enthusiast's* list of top wine terms, but 'muscular' was: 'Wines described as muscular have traditionally been linked to bigger-style red wines, including Cabernet

Sauvignons, Barolos and Super Tuscans, along with some Rhône blends. "Imagine a wine that is the exact opposite of what we have described as feminine," says Wheatley. "These are big, strong wines with lots of power and strength. Muscular means something that feels like it might put hair on your chest." '

It is notable, first, that although the basic references are to gender, wines are not referred to as male or female. It is not, then, that wines described this way are likened to one of the two sexes, but rather to a cultural overlay, to stereotypes sometimes associated with gender. 'Feminine' generally refers to qualities of delicacy and refinement that in the nineteenth century used to be considered the essence of a middle-class woman. 'Masculine', in contrast, implies a category of male characterized by assertiveness, strength, and muscularity – curiously less middle class and more working class. By extension a wine considered feminine is typically not too heavy, has delicate aromas and flavours, and is likely not to have tannins. A wine described as masculine is robust, big-bodied, and might well have firm tannins.

The website of Christopher Stewart Wine and Spirits, a Canadian liquor importer, added more information. 'Think of a masculine wine as a stereotype of a man's man; it's big (six foot six), full-bodied (two-hundred plus pounds), powerful (muscled and strong from days spent doing hard, physical labour) and most of all, it's bold. The flavours won't be hard to pick out. They will shout at you, and they will be LOUD. This is the biggest difference in the different "genders" of wine. Masculine wine is loud and intense, while feminine wine is often quiet and subtle.'

It is noteworthy that there usually is no suggestion that 'feminine' wines are better or worse than 'masculine' wines. The terms are used to differentiate wine styles, and although we may all have preferences – some of us like big-bodied, fruit-assertive reds while others prefer fruit-acid balanced reds with understated fruit – we recognize the diversity of wine styles as one of the attractions of wine itself. Nonetheless, one review in *Wine Enthusiast* magazine did express a general preference: 'When at its best, wine tends to express feminine qualities, like sexy textures, soft tannins, voluptuous fruit and delicate floral aromas.' Masculine and feminine are used more broadly in wine culture to refer to more than wine, and it has been suggested that women who make wine transfer their 'feminine' qualities to the wine they make. The implication is that male winemakers produce wine that is consistently bold, intense, and tannic. Wine bottles, too, have been gendered, with wine writers insisting that burgundy bottles, with their sloping shoulders, are more feminine than their square-shouldered counterparts from Bordeaux. It coincides with a tendency to see Burgundy's wines as 'feminine' and those from Bordeaux as 'masculine' – although even writers wedded to these terms will find transgendered wines in each region.

It is important to recognize that referring to wines by gender is not necessarily random. There are styles of wine with characteristics that are lumped into the 'feminine' and 'masculine' categories. The issue is not that the wines exist, but whether they can be labelled in gender terms. It is notable that some non-gender descriptors tend to correlate with one gender or another. We could predict that a wine described as 'big-bodied with firm tannins' would be called 'masculine'. But would we necessarily predict that a wine described as having 'floral' characteristics would be labelled 'feminine'? Perhaps. An analysis of the five million tasting notes on the Cellar Tracker website shows that 'floral' wines were more than four times as likely to be called 'feminine' as 'masculine'.

How far does the history of gendering wine go back? In 2017, Jonathan Lipsmeyer published a piece on his Gargantuan Wine blog entitled 'On Wine and Gender: A Critical History', which briefly surveyed tasting notes on wine from the Greek writers to the present. It concluded that the first example of a gendered wine was a 1920 note by the English literary critic and wine writer George Saintsbury who, in his *Notes on a Cellar Book*, referred to an 1846 Hermitage (tasted in 1886) as 'the manliest wine I ever drank'. His full tasting note read: 'Now most red wines, if not all with the exception of Port, are either past their best, or have no best to come to, at that age ... But my Hermitage showed nor the slightest mark or presage of enfeeblement. It was, no doubt ... not a delicate wine; if you want delicacy, you don't go to the Rhône or anywhere in France below Gascony. But it was the manliest French wine I ever drank; and age had softened and polished all that might have been rough in the manliness of its youth ... The bouquet was rather like that of the less sweet wall-flower.' 'Manly' seems to encapsulate all the qualities of 'masculine', so the gendering of wine in this way seems to have arrived on the scene about a hundred years ago. George Saintsbury might well have been the single original source for the gendered approach to wine, although the French-born, English-domiciled wine writer André Simon cannot have been far behind.

The use of gender terms might well have reflected the awareness of gender that came to the fore in the late 1800s and early 1900s. During the early and mid-nineteenth century a cult of domesticity in Europe and North America drew sharper distinctions between women and men. One aspect of it was the feminization of women, which portrayed them – especially middle-class women – as weak, sensitive, fragile, and in need of protection. Laws protected women (and children) from harsh working conditions in mines and factories. Marriage laws began to protect married women (in theory) from the violence and gross insults of their husbands.

At the same time, women began to invade the public sphere that had been occupied by men. They were to the fore in campaigns to improve male morality, including the often-successful campaigns for alcohol reform, and they demanded the right to vote. It is important to note that these were not necessarily contradictory trends. Women campaigned for moral reform because they saw themselves as defenders of morality and family values. And they campaigned for the vote not because they saw themselves as essentially the same as men, but because, they argued, women would bring womanly qualities of compassion and morality to governance. The issues they took up, such as drunkenness, prostitution, and gambling, were issues that affected family life.

Nonetheless, the fact that women were participating in politics in this way was new. It unnerved men and called into question gender roles, even if women espoused a limited range of issues that seemed to relate to their roles as repositories and guardians of morality. But the instability of gender roles was intensified during the First World War, when women began to take on male occupations. In Britain, women were not only employed during the war in jobs that had historically been men's – in munitions factories, ship building, and bus driving – but they began to 'act like men'. They cut their hair short, wore clothes that looked masculine and de-emphasized their hips and breasts, and began to drink in public houses in numbers never seen before.

These trends alarmed conservatives, who saw not only 'traditional' gender roles and distinctions disappearing but also feared for the future of the family and civilization itself. When the war was over, most women were fired from their wartime jobs and governments encouraged them to marry and have children to make up for the high casualties of the war. It was in 1920, at the height of this post-war period of cultural anxiety about gender that George Saintsbury restated the sharp distinctions between men and women as 'manly' and 'feminine' wines. In doing so, he used images of women and men that were being used widely in political and social discourses.

The practice was soon picked up by other writers. In the United States in the 1930s, the wine writer Frank Schoonmaker employed gender to distinguish first and second growth Bordeaux: '[Mouton Rothschild] has been called, along with Latour, the "manliest" of the red Bordeaux, and it is a fine wine by any standard.' Turning his sights on Burgundy, Schoonmaker wrote that Chambertin and Musigny were 'lighter and sometimes called "more feminine" than Chambertin'.

It is possible to amass many quotations of this sort, but the point should be clear enough that once the idea of gendering was available, many writers embraced it. For much of the twentieth century analogous notions of femininity and masculinity were entrenched in western thought – so much so that writers and their readers could accept the terms without any sense that they were facile and based on unstable and unreliable stereotypes.

As Jonathan Lipsmeyer points out on Gargantuan Wine, a critical moment came when the famous Bordeaux oenologist Emile Peynaud gave gendered descriptions scientific approval in his magisterial and influential *Le Goût du Vin*, published in 1980. In a diagram of wine characteristics that was a model for the later Aroma and Mouthfeel Wheels, Peynaud drew a line right through the middle of his wine descriptors, with one side labelled 'masculine' and the other 'feminine'. Descriptors on the 'masculine' side of the chart included rough, tannic, solid, robust, hard, firm, austere, and stiff. Descriptors on the 'feminine' side included soft, supple, sweet, unctuous, easy, gentle, and fleshy.

The use of 'masculine' and 'feminine' to describe wines seems to have waned, although it is still used by some wine writers and winemakers. It seems increasingly not merely anachronistic but actively offensive. If it arose during a period of cultural anxiety about the nature of genders and their social roles, it now exists in a different social and cultural context. Women might be under-represented in some professions (such as engineering) and over-represented in others (such as nursing), but the social distinctions between women and men are far less marked than ever before. To suggest that women are, in any meaningful sense, delicate, soft, and sensitive, and that men are sturdy, muscular, and strong is a parody of outmoded ideas. To this extent the gendering of wine, which might have arisen and flourished in specific historical circumstances, is now at odds with its prevailing cultural environment. It clings to such outmoded and discredited ideas about gender that one might as well adopt class, ethnic, or racial stereotypes of the sort that are now unacceptable in intelligent company.

WORDS ON LABELS

A separate category of wine words is those on wine labels. Labels on bottles are relative newcomers to wine, as they have generally been used only since wine has been sold at retail by the bottle. Over time other forms of labelling have been used. As we have seen, clay jars holding ancient Egyptian wines had seals that often indicated the age, quality, and texture of the wine. Age and explicit quality (such as 'good') were straightforward, and statements on seals that a wine was suitable for paying taxes or for religious purposes might well have provided knowledgeable Egyptians with enough information to identify style and quality. Quite clearly, though, there was no information on the colour of the wine nor on the grape varieties it was made from.

Some Greek and Roman amphoras carried indications of where they were from while the provenance of others could be identified by their shape, size, dimensions, and decorative features because each region produced its own distinctive amphora. Anyone who could identify an amphora would have an idea of what the wine inside was like. The authorities on the Greek island of Thasos, for example, required Thasian wine to be stored and transported in Thasian amphoras, so that a connoisseur who recognized a Thasian amphora would know, within reason, what to expect of the wine – in this case a red-black wine said to have had a strong aroma. The amphora was effectively the equivalent of a word denoting an appellation in a system where appellations denote wines made from specific grape varieties and in a certain broad style. A Thasian amphora might have conveyed as much information to a wine-knowledgeable Greek consumer in 200 BC as a bottle labelled Rioja does to an informed wine drinker today.

When earthenware vessels, such as amphoras, gave way to wooden barrels in the first and second centuries AD, the kind of wine they contained must have been written on them some way, either in words or symbols, just as on barrels in winery cellars today. Sometimes full or abbreviated information is written in chalk on the end of the barrel, sometimes it is written on paper and pasted onto the barrel, but it is always necessary for barrels to be identified in some way so that the wines can be managed, tasted, and bottled. But over a much longer period wine was sold in barrels and each barrel needed to be identified so that wine merchants and buyers knew what they were selling and buying.

When King Henry III of England bought 1,445 casks of French wine in 1243, about a thousand casks were described as top quality and the rest as mediocre and poor quality. There must have been some way of identifying which barrels were which, so that the best wine found its way to the royal table and the rest to lower courtiers or the army. Unfortunately, there is little information on how barrels were identified. Paintings of barrels of wine being loaded onto ships give no indication that they were identified in any particular way, even though they must have been.

Shipping wine in barrels was the practice for centuries and it is only in the last few decades that wine has been shipped and sold in bottles bearing labels. In 1913 bottled wine accounted for less than 4 per cent of France's wine exports (excluding champagne which must be made in bottles) and less than 8 per cent of the wine shipped from Bordeaux. Things hardly changed in the next half century: in the 1950s, only 7 per cent of the wine exported from Bordeaux was shipped in bottles. Most was shipped in barrels, then bottled at its destination.

Despite this continuity there was a major shift in the twentieth century when bottled wines were sold at retail. Until the nineteenth century consumers wanting to buy a bottle of wine would bring their own bottle to a wine merchant where the wine would be drawn from a barrel. No labels were required because consumers knew what they had bought. But with commercial bottling it was necessary to provide labels so that consumers could choose the wine they wanted. Labels are the way that we now know what is in a bottle of wine, and in fact we always choose wines to buy or drink by what is written on the label – either by the words that identify the wine or by the image and general impression that labels convey. A label that shows a château surrounded by vineyards might be thought to indicate higher quality wine than one that depicts a llama, giraffe, koala bear, or some other animal (unless it is the sheep on the label of a bottle of Château Mouton Rothschild). The typeface used on the label might convey gravitas or levity, as might the name of the wine. The line of Fat Bastard wines from the south of France (showing a hippopotamus) and the Grooner brand of Grüner Veltiner from Austria (showing a cartoon figure in a Tyrolean hat) suggest a less serious wine than many without images.

One label word that has assumed importance from the late 1800s is 'château'. Every Bordeaux estate is now known as a Château, whether or not it has an elegant building of the sort that the word implies. In the early nineteenth century, however, the top Bordeaux estates were known instead by the name of their proprietor and only two were regularly called Château: Margaux and Lafite. Cyrus Redding mentions only one château in his 1850 book, and the famous 1855 Bordeaux Classification lists only five: the First Growths Lafite, Margaux, and Latour; the Third Growth d'Issan; and the Fourth Growth Beycheville. The fact that these five were distributed over three growths suggests that there was no particular cachet attached to the word.

But clearly the word château became valued, because by the early twentieth century all the estates in the 1855 Classification were being called Château, as were a number of estates that were not included in the Classification, and several estates had begun to add Château to their names on their bottle labels. (The most prestigious Bordeaux estates began to bottle their own wines and sell their wines only by the bottle in order to combat widespread wine fraud in the claret industry in the late 1800s and early 1900s.) Before long the word Château became the default way of designating an estate in Bordeaux in the same way that Domaine did in Burgundy. Both Château and Domaine are aristocratic in implication, but Bordeaux had, arguably, a better claim to the association: nobles had owned Bordeaux's best vineyards for centuries, and many survived the French Revolution, which was not nearly as hard on the French nobility as many people believe. Most of Burgundy's best vineyards, in contrast, had been owned by the Church, especially the Cistercian order, before being sold at auction during the French Revolution – which was just as hard on the Church as many people believe.

It is not only aristocracy that the word château implies, but also a number of qualities that can be transferred to vineyards and wines: lineage, continuity, age, permanence, culture, and civilization. These values were all the more important at the end of the nineteenth century when France's vineyards were ravaged by phylloxera and when the solution involved humiliating noble French vines by grafting them onto parvenu American rootstock. Narratives of lineage, experience, and centuries-old vineyards were undermined by new plantings, and a new narrative was called for. The connotations of the château did the trick. No matter how new or old the châteaux were, they stood for history and tradition at a time when France's society, economy, and culture were experiencing vast and radical transformations. In the face of these changes, the château as a building represented stability. It has been written of Château Margaux that 'it is of the image of the vintage ... A wine long matured, a house long inhabited [it was actually built in the mid-1800s]: Margaux the vintage and Margaux the château are the products of two equally rare things: *rigour and time.*'

Château became a word that stood for quality in the popular mind, at least in the minds of many wine consumers. In the early 1890s, when a great deal of the Bordeaux wine (claret) imported into England was adulterated and blended with Spanish and other wines, a British wine trade publication wrote 'The public ... receive circulars offering Château this and Château that at apparently extremely low rates and on the strength of the name, purchase Wines, which can prove intensely disappointing.' The dismissive tone of 'Château this and Château that' suggests not only the novelty of the Château designation but also that the word was being used in a deceitful manner to cover up poor wines. Château became, however, a permanent verbal fixture in Bordeaux, and it was emulated in other French regions and outside France. There are or have been wineries with Château in their name in Canada, Australia, California, Lebanon, and Bulgaria.

If Château appears on some labels, other words appear on many more, beyond the words indicating the name of the producer, the name of the appellation, region, or country the wine is from, and the words indicating the volume of the bottle and the alcohol level – some of which are required by prevailing wine laws. Yet other words are discretionary and might or might not have any fixed meaning.

One is Reserve (Reserva in Spanish, Riserva in Italian). In some appellations it has a specific meaning and generally indicates that a wine has spent a minimum number of months in barrel (and sometimes in bottle) before being released for sale. In Chianti, for example, a Chianti Riserva must spend a minimum two years in barrel and three months in bottle. In Spain, a Reserva wine must be aged at least two years, of which at least six months are in barrel. A Gran Reserva wine must be aged a minimum of five years, at least two of which must be in barrel. These regulations (which change from time to time as wine laws are updated) are relatively new, as European wine laws date only to the 1930s. Before the word Reserva was regulated in countries such as Italy and Spain, before wine laws were introduced, wine producers had a great deal of leeway as to what they put on their labels. Almost the only regulated word was 'wine', and that was defined around the turn of the twentieth century as the fermented juice of fresh grapes, in response to perceptions of widespread wine fraud and adulteration.

There remain many words on wine labels that are either not regulated or not regulated everywhere. The word Reserve itself has precise meanings in Italy and Spain (and other European countries) as we have seen, but in much of the world it can be used by any wine producer who wants to do so. In the United States, Canada, Australia, and New Zealand, for example, wine producers tend to use Reserve to indicate a higher tier of wine than one not so designated, and it can also indicate that the wine has been aged before being released for sale. But there are no rules requiring a minimum period of ageing. In addition there is a wide range of qualified Reserves, such as Special Reserve, Proprietor's Reserve, and Vintner's Reserve. None has any legal meaning and must be counted as part of the marketing content of the label.

The same cannot be said of the grape varieties that are shown on wine bottle labels, something that, especially for New World wines, seems so normal that it seems natural. Grape varieties have been a subject of discussion for centuries, even if we often have no idea what some of them were. Part of the problem is that almost all varieties have several and, in some cases, many different names. The fact that Shiraz is also known as Syrah is well known, and there are some simple translations of some varieties, such as Verdejo in Spain and Verdelho in Portugal, and Pinot Gris in France and Pinot Grigio in Italy. Producers in other countries have a choice of the name they wish to label their wines with, and in some cases – such as Pinot Gris and Pinot Grigio (and Shiraz and Syrah) – each name has come to represent a different style of wine.

In the seventeenth and eighteenth centuries, when scientists began to categorize the plant and animal kingdoms, there were attempts to bring some order to the naming of grape varieties. To that point the same variety (perhaps different clones) was known by different names in different parts of each country. In many cases they still are: what is called Chardonnay in Burgundy (and throughout the non-French world) is known as Auvernat in Orléans and Gamay Blanc in Jura. Bordeaux's Malbec is called Cot in Cahors and Agreste in Lorraine. The range of names was much wider before the nineteenth century, and there were attempts to categorize them. In 1771 the botanist François Rozier established a vineyard near Béziers in southern France with the aim of collecting grape vines from all over the country so as to compare and categorize them. At the same time, the royal representative in Bordeaux sponsored a vineyard just outside the city where vines from the Paris area (at that time a major wine region) and other parts of France would be planted. The aim, again, was to categorize and 'to judge if there really are as many different species [varieties] as is imagined'. Given the multiplicity of names for each variety, you can be forgiven for thinking there were four, six, or ten times as many varieties in France as there really were.

The process of categorizing and settling on a national name for each variety took place in the 1800s, but over much of the century there was little change in the vineyards. Vignerons knew their vines by their local names, generally planted different varieties in the same vineyard, and picked all the grapes at the same time – some ripe, some unripe, some overripe – and vinified all the grapes, black and white, together. Their wines were field blends that represented the varieties in the vineyard and there was certainly no interest here in calling a wine by a dominant variety or by the varieties in the blend. There were some exceptions. In Burgundy the Pinot Noir grape (known as Noirien) was believed to make superior and more expensive wine, so vignerons largely kept it planted separately, although right through to the late 1800s it is clear that other varieties, including some white grapes, were planted among the Pinot Noir vines. Gamay was less prestigious, and Burgundy vignerons separated it from Pinot Noir – although there is no way of knowing how much Gamay might have crept into a Pinot Noir.

For most of France and Europe, however, vineyard plantings were fluid and pragmatic, rather than carefully regulated in terms of varieties, and it was not until widespread replanting was required after the phylloxera disaster that vineyards were replanted by variety. Phylloxera was an aphid introduced to Europe on native American vines imported for experimental purposes. It proved fatal to the European species of vine (*Vitis vinifera*), and wiped out three-quarters of the vines in France and high percentages of those in Italy, Spain, and elsewhere. When a solution to the problem was found (grafting *Vitis vinifera* vines onto rootstock of native American vines), almost all vineyards had to be replanted, and it was a time of great rationalization in European wine. Marginal regions (such as that around Paris) were not replanted, vines were planted in rows, and varieties that had not performed well were not replanted. In Bordeaux, for example, the Carmenère variety, which ripened very late and often had to be picked unripe so that it gave green notes to the flavour of wine, was not replanted.

Until the twentieth century, then, varieties were important to growers, even if they could not identify them, but consumers bought wine by geographical provenance, not by variety. Sometimes the country of origin was enough information, but region was also important, especially when wines came from regions that were considered prestigious: Champagne, Burgundy, and Bordeaux in France, the Rhine and Mosel Valleys in Germany, Chianti and Montepulciano in Italy, for example. In Europe regional and district names were more important than grape varieties, and wines were known either by broad regions or by sub-regions (sometimes even smaller districts) within them. When appellation laws were introduced, appellation names were dominant, and in Europe's three main wine-producing countries, wines became known as Rioja, Bordeaux, Chianti, and so on.

In Germany, by contrast, grape variety (almost always Riesling) was dominant, and grape variety was also eventually permitted on the labels of wines from Alsace as it moved back and forth between German and French control between 1870 and 1944. In the New World, where there were at first no wine laws, producers could label wines as they pleased and it pleased some of them to adopt the names of prestigious European appellations or wine styles. California and other wine-producing states, along with Canada, Australia, South Africa, and New Zealand, produced fortified wines labelled Sherry, Port, and Madeira; sparkling wines labelled Champagne; and table wines labelled Rhine Wine, Burgundy, Hock, and Claret. American wineries began to label their wines by grape variety only in the 1930s, and other New World producers slowly followed suit.

Labelling by variety is, then, quite a recent phenomenon, but it has been expanding. In France and Spain, especially, wine laws have been relaxed to allow producers to show the names of varieties as well as appellations. There are now Riojas showing the name Tempranillo, and Bordeaux wines showing the names of Cabernet Sauvignon and Merlot. These changes have largely been a response to market challenges posed by New World wines, which are almost always labelled by grape variety. There is also recognition that as wine consumption falls in Europe, European wine producers must sell more and more of their wines in the New World, where consumers are accustomed to buying wine by grape variety.

Still, there are some regions that resist selling by variety. One is Champagne, whose sales are robust enough that relabelling is hardly necessary. Others are well-known Italian regions such as Chianti and Barolo. Although some New World wine labels eschew variety in favour of a brand name, only one generic, non-varietal name is widely used, and that is Meritage. Meritage wines are blends of the grapes approved in Bordeaux. They were commonly referred to as 'Bordeaux blends', but when it became illegal to use that term, to protect the Bordeaux brand, the word Meritage was devised. Information on the grape varieties in a Meritage wine can be printed on the back label, and whether the Meritage authorities will allow them on the front label, as Bordeaux does with mass-market wines, remains to be seen.

6

WINE AND THE TABLE

At the 2013 Sommelier du Monde competition in Tokyo, contestants were asked to describe and identify four wines and to suggest food pairings for each. One contestant identified a wine as a Nebbiolo from Piedmont (it was a Côtes du Rhône) and recommended serving it with 'roasted lamb with a red wine sauce, and potatoes with black truffle salt'. Another contestant identified a wine as a Grüner Veltliner from Austria (it was a Chenin Blanc from India) and suggested serving it with 'sautéed shrimp with pancetta and orange, on a bed of wild rice' or a 'filet of pickerel, pan-fried, served on some herbed ravioli with a dill and grapefruit beurre blanc'.

Such exacting food pairings reflect a modern preoccupation with precision in wine and food matching. As descriptions of wines have become longer and more complex, as descriptors of aromas and flavours have been piled on top of one another, so there has been pressure to suggest food pairings that are equally complicated. For many wine writers, especially in North America, it is no longer enough to suggest eating white fish or red meat with a particular wine; it is necessary to be precise as to the kind of fish, bird, or animal, to specify the cut, and to describe in detail the method of preparation, the condiments, the sauces, and the accompaniments.

This style of wine and food matching, whose complexity probably makes it of interest and value to a very small number of people, has an equally shallow history, as it seems to go back no further than the 1980s. During the preceding thousands of years that wine has been available, the history of drinking wine while eating food was largely characterized by informality and promiscuity: given some wine – any wine – a person would be happy to drink it with whatever food happened to be available, and diners seemed to care very little about which wine – red or white, light or full-bodied, this variety or appellation or another – they reached for as they ate. It might well be that some patterns or rationales underlay the apparent randomness of foods and wines that we know were consumed together, but with few exceptions it is very difficult to discern them. For the very reason that precise food and wine matching was not important, hardly anyone bothered to record the precise wines they consumed during their meals. But what is interesting is that they were far more likely to describe the food in detail than the wine.

WINE AND FOOD IN ANCIENT SOCIETIES

For wine to be carefully paired – or not – with food, both must be present on the table, and even though that might seem perfectly natural to us, it has a history in its own right. We have no idea of how early in human history food and wine began to be combined, but we can assume that food was for a long time consumed without wine; water must have been the first beverage at what passed for the prehistoric table. The earliest evidence of wine dates back to northern China about 9,000 years ago, when grapes were part of a fermented beverage that included rice and honey. The earliest known winemaking facility dates back about 8,000 years in the southern Caucasus region of Georgia. But only much later do we get clear evidence of food and wine existing in the same locations. In many of the earliest sites where evidence has been found – in Georgia, China, and in the Zagros mountains on the border of modern Iran and Iraq – wine is more likely to be associated with religious occasions, such as funerals. This is not to say that food was not consumed on these occasions, and in fact the funeral banquet of King Midas which took place about 700 BC (see below, p. 161) included both food and drink.

WINE AND FOOD

At the same time, most ancient representations of wine drinking show it happening without food. Many Egyptian depictions, for example, are of parties where participants drank beer and wine, apparently without eating food at the same time. That might go some way to accounting for depictions of drinkers at these parties vomiting, passing out, and having to be carried away. The Greek symposium, an occasion when elite males gathered to drink diluted wine all night, did not include food but did follow a meal. After a banquet without wine, the men separated from the women and went to a room that was dedicated for the symposium. For the following hours, until dawn, they drank watered-down (and thus low-alcohol) wine, but on full stomachs. This was not unlike the eighteenth-century (and later) English upper-class practice where the men separated from the women after a meal and went to a separate room to drink port. The difference was that the ideal of the Greeks' symposium was to drink but remain relatively sober, while eighteenth-century English port-drinking men aimed to get drunk and revelled in their intoxication.

The Roman version of the symposium, the convivium, did include food, so it was an occasion where wine and food were consumed together – and where women were sometimes admitted. We have sometimes generous accounts of the food that was consumed at convivia, and meals were often replete with many dishes – sometimes despite Roman sumptuary laws that stipulated that sows' udders should not be eaten and that no meal should include more than one winged creature, and that the creature should not be fattened by force feeding. In a rare surviving dinner invitation from about 55 BC, the Greek philosopher Philodemus invited his Roman friend Piso to a meal but specified that they will have to forgo delicacies such as sows' udders and wine from the island of Chios – a highly prized wine at the time. It is frustrating that while we know what Philodemus and Piso did not eat and drink, we do not know what they did.

Despite these prohibitions, sows' udders ranked as delicacies at some convivia, along with such prestigious dishes as fresh shellfish and mullet and more pedestrian items of meat, fish, fowl, fruit, and cheese. It is not clear whether wine accompanied the food or followed it. In one wall painting at Pompeii, as John H. D'Arms put it, 'the painter has represented the banquet as having reached its final, sympotic phase: there are no signs whatsoever of any foods, and the figures are deep into the *commissatio*, post-prandial carousing'. Other paintings show banqueters drinking and displaying drinking cups, with more drinking paraphernalia on tables and servants moving through the room, dispensing wine. Food and drink might have been consumed at the same time, but representations generally show one or the other and in great detail. Foodstuffs occasionally appear in drinking scenes, but 'when they appear at all, are usually unidentifiable'. All this suggests that in cultural terms, the consumption of wine and food together was not important.

There is some evidence that the Romans came to combining wine and food relatively late. For many centuries their diet was primarily liquid and took the form of *puls*, a porridge or gruel made from emmer, a hulled wheat known in Italy as *farro*. Because of the difficulty of making bread from emmer, it made a late appearance in Rome, with the first bakeries being established between 171 and 168 BC. The shift from wet to dry food as the staple of the Roman diet might explain the increased popularity of wine, as it is necessary to accompany bread with liquid in a way that is not so with gruel. From the end of the second century AD, bread and wine were firmly paired in the Roman diet.

Bread and wine were, in fact, commonly consumed together for thousands of years. There have been times, such as the seventeenth and eighteenth centuries, when bread was the staple diet of the mass of Europe's populations – they derived the bulk of their calories and nutrients from it, and they spent most of the money available for food on it. In those parts of Europe where wine was relatively inexpensive, bread and wine must have been the default pairing. But we should also bear in mind that wine was not consumed by all Europeans. It was more commonly drunk in southern Europe, where grape vines grew easily and wine could be produced cheaply. In much of northern Europe, on the other hand, wine was more expensive because little could be supplied from local sources and most had to be shipped over long distances, which added to the price at its destination. Here, only the better-off strata of society could afford wine.

And we should always remember that throughout Europe, right through to the twentieth century, extreme poverty was extensive, and that the poor had no option but to drink water, no matter what its quality and whether physicians advised against it. Moreover, although adult men with the means to drink wine might have done so often, even daily, other demographics probably abstained or drank wine rarely. Children were advised not to drink wine for reasons based on the humoral understanding of the human body, and there was a general social objection to women drinking wine for fear that they would become intoxicated and sexually careless. Because women and children made up the majority of Europe's populations, wine drinking on anything like a regular basis, with or without food, was very much a minority practice there from the Middle Ages until the twentieth century.

That said, wine found its way to the tables of the middle and upper classes of Europe from the Middle Ages onwards. Some of the evidence lies in paintings and other visual representations, as we shall see later in this chapter, but there are also some descriptions of meals that comprised food and wine. It is not surprising that most involve banquets and the upper classes, as these are the dining occasions that were more likely to be recorded in documents that were most likely to have survived. Meals further down the social scale were rarely described, although there are odd exceptions. For example, in a divorce hearing in the Norman city of Rouen during the French Revolution it was noted that the couple had separated and then got back together, and that to make their 'reunion' known they had invited their neighbours for a meal with wine. (Clearly the event was not enough to seal the reunion, as they found themselves divorcing soon afterwards.)

As for banquets and feasts, where we expect wine always to have played a major role, Ken Albala notes that in the first two centuries of the Early Modern period the culinary literature was 'surprisingly reticent' on the subject of wine. There are references to wine in food preparation and discussions of the staff who would serve wine, but very little on specific grape varieties and on styles of wine. In this respect writers on the practicalities and etiquette of dining tell us far less about wine than physicians who wrote about the effects on wine on health. It is, of course, possible to extrapolate dining practices from medical advice. If physicians recommended against drinking wine that had been cooled by ice or snow, then diners might have avoided cooling wines this way at the table. But there is no certainty that medical advice related to eating and drinking was any more conscientiously followed in the past than it is today.

Ken Albala gives examples of how 'the concerns of health and gastronomy could directly clash'. Physicians warned against drunkenness and the diseases it could cause, including weakening the ability to procreate; against drinking chilled wine; against adding things such as sandalwood, aloes, and musk to wine because they caused headaches; against eating fruit at the end of a meal; and against drinking wine while eating peaches because the wine prematurely forced the fruit into the veins before it could be digested. Yet these 'were all common courtly practices at the time', Albala notes. Fruit and wine, which for centuries was considered a problematic pairing, was almost always served toward the end of a meal to refresh diners' palates.

A more general example of medical advice is the question of excess, in this case excess in both drinking and eating. Physicians and others had warned against excessive drinking for thousands of years, but in the Early Modern period these warnings intensified and were supplemented by strong advice against gluttony in respect of food. But lavish feasts, which established their hosts' social worth, were lavish because of the sheer amount of food and drink that was provided, as well as its variety and richness. Many such meals included a staggering range of meat, fish, and fowl, not to mention fruits, nuts, and other items. The offerings were generous; to say that the guests ate well is an understatement, and, in the eyes of physicians, they overloaded their digestive systems perilously.

Wine had historically been touted as an aid to digestion, but drinking too much wine with too much food – as seems to have been the general practice at banquets – only made things worse. Physicians argued that wine, a warm beverage in the humoral way of understanding the human body, added intolerable heat to the already-warm process of digestion. It produced vapours that rose into the brain, overwhelming diners and making them become confused and incoherent. The suggestion here is that the symptoms we associate with drunkenness might result from drinking too much wine or from drinking wine moderately while eating too much food. This would not be drunkenness as we commonly understand it – the result of drinking alcohol to excess.

The issue of consuming wine and food at the same time raises the question of whether some wine and food pairings were common or thought desirable in the past. (The term 'wine pairing' has come to mean not simply drinking wine with food but a particularly good or successful combination of a particular wine with a specific food.) Some records of meals are fascinating, but they throw little light on our subject. An example is the remains of a lavish meal consumed in about 700 BC and thought to have been the funeral banquet of King Midas. A burial chamber in an artificial mound, located in Gordion in central Turkey (formerly the capital of the Phrygian empire over which Midas ruled), contained the skeleton of a 60- to 65-year-old male in a log coffin, surrounded by the residue of a banquet. There were three 150-litre vats to hold liquid, more than a hundred drinking bowls, bronze plates, and other dining paraphernalia. It suggests a larger gathering than the chamber could have accommodated, and so the meal was probably eaten outdoors.

As for what the guests ate and drank, chemical and botanical analysis of the residues showed both the food and the beverage were combinations of ingredients. The food was a stew of goat or sheep meat that had been marinated in oil, honey, and wine before being grilled. It was then mixed with lentils and cereals and additionally flavoured with herbs and spices. This stew was accompanied by a beverage that was no less complex: a mixture – although 'blend' is probably a more positive word – of wine made from grapes, beer made from barley, and mead (honey diluted with water and then fermented). It is not clear whether these ingredients were co-fermented or made individually and then blended. If the three 150-litre vats were full of this beverage and there were as many guests as drinking bowls (a hundred), each guest could have had more than four litres and the banquet might have been quite lively.

Of course, we can only guess what the food and the drink tasted like. For both it would have depended not only on the flavours of each ingredient but also on the proportions of each. More mead would have sweetened the beverage, more herbs and spices would have intensified the flavours of the goat/sheep stew. What we do not know is whether the drink and food were in any sense prepared so that they 'paired' well together, or whether each was prepared independently on the implicit assumption that all that was required was a tasty beverage and tasty food. It is foolish to assume that the preparation of food and drink (or any other aspect of culture) in early societies was intuitive rather than deliberate, or crude rather than sophisticated, but in many cases (such as this one) we simply do not have evidence either way.

The classical period does not produce a lot more information. The Greek and Roman authors tell us a lot about food and even more about wine, and although they might well consume both together at times, they seldom commented on any combinations as being particularly appropriate. The Greek custom in some cases (such as symposia) was to eat food and then to drink wine afterwards, thus clearly separating the two. Greek and Roman descriptions of wines often provide information on their colour, weight, and medical properties, but they are silent on the food they go best with. To make a point that will be expanded upon toward the end of this chapter, the long historical silence about combining specific wines and foods reinforces the distinctiveness of the modern preoccupation of food and wine pairing.

WINE, FOOD, AND HEALTH

To this point we have generally assumed that pairing food and wine means looking for similarities or contrasts in their flavours and textures. But Greek and Roman physicians and their Arab counterparts set up other criteria to consider when they developed the humoral system, described more fully on pp. 8–14. Briefly, the strength and balance of each of the four humours in a body contributed to the individual's physical and emotional wellbeing, and each humour was located on two axes: dry–moist or cold–hot. A healthy person was one whose humours were at the right strength and in balance with one another. But there was no single, universally correct balance, and there were variations among individuals, no matter what their age and gender, so that each person had their own unique humoral composition. When an individual's humours became unbalanced in terms of what was appropriate for them, they became physically or emotionally ill, and the aim of the physician was to rebalance the humours so as to restore the patient to health. It was a complicated process, as the physician needed to ascertain each patient's correct balance in order to restore it and then to prescribe ways of achieving that goal.

Diet was critical to humoral medicine or therapy because every item of food and drink was given a value on the warm–cold and dry–moist scales. Wine and meat, for example, were warm, while beer and most fruit and fish were cold. These values of warmth and coldness did not reflect the physical attributes of the beverages and food, but rather the contribution they made to the individual humours. Wine, for example, boosted the role of blood in the body because both wine and blood were warm and moist, and that would be useful where a patient was cold and clammy. In the case of an illness accompanied by a fever that heated the body, cold foods, such as beer and fish, might be prescribed to counteract the body's excessive warmth.

In *The Taming of the Shrew* (Act IV, Scene I), William Shakespeare provides a practical example of the relationship between the humoral theory and food. Petruchio pretends to be disagreeable and angry so as to demonstrate to his wife, Katherina (the 'shrew', or an unpleasant woman), what it is like to be in her company. In humoral terms, being disagreeable was to be choleric, a disposition that reflects the dominance of yellow bile, also known as choler, in the body. Shakespeare has Petruchio berate the servants for serving over-cooked mutton (meat from an older sheep) which is classified as a choleric food, to two people who are already choleric. When Katherina suggests that he is over-reacting, Petruchio replies:

> I tell thee, Kate, 'twas burnt and dried away.
> And I expressly am forbid to touch it,
> For it engenders choler, planteth anger;
> And better 'twere that both of us did fast,
> Since of ourselves, ourselves are choleric,
> Than feed it with such over-roasted flesh.

Here Petruchio states that he was expressly forbidden, perhaps by a physician, to avoid 'choleric' food because it would only intensify his irritability and anger. He goes on to say that because they were both inclined to be choleric, it would be better for them to eat nothing rather than to tuck into the overcooked mutton.

It is not difficult to see how this humoral theory affected wine and food pairing, at least from the perspective of physicians. Wine was a warm beverage (although some wines were warmer than others) and it was important not to pair it with too much warm food that might overwhelm the body with warmth. Assuming that a diner's humours were in balance (that is, that they were not ill) a meal that was balanced would reinforce their wellbeing by not upsetting the equilibrium. If the meal included fish (which was cold and moist) and fruit (which was also cold), it made sense to drink wine, whose warmth balanced their humoral coldness.

Allen Grieco notes that some Italian proverbs from the Early Modern period capture some of these pairings, even if they lose some of their catchiness in translation: 'sui pesci, mesci' ('with fish, drink wine'), 'costa di vacca e vino senz'acqua' ('cows ribs and wine without water'), and 'pesche, peri e pomi vogliono vini buoni' ('peaches, pears and apples require good [strong] wines'). Similar proverbs existed in seventeenth-century France, where pears were thought to be very difficult to digest. One proverb advises 'after pear, drink wine', and a Breton proverb direly predicts that 'if pears are not followed by wine, they will soon be followed by the priest'. The stress here is on wine as an aid to digestion, but these proverbs emerge from a culture where the humoral system was the principal basis of understanding the body's functions. We might also note that pears were considered 'feminine' and that this quality could be counteracted by drinking a 'masculine' wine.

An important characteristic of wine in the humoral system, remember, was that it was understood as having gradations of heat, whereas nearly all other beverages and foodstuffs were attributed a single value: they were either warm or cold. By the Middle Ages, sweet and rich wines were considered warmer than lighter, more acidic wines, and there were even more nuanced scales of warmth. In the mid-fifteenth century one physician wrote that 'small' wines (possibly meaning wines with low alcohol) were warm in the first degree, more powerful small wines were warm in the second degree, wines made from Grenache, Malvasia, and certain other grape varieties were warm in the third degree, and eau-de-vie (made from wine) was warm to the fourth degree.

These gradations of warmth made possible a more precise pairing of wine with food, with the physician playing the role of the modern sommelier. If the food was a combination of warm and cold ingredients – such as meat, fish, vegetables, and fruit, where the cold was predominant but did not monopolize the meal – it was possible to calibrate the heat provided by the wine by selecting one that was more or less warm. This is vaguely analogous to the modern practice of pairing food with wine made from a specific grape variety or in a specific style. But although you might have heard a sixteenth-century physician advise that 'you should drink a Grenache with that meal', it was the degree of warmth that was in play, not the grape variety in itself nor the wine's match with the flavours, weight, and texture of a dish.

The humoral approach to food and drink reflected the dominant paradigm of understanding sickness and health and the functioning of the human body for more than two thousand years. Yet we should not assume that during that long period everyone designed their diets in light of their humoral composition. For the mass of people, many of whom were poor (the indigent and working poor could easily make up a third of the population) the daily diet was not so much a matter of choice but a matter of eating whatever was available.

WINE, FOOD, AND CLASS

Bread or gruel were the staple foods for most Europeans until the nineteenth century, and wine might have been widely consumed in wine-producing regions where it was relatively inexpensive because the price did not include the costs of shipping. But beer was cheaper than wine everywhere and in northern Europe, where viticulture was difficult, wine consumption was restricted to the better-off sections of society. Even though it is widely believed that everyone in Early Modern Europe drank beer and wine because the water supplies were thought to be dangerous, many people – perhaps most people – must have drunk only water as their means of hydration. The poor could not afford wine or beer, but water – whether or not it was safe to consume – was free. Physicians insisted that children, who made up a much larger part of the population than they do today, should not drink wine because it was warm and would overheat their already-warm bodies. There was a general male preference that women should not drink wine or beer in case it loosened their inhibitions and led to fornication or adultery. These three categories – the poor, women, and children – must have accounted for at least three-quarters of the population. It means that in wine-producing regions at the very most a quarter of the population (financially viable adult males) drank wine, and that fraction would have been much smaller in parts of Europe where only imported wine was available. It made drinking wine very much a minority activity, and concern for the food that it accompanied even more limited than today.

In addition to the humoral values that were attributed to individual foods, there were cultural and social values in that some foods were considered more appropriate to the upper classes and others to the lower orders. In many cases it was a matter of cost and availability. The swans, ducks, capons, and other unfortunate birds that found themselves decorating banquet tables were beyond the reach of any but the wealthy. So were the rich desserts and other accompaniments. In general terms the mass of the rural population supplemented their cereal-based food with a little meat – often pork, as pigs could be kept more easily than other animals because they scavenged for food.

Beyond considerations of cost and availability, the Church imposed restrictions on the foods that could be eaten at certain times of the year. Dairy products were especially problematic, and Ken Albala speculates that for perhaps a third of the year butter and cheese were forbidden or could be consumed only by special dispensation from the Church. Some cities purchased global dispensations for their inhabitants. Bans on consuming dairy products were a particular hardship in northern Europe and elsewhere where dairy cattle were common, and substitutes, such as olive oil, were expensive. There were frequent complaints about having to purchase substitutes when butter and other animal fats were plentiful and relatively inexpensive.

In various ways, then, for reasons of cost, health, cultural value, and religion – not to mention the basic seasonality that limited the availability of foodstuffs – the diets of the great majority of Early Modern Europeans were relatively restricted. If cereals prepared in various ways, mainly as bread and gruel, were the staple ingredients of the diet of the mass of the population, that was what wine was drunk with, and any advice regarding other foods and the various styles of wine was largely irrelevant.

STYLES OF WINE

Yet another consideration was the style of wines that were popular at any given time. Today most of us are used to having access to a wide range of wines – wines from many countries, made from many grape varieties, varietal and blended wines, and wines of several colours and styles. For most of the past, the selection of wines was much more restricted. In much of France, for example, the dominant wine style from the Middle Ages to the nineteenth century was a light-coloured, light-bodied, and relatively low-alcohol (about 10 per cent) red. This style of wine, often made from both red and white varieties, was known as clairet in France and claret in England, where it became synonymous with red wine from Bordeaux. Clairet was, however, the default style in much of France, no matter which grape varieties were grown in different regions. There were other styles – white wines and weightier reds – but clairet was the most common.

Clairet was also said to be a style of wine that was most suitable for those who did not live by labour. The French agronomist Olivier de Serres, who wrote extensively on viticulture and wine, noted in 1600 that 'good, full-bodied red and black [deep red] wines' were 'appropriate for working people … and greatly sought after by them as much as white and clairet wines are by people of leisure'. A few years later Jean Liebault, a physician, wrote that 'red wine nourishes more than white or clairet and is more suitable for those who work hard because work and vigorous exercise neutralize any of the disadvantages that red wine has'. As for the dark red wine that was commonly referred to as 'black wine', 'it is best for vignerons and farmers because once digested by the activity of the stomach and work, it gives more solid and plentiful nourishment and makes the man stronger in his work'. Even if these heavy wines weighed on the drinker and made his blood 'thick, melancholic, and slow-flowing', there was no cause for concern because manual workers were earthy, thick, and slow anyway, In contrast, Liebault wrote that clairet and white wines passed easily from the stomach to the liver, producing rich blood and rejuvenating the heart and brain.

The dominance of clairet in France and also in England, where it became very popular from the thirteenth century onwards, made it the default wine at the tables of the better-off. If there was any pairing to be done, it meant starting with clairet and calibrating the food, rather than matching wine to any dish being served. This is not to say that all clairets were the same. They were made from various grape varieties that included both red and white because until the twentieth century most vineyards in Europe were planted in a number of varieties. Varieties were not reliably classified until the nineteenth century, and for the most part they were not planted separately in Europe until the extensive replanting that was required after the phylloxera disaster of the late 1800s and early 1900s.

Until then, wines were generally field blends of several varieties – wines made from the varieties as they occurred in the vineyard, with the varieties co-fermented. Some varieties ripened before others so that each vintage, with its unique weather conditions, produced a different combination of ripe, over-ripe, and under-ripe grapes. When we say that the default wine was clairet, then, we do not mean that the wine was consistent in flavour, body, texture, and alcohol; it varied from year to year, place to place, and batch to batch. There was also variation in colour, although within an acceptable range because colour was important; winemakers would add dark red wine to deepen clairet or white wine to lighten it, all with the purpose of obtaining a colour that clairet drinkers considered acceptable.

PAIRING WINE AND FOOD

The higher one's status and wealth, the more likely one was to drink wine and the greater the range of wines one had to draw from. To this extent, the better-off had at least the opportunity to select different wines to pair with food if they wanted to. In the seventeenth century the English diarist Samuel Pepys recorded his wine purchases and the contents of his cellar in considerable detail, and described many of his meals in equal detail. But it is telling of the unimportance of precise wine and food pairing that Pepys usually failed to bring the two together.

As far as his cellar was concerned, Pepys listed casks of wine from Spain, Malaga, and the Canary Islands, as well as claret, sherry, and an unidentified white wine. Recording the cellars of his acquaintances, Pepys listed even more, including champagne, wine from the Rhine Valley, Greece, Syracuse, and Florence.

It was Pepys who famously first recorded the arrival in London of wine from the Haut-Brion estate from the Graves district of Bordeaux – the estate responsible for the First Growth wine in the 1855 Bordeaux Classification. On 10 April 1663 Pepys wrote that he had gone to the Royal Oak Tavern 'and here drank a sort of red wine, called Ho Bryan, that hath a good and most particular taste that I never met with'. It is a frustrating tasting note because it does not tell us what made the flavour of that Haut-Brion (perhaps a young wine from the 1662 vintage) so 'good and most particular'. Something about it made it stand out from the other clarets that Pepys must have been used to drinking, but we do not know what it was. But it was likely that he drank it at about noon and without food, as the entry in his diary for that day continued with 'home to dinner', a reference to the midday meal.

Pepys often listed the wines and other beverages he drank, but seldom described their qualities. In 1661 he writes of taking an acquaintance to a tavern 'and there did give him a tankard of white wine and sugar', a common practice in England in order sweeten wines, but not a description of the wine itself. In 1666 he refers to 'burnt claret', which could mean it was fortified with brandy ('brandy' comes from the Dutch word for 'burnt wine'), was distilled claret, or claret warmed by the fire. But Pepys rarely mentions combining specific wines with specific foods, although occasionally he came tantalizingly close. The hundred or more guests at the reception that preceded his brother's funeral in 1663 were served 'six biscuits apiece, and what they pleased of burnt claret'. Later that day, Pepys and a few others went to his brother's house and ate oysters, cake, and cheese, but there was no mention of wine. On a hot day in June, 1661, Pepys noted that he and some others stayed outside until midnight, 'drinking great draughts of claret, and eating botargo [cured fish roe] and bread and butter'.

For the most part, though, Pepys describes his more elaborate meals by listing all the foods but either ignoring the wines or describing them vaguely as 'many wines' or 'wine of all sorts'. In 1662, for example, he invited people to dinner and 'I having some venison given me a day or two ago, I had a shoulder roasted, another baked, and the umbles [liver, kidneys, and other organs] baked in a pie'. There was no mention of wine but, knowing Pepys (who was not at that time in one of the phases where he was trying to give wine up) it must have been present; he notes that 'we were merry as I could be in that company'. Pepys invited his father, brother, uncle, and cousins to breakfast in 1660: 'I had for them a barrel of oysters, a dish of neat's tongues [beef tongues], and a dish of anchovies, wine of all sorts, and Northdown ale.' Specifying the regional ale that was consumed with the varied foods trumped the need to name the wines.

Although there are few reliable descriptions of the specific foods and drinks at individual meals, household accounts can give us a glimpse into what some better-off people ordered. In January 1784 the Duke of Saulx-Tavanes, whose country estate was located only a few kilometres from Dijon, in Burgundy, ordered the following items of food and drink:

Turkey with truffles	Rum from Jamaica
Chicken patties of Rouen	Cognac
Sauerkraut of Strasbourg	Muscat wine from Toulon
Olives of Marseille	Malaga wine
Rocquefort cheese (in a pot)	Rhine wine
Anchovies in oil	Bordeaux wine
Spiced bread of Rheims	Mocha coffee
Prunes of Tours	Cayenne coffee
Levant rice	

There was plenty of variation and many exotic items in this one month's order, which clearly did not represent the whole range of foods in the duke's larder or the wines in his cellar. There is no inventory of all the food, which was fairly transient, but we do have a record of his cellar. It was dominated by 240 bottles of wine from Beaune (which was not far away from his estate) and a similar number from the Médoc, in Bordeaux – presumably most of them clairet. They were supplemented by several hundred more bottles from Champagne, Malaga, Smyrna, Cyprus, Montliban, and Tokai. He also bought wine by the barrel, such as the cask of Bordeaux wine he purchased in 1787. Clearly, there was the possibility of some imaginative food and wine pairing, but if it did occur, the duke's records are silent on it.

In some situations, wine and food pairing was limited by circumstances. When Bishop Nicholas Ridley and Archbishop Hugh Latimer were imprisoned in Oxford in 1555–56 prior to being executed, the bailiffs who organized their meals kept careful records so that they could have their expenditures reimbursed. The menus that are described are notable for the variety of foods the prisoners were served, and it is clear that there was an attempt to provide them with diets appropriate to their social rank. So fastidious were the bailiffs on this point that they ensured they spent more on the archbishop's meals than on the bishop's. In the first half of October, 1555, they spent 1,473 pence on Archbishop Cranmer's food and drink, a good third more than they put out for Bishop Ridley (1,102.5 pence). And although ale and wine were served with both main meals of the day (dinner and supper), Cranmer's wine cost 6 pence a day, while Ridley's cost less than half that.

Wine is prominent at the meal table of a middle-class Dutch family in the eighteenth century. Engraving by T. Houbraken after C. Troost.

Again, as so often in the records, the foods are described in rich detail. There were eighteen different freshwater and ocean fish and sea foods, including pickerel, herring, plaice, mussels, and oysters; ten kinds of meat (such as bacon, beef, calf's head, and marrow bone); and nine sorts of 'fowl' (including lark, capon, duck, and plover). Other items included cheese, eggs, fruit, and desserts, together with butter and marmalade. Bread was served with every meal. But in contrast to the precise description of the food (which was needed to justify the cost), the omnipresent drink was described simply as 'wine'. Although the records show that fish and meat were not served together at meals, there is no hint that the wine on each occasion was any different – that white was served with fish, red with meat. It is quite likely that claret was served with all meals, but we cannot know for certain. The only hint of a relationship between meals and a wine style was that when caudel (a sweet wine-based punch) was served, it came after the meal, rather than with it.

Workers who were provided with wine as part of their pay were limited to the wine that was provided to them. A striking example of wine rations comes from the Arsenal, the ship-building facility of Venice, in the seventeenth century. The wine provided to workers throughout the working day was a large part of the Arsenal's budget, partly because it had to be shipped from further down the Italian peninsula. Because the wine was diluted to a ratio of one-part wine to two-parts water before being served, local wines from the Veneto and the northern Adriatic were too weak and wine was shipped from the south, where it was more robust and higher in alcohol. Consumption rose dramatically in the early 1600s, from 3.2 litres per worker in 1615 to 1619 to nearly 5 litres in the late 1630s, but an inquiry showed that much of the extra was being consumed by family members and outsiders who came to the Arsenal for the free wine. In the winter months, when the workers stayed in the Arsenal for their lunch, this wine was part of their meal. It seems to have been a substantial part, for when managers carried out a survey they found that workers who went home for lunch consumed 20 per cent less wine.

The wine that the Arsenal's workers drank was the same throughout the year, but popular medical works sometimes suggested seasonal styles of wine. In winter, reads one English guide, 'they drynke ofte stronge wynes', while another recommended that in spring one should 'drinke temperate wine, beere or ale, so that they be not to stronge, ne oversweet. For in this time all sweet things ought not to be used.' If such medical advice were followed, it would mean that 'temperate' (less strong, less alcoholic) wine would be drunk in the summer and autumn when fresh vegetables and fruit were available. During the winter, when menus might be more dominated by meats and salted produce, heavier wines would come into play.

A final criterion of wine and food pairing that was probably important in the past is provenance. One of the common formulas for wine and food pairing today is to drink the wines with the foods that come from the same region. This seems a straightforward matter in some cases. For example, Muscadet, the white wine made (now) from the Melon de Bourgogne grape variety in regions near the mouth of the Loire River, is a classic wine for pairing with fish and crustaceans. It is easy to see that the wine might have been made to pair with the fresh-water fish of the Loire or with the fish and seafood from the Atlantic Ocean. Similarly the red wines of northern Italy are often said to be perfect matches for the richer meat and pasta dishes of the region, while Malbec, the signature wine of Argentina, goes well with the beef that is so prominent in the Argentine diet.

For reasons of cost, if nothing else, it makes sense to think that people in the past ate and drank locally – that what they consumed was grown, raised, and produced in the area where they lived for the simple reason that local produce was less expensive than produce that had to be transported to its destination market. That meant that people living near the sea or rivers ate more fish than people living far from water, and that people living in the Mediterranean area consumed more olive oil than their counterparts in northern Europe. It must have been the same with wine, too, and for the same reason: that, all things being equal, local wine was less expensive than wine produced elsewhere. Drinking the wine and eating the food from the same district or region, a sometimes helpful guideline for wine and food pairing today, was simply a financial imperative in earlier times.

REPRESENTATIONS OF WINE AND FOOD

Perhaps paintings and other portrayals of meals, tables of food and drink, and banquets can throw some light on food and wine pairings. Items of food and drink were also popular subjects for still-life artists, and meals of various kinds provided focal points for depictions of social interactions of many kinds. Wine frequently figured in these representations, and their contexts might illuminate contemporary food and wine pairings. But there are limits to the usefulness of art in this respect. First, we must assume that the wine and food were represented accurately when it was painted from a subject, such as a still life. Even then, it is possible that a painter might modify the colour of a wine for aesthetic or painterly reasons – to whiten or lighten a dark red wine so that it stood out more effectively against a dark background. Wine was flexible, in this sense, as various colours were known to the artist's audience; it would have been far less feasible to tamper with the colour of fish, bread, or fruit. As for images based on imagination, such as representations of the Last Supper, it might well be that the food and drink reflected the habits of the time of the painter, but we really have no way of being sure.

Another limitation of the use of paintings for exploring food and wine combinations is that unless there is supplementary information, we can generally learn no more about the wine than its colour or hue. There were white wines and red wines in paintings, and sometimes the hues are significantly different: white wines are sometimes watery and transparent and sometimes golden and almost opaque, while reds can be light and translucent or a deep opaque ruby. Occasionally, beads of condensation on a glass or carafe alert us to the likelihood that a wine was served chilled. What we cannot tell from paintings, however, is how dry or sweet the wines were, whether they were intensely or lightly flavoured, what they tasted like, and whether they were fresh and fruity, tannic, acidic, or oxidized.

In some cases we might want to leap to assumptions, such as that a golden-coloured white wine accompanying a sweet dessert was a sweet white wine, that a transparent white wine with fish was dry, and that a red wine on a table with roasted game meats was full-bodied and somewhat tannic. These are matters for the eye and the imagination, but the evidence we can glean from a few dozen representations discussed here (a very small and unscientific sampling of the vast corpus of food-centred art) suggests that we cannot draw any firm conclusions. The food and wine pairings in these representations (most painted between 1500 and 1800) seem no more systematic than those described in the literary sources of the period.

Food and wine without a table: a Roma family enjoying a meal of bread, soup, and wine. Eighteenth-century engraving by Francus Pedro after Francus Maggiotto.

Overall, these paintings show no clear patterns in their combinations of food and wine. The major exception was oysters, which were almost invariably shown with white wine. For example, Pieter Claesz's *Still Life with Oysters and Goblet* (1642) shows a plate of shucked oysters, a lemon, bread, and a goblet of chilled white wine – 'chilled', because there is condensation on the outside of the glass. The pairing is such that it could be a photograph from a modern table, where white wines such as Chablis, Muscadet, Chenin Blanc, or Albariño – all suitably chilled – are common wine pairings with oysters.

Oysters were long considered to be common or base food – food appropriate for the masses but not for the upper classes – and they were probably consumed by many ordinary folk with beer or water, rather than with wine. But in the seventeenth century their cultural status rose and they are shown in Claesz's painting in a context suggesting they were on the table of a well-off household. In seventeenth-century Holland, only wealthier people ate off pressed white tablecloths and the kind of dishes shown in the painting, and only they would have drunk chilled wine. Claesz used essentially the same wine (judging only by appearance) in other food-centred still-life paintings that featured such items as crab, lobster, and turkey pie. Perhaps it was nothing more than the wine he drank as he painted.

Oysters and white wine also appear in William Hogarth's *The Banquet* (1754), one of four paintings illustrating an electoral campaign. In this one, which is all about the gluttony of the governing Whig party, a portly man wearing a wig that has slipped askew has fallen ill after eating many oysters (the shells are on the table in front of him). That the company at the table are drinking white wine is shown by a boy-servant emptying a cask of white wine into a vat beside the table. A bowl floating in the wine and another nearby make it clear that this wine is being poured out generously to everyone at the table.

Perhaps the best-known representation of oysters is *The Oyster Lunch* (about 1735), by Jean François de Troy. In an elaborate salon a group of wealthy men have gathered for lunch. A servant shucks oysters, with the shells piling up, while the guests enjoy them with bread. The sole wine in the scene is champagne, being served from the bulb-shaped bottles typical of the eighteenth century, and the painting shows some of the men looking upward as their eyes follow the trajectory of a cork that has been popped. Beside the table is an ice chest containing more bottles of champagne, with only their necks showing above the water. Despite the title, this painting seems to be as much about the champagne as about the oysters, and it certainly emphasizes the pairing of the two.

If oysters and other seafood seem to have attracted white wine, there seems to have been no universal rule to show people drinking white wine with fish. The early sixteenth-century painting *St Benedict Feeding the Monks* (a fresco in the Abbey of Monte Oliveto Maggiore in Siena) shows Saint Benedict and five monks, each with bread and a plate holding two small fish that are reminiscent of sardines. There are three carafes on the table, only one of which contains liquid, and it is clearly red wine. Four of the monks have glasses of red wine or the residue of red wine. Perhaps significantly, Saint Benedict himself has no wine, as it was his view that monks should not drink wine, with or without food. We have no idea if sixteenth-century monks looking at this fresco were taken aback by the combination of red wine and fish. Perhaps they were accustomed to drinking red wine with everything or perhaps it was *de rigueur* to paint wine red in religious images because red wine evoked Christ's blood.

Annibale Caracci's *The Bean-Eater* (1585) is rare among portrayals of tables as it shows a man of the lower classes eating. This meatless meal consists of a bowl of beans, bread, salad, and some green onions. For drink there is a ceramic pitcher and wine glass containing pale red liquid that was probably clairet. A similar representation, *The Peasants' Meal* (1642) by Louis Le Nain, shows three peasant men sitting around a table, eating bread (the staple of the peasant diet) and drinking light red wine, undoubtedly clairet. The three Le Nain brothers painted several pictures of peasant families, each showing men and women drinking clairet with bread.

As suggested earlier, representations of the Last Supper are probably among the least useful genres for giving an idea of contemporary dining practices because they were more intensely allegorical than representative. But they consistently show the wine as red, no matter what food is displayed on the table. Domenico Ghirlandaio's fresco in Florence, for example, shows the disciples drinking red wine while eating bread, cherries, and apricots. Other paintings of the Last Supper include fish, the symbol of Christ, and lamb, which was historically sacrificed and was an allusion to the sacrifice of Christ at the crucifixion.

No doubt the wine was consistently red because it was at this meal (a seder) that Christ told the disciples that the wine symbolized his blood: 'Then he took the cup, gave thanks and offered it to them, saying, "Drink from it, all of you. This is my blood of the covenant, which is poured out for many for the forgiveness of sins".' White wine would not have had the same visual effect of reinforcing the message. Yet there are representations of Jesus eating that show white wine on the table. For example, Michelangelo da Caravaggio's *The Supper at Emmaus* (1599) shows a carafe and glass of white wine, along with a chicken and a bowl of fruit, such as grapes and apricots. The other notable episode that connects Jesus to food and wine was the wedding at Cana, where he performed the miracle of turning water into wine. It is implied that wine was consumed throughout the meal, because its running out was the reason Jesus was asked to create more. This must have been white wine, because there was apparently no difference in colour from the water to the wine: the observers had to taste the liquid before they knew it was wine.

As for sweet courses, wines are shown in varying colours. In Lubin Baugin's *A Meal of Wafers* (about 1630), the sweet wafers *(gaufrettes)* are accompanied by a glass of wine that is deep amber in colour. It is suggestive of a sweet wine, such as a Sauternes or other late-harvest wine, but of course we cannot gauge its sweetness from the painting itself.

THE NINETEENTH AND TWENTIETH CENTURIES

In more recent times, until very recently, there has not been much more interest in matching food and wine. Victorian books on cooking, such as *Mrs Beeton's Book of Household Management* (first published in instalments between 1859 and 1861) discussed cooking and the presentation of food at length, but devoted little space to wine. In the chapter on beverages Mrs Beeton starts with tea ('the cup that cheers but not inebriates') and coffee, but also gives recipes for making wine from cowslip, elderberries, ginger, and gooseberries. There is a recipe for 'claret-cup', a refreshing and low-alcohol beverage which included a bottle of claret, a bottle of soda water, sugar, and ice, as well as recipes for mulled wine and hot punch.

The longest discussion of wine in Mrs Beeton's classic book was in terms of the duties of the butler, who was not only responsible for the preparation of the dining room and table, but also served the first dish and oversaw the meal. But the 'real duties' of the butler were in the wine cellar, where he was expected to advise his master 'as to the price and quality of the wine to be laid in': 'Nothing spreads more rapidly in society than the reputation of a good wine cellar, and all that is required is wines well chosen and well cared for.' Much of the wine was purchased in casks and Mrs Beeton gave instructions on fining and bottling, as well as ageing. Old port was ready to drink within five or six months of bottling, 'but if it is a fruity wine it will improve every year'.

With a cellar such as this, a well-off person would have the wherewithal to pair wines with foods which Mrs Beeton hints at when she suggests the order of service at a 'gastronomist's' dinner party: 'The order of food is from the most substantial to the lightest. The order of drinking wine is from the mildest to the most foamy and most perfumed.' This suggests serving the lightest wines with the heaviest dishes, and drinking champagne (it would have been champagne) and sweeter wines at the end of the meal, either with dessert or after. She spends pages providing sample menus for dinners with varying numbers of guests and dinners at different times of the year. Yet although these multi-course efforts are set out in some detail, there is no mention of any wine – or of any beverage, for that matter.

'Indulge the true ambition to excel, In the best art, the art of living well.' Living well appears to include a standing rib of beef and a bottle of wine, even if it does lead to gout. Eighteenth-century etching by Thomas Best.

If some cookery books dealt with wine, it was a rare book on wine that mentioned food. When Robert Druitt, an English physician, published his *Report on the Cheap Wines of France, Italy, Austria, Greece,*

Hungary, and Australia in 1865, he subtitled it *Their Use in Diet and Medicine.* But there is little in the way of useful detail. For burgundy, for example, Druitt writes, 'as with Claret, there is abundance of good, cheap wine, suited to every pocket, which ought to be introduced at dinner and evening parties, instead of vile Hambro' sherry and to be ordered for the invalid whose appetite needs a whet.' More substantial, if still brief, is Druitt's discussion of Hungarian wines: 'If a man dines on a single joint [of meat], he would prefer a bottle of Erlaurre or Ofner; if he has a complex repast, he would drink these light wines with his fish or entrées.' Elsewhere the references to wine and food pairing are open to interpretation. Druitt writes of a Cape (South African) port with an alcohol level of 36 per cent that 'one eighth of a bottle is all a man need drink with the most savoury parts of his dinner'.

Druitt mentions specific pairings several times in his book. He suggests that Volnay, from Burgundy, should be drunk 'in the middle of dinner with roast meat, or, still better, with hare or other game.' Writing of Bordeaux, he suggests that 'one thing that would go with its greater use ... would be the custom of drinking it in its proper place *during dinner* as a refreshing and appetizing draught, to entice the languid palate to demand an additional slice of mutton.' He even advocated giving children wine to stimulate their appetites: 'All kinds of problems could be avoided if, when the governess had said "Miss Jeannie won't eat her mutton," the physician had said, "Give her some kind of light, clean-tasting, sub-acid wine – Bordeaux or Hungarian – let her sip this, *ad libitum*, at dinner, so that it might tempt her to relish her mutton".'

We can discern here some movement toward pairing specific wines with specific foods, but the examples seem crude and vague when compared to the precision of modern wine and food matching guides. We need to remember that the nineteenth-century books on wine and other alcohols were written as the temperance movements were gaining strength. Even in England, where these were far less influential than in the United States, they helped create an atmosphere less friendly to drinking wine with meals.

One pairing that became increasingly popular in the twentieth century is wine with cheese. Cheese is an odd food because although it has become a very popular part of dining in western societies – where specialist stores and artisanal producers have proliferated since the late 1990s – it was often unvalued until the early 1900s. This is true even in France, the home of Brie, Camembert, Roquefort, and other regional cheeses that have become as close to becoming household cheese names as England's Cheddar and Stilton. Kolleen Guy's research on terroir suggests that the pungent smells given off by fermenting cheeses were, until the late nineteenth century, unacceptable to the French urban classes. Not only the famously smelly French cheeses, such as Époisses, were implicated here; almost all cheeses smelled or outright reeked of the countryside and the peasantry – in short, of the terroirs, the places they came from. To this extent, because terroir still carried a negative meaning, cheeses were rarely part of the diet of France's growing middle class.

For this reason, most of the cheese produced in France was consumed in the countryside, where it was made. It was a local product for local consumption, not one to be widely traded. The exceptions were a few 'noble' or bourgeois cheeses, such as Cantal and Roquefort, that were considered delicacies and found their way onto fashionable tables. (The Duke of Saulx-Tavanes, mentioned earlier, included Roquefort in his food order in 1784.) Otherwise, Guy writes, 'cheese was a food for peasants, herdsmen, woodsmen, and savage people who verged on the animal condition'. Cheese had long been denounced by physicians, who tended to see it as putrified milk and as a 'dead food'. It was fatally associated with peasants: it was tainted by being made by peasant women and shaped by their grubby hands, and one physician averred that cheese took on the 'dark and bilious destiny fermented in peasant blood'.

Sometime in the 1800s, however, there was a sea change in urban French attitudes toward cheese. The reason is not clear, but a more conservative approach to gastronomic variety gave way to a willingness to experiment. The consumption of Camembert (which had been invented in the early nineteenth century) in Paris doubled between 1886 and 1894, and sales of Livarot and Brie rose significantly in the same period. Camembert and Brie are relatively low on the aroma scale, which might explain their early acceptance, but Livarot is definitely pungent – if any cheeses smelled of peasants in the mind of the bourgeoisie, Livarot would have been among them.

The long resistance to cheese by the French contrasts with the cheese trolley, with its array of dozens of cheeses, that is rolled up to tables in many fine French restaurants today. The history of cheese, however, alerts us to the fact that cheese is a relative newcomer as a pairing for wine. As a food and a beverage now commonly consumed together, cheese and wine are generally thought of in generic terms: any cheese goes with any wine. If, in practice, most people drink red wine with cheese – any cheese – the wine-and-cheese formula shows awareness of a pairing, but in a very generic way.

The same is true of a popular wine and food pairing guideline: that one should drink white wine with fish and white meats and red wine with red meats. The fact that this has become widely known suggests that there is a general awareness, at some cultural level, that one should not pair wine and food haphazardly, but rather give some thought to the pairing. It is impossible to say quite how extensive this awareness became in the twentieth century, but it is safe to say that until relatively recently the great majority of people who drank wine with a meal at home were content to drink any style of wine, no matter what the food on their plate. Restaurant meals were another matter, of course, because diners had to choose food from the menu and wine from the wine list.

MODERN WINE AND FOOD PAIRING

Only toward the end of the 1900s was there a significant change in attitudes toward food and wine, and then it occurred as part of an overall change in the culture of wine. From the 1970s wine writers (who more and more called themselves 'wine critics') began to write about wine in much more precise ways than ever before. As noted, influenced by writers such as Robert Parker (see p. 140), they began to give wines scores, rather than simply describe their positive and negative qualities and leave it to readers to decide if they might enjoy the wines. They began to describe wines in increasingly complex ways, and to focus on flavours rather than on overall style.

The modern wine and food pairing paradigm emerged from this shift in attitudes toward wine. It was no longer enough to suggest drinking white wine with fish and red wine with meat, especially when some fish (such as salmon) were more red than white, and some meats (like chicken and pork) were more white than red when cooked. Nor was it enough to suggest drinking Pinot Noir or Gamay with salmon or Chardonnay with chicken or pork. Just as precision imbued the way wines were described and evaluated, so wine and food pairing needed to be precise.

The shift in wine and food pairing was also associated with the rise of the sommelier. The name sommelier was originally used to refer to the man (it was always a man) who looked after loading beasts of burden with the food and other supplies of a king or noble who was starting off on a journey. Over time the scope of the word changed and by the twentieth century it was restricted to the functions of maintaining a cellar and serving wine in a restaurant. These were essentially the functions of a nineteenth-century butler, making a modern sommelier a sort of public butler.

One of the prime functions of a sommelier is to help diners identify an appropriate wine pairing for the food they have decided to eat. Courses on the way to pair wines and food are integral parts of sommelier programmes offered by institutions such as the Court of Master Sommeliers, but not of more academic programmes delivered by the Institute of Masters of Wine, which has no practical wine-service component.

There is now a solid corpus of writing on food and wine pairing, and it has of course become embedded in the training of sommeliers because their duties include not only creating and maintaining wine lists but also advising diners on wines that would go well with the food they have decided to eat. (It is noteworthy that when presented simultaneously with a list of food – the menu – and a list of wines, the great majority of people choose the food first, and then think about wine that might go well with it, rather than vice versa.) For those eating at home or in another situation where they find themselves without the benefit of a sommelier, there are innumerable books, websites, and apps that offer advice.

Wine and food-pairing advice is integrated into many books on wine (though fewer on food), and there are books dedicated to the subject, with titles such as *Wine and Food: Perfect Pairings Every Time* and *Food and Wine Pairing: A Sensory Experience.* In *Wine and Food*, Jane Parkinson suggests Sauvignon Blanc or a rosé to go with crab: 'Dressed crab, crab salad, crab cakes; it doesn't matter what the dish, one of these two wines usually comes up a treat with crab.' As for smoked chicken, a Chenin Blanc aged in oak does the trick: 'A smoked chicken tastes more of smoke than chicken, so an oaked Chenin Blanc from South Africa is a lovely match to pick up on this smoky flavour.' A creamy chicken pie with its pastry coating, on the other hand, calls for a 'full and frank style' of Chardonnay, and Jane Parkinson suggests looking for one from California, the Limarí Valley (Chile), or Mendoza (Argentina).

Some pairing guides offer puzzling advice. One popular Canadian website suggests that 'roast chicken' should be paired with sauternes, cognac, bergerac, or red bordeaux. But for 'roasted chicken' (the same food), the pairing tool proposes bergerac, red bordeaux, bardolino, red burgundy, and Pinot Meunier. There is no indication of whether the red or the white wines of Bergerac are intended here. Another pairing guide, a book this time, suggests that mahi-mahi, a fish with 'firm, meaty, almost sweet flesh' goes 'best with "white" wine'. The suggested wine is a Pinot Noir.

Wine has had an uneven presence at the table in terms of both frequency and the character of its presence. There is a long history of drinking wine and eating food at the same meal, especially among better-off sections of many societies. But there are limitations when it comes to people in general, because in most places at most times only a small percentage of the population, almost all concentrated in the adult male demographic, drank wine. But it is wise to remember that many people who can drink wine with their meals choose not to.

Although the common image of the French family sitting down to dinner includes wine on the table and the children having a small glass of diluted wine – lore has it that this is how French children learn to drink responsibly – the frequency of wine appearing on the French dinner table has declined significantly in the last few decades. In the 1950s a third of French people had a glass of water, not wine, at hand when they sat down to their evening meal. By the 1990s that was true of three-quarters of them – and the rate of water drinking has increased and the rate of wine drinking has declined since then. These trends go with a steady increase in the rate of bottled water consumption in France, an increase from 20 litres per capita in the 1950s to more than 150 litres in the early 2000s.

As wine consumption declines in the old wine-drinking societies (Italy, France, and Spain) wine at the table has probably become more common in North America, Australia, and Britain, where wine has in recent decades become more integrated into cuisine and has become a lifestyle drink. Greater familiarity with wine and interest in wine have promoted more awareness of the relationship between wine and food and taken it to a degree unprecedented in the longer history of wine.

7

WINE AND WAR

One panel of the Bayeux Tapestry, which shows the invasion of England in 1066 by a Norman army led by Duke William ('the Conqueror'), depicts the wine brought along for the occasion. It is an image of a barrel on a cart, with the embroidered caption *carrum cum vino* – a cart with wine. If the caption is minimalist, the single cart was representative, for the Norman army undoubtedly brought many such carts loaded with barrels of wine, even though we have no way of knowing how many. Nor do we know where the wine came from and what its precise purpose was. It was probably from northern France – perhaps even from Normandy, as wine was produced even there until the late eighteenth century and possibly longer – but it more likely came from the extensive wine-producing regions closer to Paris or from the Loire Valley. As for the uses of the wine, some might have been good quality wine for Duke William's kitchen and table, but the bulk was undoubtedly *vin ordinaire* destined for consumption by the soldiers.

What the Bayeux Tapestry illustrates is an example of the role of wine in war in Europe, where it has frequently been part of military rations. It is true that, rather than haul their own wine, the Norman soldiers might have seized the wine (and ale and cider) that was produced in the English territories they were about to occupy. The Domesday Book, a survey of rural land and property in England carried out two decades after the Norman occupation, listed forty-two vineyards – some of which might, of course, have been planted by the Normans themselves in the intervening years.

Bringing their own barrels in 1066 (an early example of BYOB) was not necessarily a comment on the quality of English wine, but the Bayeux Tapestry shows that the Norman army had a sophisticated supply train to ensure that soldiers had the weapons, food, and drink they needed. This runs counter to the common view that in the past European armies always lived off the land, seizing or requisitioning supplies as they went. Instead, there is ample evidence that during the Middle Ages armies expecting to carry out a long campaign were likely to carry their own supplies with them and be resupplied from a base at the rear, rather than engage in raiding actions that might or might not secure enough rations for the soldiers.

This is not to say that soldiers would not – with or without authorization, systematically or opportunistically – help themselves to the produce available in regions they passed through. But this foraging as a pattern of supply was far less common than often thought. Wine was certainly high on the list of desirable rations, and it might well be seized from cellars when armies were campaigning or passing through wine regions. But there were dangers to soldiers' foraging for wine, notably the possibility that they would drink it on the spot and be unable to march (or fight) until they recovered. It was another reason for armies to take wine with them and dole it out in measured volumes on a daily basis: they could control their soldiers' drinking.

WINE AND WAR IN THE ANCIENT WORLD AND THE MIDDLE AGES

Wine was the drink that kept a number of European armies going, and there is continuity in this respect for some two thousand years, beginning with the well-documented wine rations provided to the soldiers of Ancient Greece and Rome. Military rations of wine reflected the simple reality that wine of some quality or other was integral to the daily diet at all social levels in these cultures. Greek soldiers were typically given a daily ration of between 0.5 litre and 1.3 litres of wine – the range reflecting some uncertainty about modern equivalents to Greek measures of volume. Some scholars suggest that the higher volume would be consumed not only by the soldier but also by his dependants. Moreover, in all cases like this, when we think about alcohol rations provided to soldiers, we must bear in mind that the alcohol level of wine was almost certainly much lower than is common today. The wine provided to French soldiers in the First World War was pegged at 10 per cent alcohol, and it is very unlikely that the wine provided to Greek soldiers was as strong or stronger than this to start with. What they drank – what everyone drank in Greece and Rome – was poor wine diluted with water, so the actual ration was that much lower in alcohol.

Roman soldiers enjoyed, if that is the word, low-alcohol wine as part of their rations. Rather than savour the quality wines praised by Pliny and Cicero, soldiers downed a wine derivative called *posca*, made by diluting sour wine with water. Depending on the translation, it is variously referred to as wine, sour wine, and vinegar. Whatever it is called, *posca* must have been light-coloured (perhaps the fashionable *oeil de perdrix* hue of many modern rosés), somewhat sour and flavourless, and very low in alcohol – not to mention inexpensive, which made it attractive to the authorities for bulk purchase and mass distribution as a military ration. It is probable that Roman soldiers received about a litre of *posca* a day, not an alarming volume because the alcohol level must have been very low, perhaps as little as two or three per cent. Even so, *posca* was preferable to water because it was derived from wine, which was considered a healthy beverage.

It was *posca* that, according to the New Testament, Roman soldiers offered to Christ on the cross, either (depending on interpretation) to mock him or to help alleviate the agony of crucifixion. After tasting the *posca*, Christ refused to drink it, but scholarly interpretations suggest that he did so for reasons other than its quality, although it was far inferior to the wine Jews in Palestine might ordinarily have drunk. The wine Christ conjured from water at the wedding at Cana was reported to be high quality, and the wine served at the Last Supper (a Jewish seder) would certainly have been good-quality, first-press, undiluted wine, not *posca*.

Posca was the daily ration in the Roman armies but soldiers who were sick or wounded received ordinary wine because of its therapeutic properties (see pp. 6–8). In these circumstances, wine was provided as a medicine rather than a daily beverage. Soldiers were also permitted to purchase wine to supplement their *posca* allowance, and some were clearly keen to do so. When the Roman consul Metellus arrived in Africa in 109 BC he found that the soldiers garrisoned there had stolen local slaves and livestock in order to barter them for wine. A few years later, Herod provided wine and other necessities to Roman soldiers besieging Jerusalem after they threatened to mutiny if they did not receive adequate supplies.

Wine rations were more likely to be found in the armies raised in wine-producing regions, where wine was plentiful (in good years) and relatively inexpensive because it did not have to be shipped over long distances to the armies. The Romans quickly extended viticulture and winemaking throughout their European empire, and although it might not have been a primary purpose, this gave their armies ready access to wine depots almost everywhere.

Yet wine was sometimes provided to soldiers from ale-drinking countries. Perhaps that can be explained by the fact that it was more efficient to transport wine: even though the alcohol level was very likely no more than 10 per cent, it was considerably higher (perhaps two or three times as high) than the alcohol level of ale. A barrel of wine thus contained far more alcohol than a barrel of beer. In 1282, for example, King Edward I of England bought 600 barrels of Bordeaux wine for his ale-drinking soldiers who were fighting the Welsh. A few years later his son, Edward II, ordered 4,000 barrels of Bordeaux wine for his military campaigns in Scotland. Red wine from Bordeaux (known generically as 'claret') was widely consumed by the better-off classes in England in the Middle Ages, and it could be that ordinary soldiers were supplied with wine instead of the ale that was their usual drink rather than engage in raiding actions, because wine was a more efficient way of delivering alcohol.

There are no very precise statistics on the size of military wine rations in the Middle Ages, but a French plan of campaign from 1327 specified daily rations for a fighting soldier as about 0.6 of a litre of wine, 107 grams of meat, and just over a kilo of grain for making into bread. The total was about 3,350 calories, of which the wine would have contributed about 500. The rations of sailors in the Venetian fleet at about the same time included 715 grams of biscuit, 536 grams (just over half a litre) of wine, and 52 grams of salt pork, for a total 3,915 calories, to which the wine would have contributed about 450. Wine was not a major part of the nourishment provided by military rations, then, but it probably contributed disproportionately to morale.

By the end of the Middle Ages growing anxieties about the safety of water supplies, which were increasingly polluted by industrial, human, and animal waste, made it that much more desirable to provide soldiers with beverages that were safer – and beverages containing alcohol eliminated some of the bacteria commonly found in water. This was especially important in sieges, when attacking and defending soldiers might stay in one place for days and weeks at a time, exposing local water sources to pollution by human and animal waste – not to mention by decomposing bodies and carcasses – and fostering the spread of water-borne epidemic diseases. In 1418, for example, the supplies 'for the refreshment of the army' sent to soldiers carrying out Henry V's siege of Rouen included thirty large barrels of sweet wine. In 1470, when an army led by the Duke of Lorraine laid siege to Châtel-sur-Moselle, ninety-one barrels of wine (about 43,000 litres) were delivered to the soldiers.

Wine was no less important to the garrisons defending besieged towns because their water supplies could be compromised or exhausted. When the Norman/English army (perhaps now supplied with ale for the English soldiers, as well as wine) of Duke William of Normandy (who by then was also King William I of England) laid siege to Exeter in 1068, the town's two wells ran out and the garrison survived on wine until being forced to surrender. A supply of water was obviously essential to defenders at a siege and attempting to cut them off or pollute them were common tactics. When Barbarossa besieged Tortona in 1155 he dumped rotting human and animal corpses into the spring that provided the town with fresh water. Unable to sustain themselves on water, the town's defenders soon surrendered.

We should note that the purpose of giving soldiers an alcohol ration at this time was not only safety, but also to boost morale and courage before battle, as rum and brandy were often used in the First World War. Using alcohol for that short-term purpose was not unknown earlier. The eminent British military historian John Keegan suggests that among the prime factors that sustained men in battle, 'drink is the most obvious to mention'. He writes of the Battle of Agincourt (1415) that 'the English, who were on short rations, presumably had less to drink than the French, but there was drinking in the ranks on both sides during the period of waiting [before battle] and it is quite probable that many soldiers in both armies went into the mêlée less than sober, if not indeed fighting drunk'.

Wine might well have fortified fighting spirits, but for the most part it was considered a healthy beverage that helped to sustain soldiers whether or not they were actively engaged in fighting, and it was regarded as an integral part of the soldier's diet. For example, in the early 1400s the guards at the Château de Custine, on the Moselle River, received a daily ration of two litres of wine – more than one might think appropriate for soldiers who had to remain alert, even if the alcohol level was low compared to modern wine.

Scene of a sixteenth-century military engagement prominently showing wine barrels. Engraving from Paracelsus, Opus chyrurgicum, des weitberumbten Hochgelehrten und Erfarnen (1565).

Even though wine appears to have been provided to soldiers as they campaigned, there is little doubt that they must often have helped themselves, informally, to any they came across. Civilian populations were generally caught up directly in wars (the First World War was on the whole a notable exception) and at the very least suffered their economic impact. Sometimes hostile armies destroyed communities and their crops and livestock, sometimes the inhabitants themselves destroyed their reserves, crops, and livestock in the face of an advancing army so as to deprive it of resources. In wine-producing areas, these reserves included barrels of wine and the crops included the vineyards.

Froissart's chronicle of the Hundred Years War, for example, recorded that 'Now the Earl of Buckingham and the van and rear guards were lodged at Toury in Beauce and the surrounding area, and their foragers found provisions in great abundance. They also had the run of the land of Gâtinais [at the eastern end of the Loire Valley], and from the abbeys and fine houses they had extorted wine which they had loaded onto carts in casks, bottles and barrels, from which they derived no small comfort.' Communities would have better stocks of grain and wine soon after the harvest (in September–October) than later and, if the timing was right, armies that pillaged wine-producing villages could seize enough wine to supply them for weeks and months. Extortion was also a possibility. The same chronicle notes that 'The Lord of Fitzwalter made himself known to the Lord of Viévy [near Blois, in the Loire Valley] and entreated him to send him some of his wine out of courtesy, and his land would be spared from being burnt and overrun. The Lord of Viévy sent him a vast quantity along with thirty white loaves, for which the Lord of Fitzwalter was very grateful and stood by his assurance to him.'

WINE AND WAR IN EARLY MODERN EUROPE

If the Lord of Viévy's vineyards and other land were spared, others were not so fortunate. European wars in the Early Modern period involved civilian populations as much as armed forces. Many armies carried out scorched earth practices, destroying crops and wrecking vineyards. The Hundred Years War, which was fought across Europe, together with the many regional conflicts of the Early Modern period, not only devastated vineyards in many regions but also reduced the size of the population. Smaller populations meant a lower demand for all goods and services, including wine, and a shortage of labour made it difficult to sustain viticulture. Wine villages were particular targets for what are perhaps obvious reasons. During the French invasion of Spain in 1808, an officer wrote 'In the end Villafranca was literally plundered, and the drunkenness that prevailed ... led to the most shameful incidents.'

If military action did not lead to the destruction of vineyards or the pillaging of wine, it could easily interfere with the wine trade. In the mid-1700s the Seven Years' War appears to have disrupted normal patterns of trade. In 1761 the priest in Burgundy's Volnay district, concerned for the income he derived from the parish's vineyards, complained about the war the French were waging at the time. It had so depleted France of cash, he wrote, that soldiers and civilians alike were unable to pay for the wine they were accustomed to drinking. Moreover, he wrote, the war had played havoc with the wider wine trade, such that foreign merchants had simply stopped coming to Burgundy to buy wine to ship to more distant European markets. Because they did not have to contend with these outsiders, local merchants were able to pay low prices for wine.

But there were also surprising exceptions to these expectations. One might have thought that the occupation of much of Portugal by the Spanish and French during the Napoleonic Wars would have had an adverse effect on the exports of port. But the extensive vineyards of the Douro Valley were generally ignored by the invading forces. Spanish troops largely confined their activities to Oporto, and did not penetrate the Douro Valley. Even in 1808 when the Portuguese began to organize resistance and the French sent forces into the wine-producing districts of the valley, there was little effect on the vines. The likely reason is that the slopes where the vines were planted were so steep that soldiers were unlikely to traverse them. After the war there were reports of vineyard damage, but they are hard to verify. Nor was the port trade seriously affected, despite the fact that the conflict disrupted vineyard routines. Men between eighteen and forty years of age were conscripted into the Portuguese armies and horses and boats were requisitioned, but the production of port remained steady. And although most of the English merchants, who had been responsible for the bulk of port exports, left Oporto soon after the French army arrived, their activities were taken over by Portuguese nationals. Exports of port to England fell slightly in 1807 and 1808, the first years of French occupation of Portugal, but they picked up soon afterwards. Some convoys of ships carrying port to England were escorted by ships of the Royal Navy.

At the very same time, Europe's wine trade generally was disrupted by the Continental Blockade, imposed by Napoleon to deny Britain imports from its European trading partners. It seems to have been largely successful, despite a small but steady smuggling industry that sprang up to ferry luxury goods (including wine) from France to England across the English Channel.

A century earlier, the Bordeaux wine merchants and their English customers appear to have found a more ingenious way to ship large volumes of wine despite the trade embargo imposed when their countries were at war. The volatile relations between France and England in the late 1600s and early 1700s meant that trade was an on-again, off-again affair. France exported wine to the English market during a time of peace from 1697, but by 1703 the countries were at war again and trade ceased. When this had happened in the past, English claret drinkers had had to find alternatives, but this time massive volumes of highly valued French wine found their way onto the English market – wine that had been captured from French ships in the English Channel by English privateers, privately owned ships authorized by the government to seize enemy vessels.

This wine in these seizures was from Bordeaux estates highly prized in England, such as Haut-Brion, Margaux, Langon, and the estate of Arnaud de Pontac, but it also included some from Châteauneuf-du-Pape. Once ashore in England, the wine was purchased at auction by London merchants and they in turn sold it to their wealthy clients. The Earl of Bristol was one, and his accounts show that he bought a hogshead (a barrel of about 240 litres) of 'Margoose [Margaux] claret' in 1703, 'three chests of wine from Avignon [probably Châteauneuf-du-Pape]' in 1704, '3 hogsheads of wine, 2 of Obrian [Haut-Brion] and 1 of white Langoon [Langon]' in 1705, and '2 hogsheads of Obrian wine' in 1707.

Ultra-premium wines such as these fetched good prices. In 1705, three auctions of a total of 738 barrels of wine from Haut-Brion, Pontac, and Margaux brought in more than £40,000, an average of £54 each. Clients who bought these barrels would have paid more, of course, after the merchants' mark-up. These prices were far above what were common and represented the scarcity value of claret (and other French wines) during the embargo. The wine might well have been on its way to ports in northern Europe, where French wine was shipped in the normal course of events, but so much was seized by privateers and sold on the English market that we are entitled to suspect that the 'seizures' were planned. It seems unlikely that Bordeaux merchants would willingly have continued to bear the losses sustained by the activities of English privateers, who kept most of the proceeds of the auctions. We can only speculate, but there might well have been an arrangement by which the French sailed their ships into the Channel, where their cargo of wine was 'seized' and later sold, with the privateers returning some of the proceeds to the French merchants for their thoughtfulness in sailing their wine close to the English coast. If the Bordeaux merchants received only a third of the proceeds of the auctions, which were inflated prices in any case, they would have done quite well, and certainly much better than they would have had they not been able to access their English clients at all.

Over the longer term, the disruption caused by war, together with shifting alliances, led to changes in the wine trade. In 1703, for example, England and Portugal signed a treaty (the Methuen Treaty) which gave Portuguese wine – most of it the fortified wine, port – preferential treatment as an export to England. It guaranteed that Portuguese wines would always be levied at a lower rate of duty than French wines, and it underpinned the popularity of port in the 1700s, first among the middle classes, then among upper-class men.

Throughout these wars, soldiers continued to be given rations of alcohol. Depending on the army, the rations were in the form of beer or wine, and – after distilling became commercial in the 1500s – of brandy or other spirits. From the mid-1600s the Royal (English) Navy began to give sailors a daily measure of rum (diluted with water) that was sourced from the sugar plantations of England's Caribbean colonies.

WINE, WAR, AND RESTRICTION

Only when nineteenth-century temperance campaigners began to challenge what had been the largely unquestioned benefits of alcohol were there serious reconsiderations of the practice of providing wine and other alcoholic beverages to soldiers. Just as temperance and prohibition movements initially had more influence in the United States than elsewhere, so the American army experienced the first impact. American soldiers had been given a ration of whiskey since the War of Independence but under pressure from temperance organizations and many in the military command the American army went dry in 1834, making it the first Western army to give up alcohol rations during both peace and war.

Wine and the Crimean War. 'A Christmas Dinner on the Heights before Sebastopol.' Soldiers enjoy a meal with bottles of wine and more wine chilling in a bucket of ice. 1855 lithograph by John A. Vinter after William Simpson.

During the 1800s and the early 1900s up to the First World War, many governments were under increasing pressure to stop providing soldiers with alcohol. Temperance advocates argued that by giving soldiers alcohol rations, the state was complicit in turning healthy young men into what became known by the 1860s as 'alcoholics'. Some physicians and serving officers argued that alcohol was responsible for most military indiscipline and inefficiency. A British naval officer told a parliamentary committee in the late 1850s that during the Crimean War 'almost every accident that I witnessed on board ship was owing to drunkenness. Drink was more dangerous than gunpowder.'

Even then, some opponents of alcohol in the military thought there was a role for it in circumstances when soldiers were under extreme pressure. Edmund Parkes, a professor of military hygiene, studied British soldiers in the Ashanti campaign of 1874, and expressed doubts that alcohol did any good in a general sense. But he thought that it might be given to soldiers in 'emergencies', such as at the end of a march or when 'after great fatigue a sudden but short exertion is required'.

To test the suggestion that alcohol had a negative effect on efficiency, several armies carried out experiments before the First World War to see if it really did impair skills such as gunnery accuracy and stamina on route marches. The French army carried some out in which they monitored soldiers who drank either beer or wine as part of their rations. Other armies compared soldiers who had consumed alcohol with soldiers who had not, but the idea of the non-drinking soldier appears to have been inconceivable to the French military authorities. They were probably more realistic and the results of their experiments were, to their minds, conclusive: soldiers who drank wine were more accurate marksmen than those who drank beer. As for efficiency, a study of soldiers sent on a route march in Bordeaux (of all places) showed that soldiers who drank wine were 'less tired and went along the road singing and chanting', while those who drank beer were 'sluggish [and] marched with a heavy step'.

These conclusions, which paralleled the contemporary French stereotypes of the vivacious, happy, wine-drinking French and the stolid, dull, beer-guzzling Germans, were great news for the French military. In the years before the First World War they were expecting to go to war with Germany, and in the light of these findings they could anticipate an easy victory by their agile, wine-infused soldiers. But the German army's experiments, which compared the marksmanship of soldiers who had drunk spirits (not beer) with those who had not – the experiment involved firing 36,000 rounds over sixteen days – indicated that alcohol consumption had no negative effect on accuracy.

The First World War provided the first opportunity to put temperance ideas to the test in the context of an armed conflict, the subjects being the millions of young men who found themselves beyond the constraints of family in particular and free of social surveillance more generally. For many, perhaps most, it was their first time away from home, and they found themselves in situations where alcohol consumption was the norm. This is not to say that the military authorities opened the floodgates to unrestrained drinking, because in fact most tried valiantly to limit alcohol consumption (especially of distilled spirits) by their troops. For all that the military commands had contested arguments that alcohol was harmful to military efficiency and discipline, they had no desire to test its boundaries.

The most radical position on alcohol was taken by the Russian government, which not only prohibited sales of alcohol (which meant vodka) during mobilization in August 1914, but also banned the production, sale, and consumption of alcohol by Russians for the duration of the war. This policy of total national prohibition, which preceded America's far better-known policy by six years, was later continued by the Bolshevik government after the Revolution of 1917. In the short term, however, Russian prohibition had a significant impact on the war. Germany's Shlieffen Plan for opening the war provided for committing massive forces against Belgium and France and achieving quick victories there before moving troops east to confront the Russian army, which was notoriously slow to get into the field – partly because of the heavy drinking that accompanied mobilization. But the German plan to encircle Paris failed and without alcohol the Russian army mobilized far more quickly than expected.

In theory, Russia's prohibition policy meant that in 1914 it would field a dry army supported by a civilian economy that would be all the more productive because workers would be entirely sober. In reality, illegally produced vodka (*samogon*) quickly filled the alcohol void, and the Russian military and civilian war effort was as well lubricated as if prohibition had never been imposed. The imperial court of Tsar Nicholas II participated in the illusion of prohibition. Although the Tsar declared that he, his family, and others in the court in Saint

Petersburg would set an example by abstaining from alcohol during the war, wine flowed in clandestinely from other parts of Europe. In 1916 a ship carrying supplies to the imperial court was sunk by a German submarine in the Gulf of Finland. Its cargo was salvaged in 1998 and was found to include more than 2,000 bottles of Heidsieck Monopole Champagne from the 1907 vintage. (Most of the bottles were in good condition after eighty years on the cool dark seabed.)

WINE AND THE FIRST WORLD WAR

The most effectively wine-fuelled army of the First World War was the French. Even though French soldiers did not have a regular daily ration of wine before the war – although officers could dole out wine as they saw fit – a ration was established only a month after the conflict began. The ration, which was in part inspired by the gift of 20 million litres of wine by Languedoc producers to French military hospitals, began at a quarter of a litre of wine a day. It was soon increased, however, to half a litre, which could be increased when soldiers experienced extraordinarily trying conditions. Sometimes French troops were given brandy before going on the attack – which shows alcohol being used as a nerve-stiffener as distinct from the generally health-giving purpose wine was expected to serve. Occasionally, when supplies of wine were interrupted, other alcoholic drinks were supplied, and there are reports of champagne being distributed on Bastille Day in some years. But these were exceptions. Wine was the daily drink of French soldiers and the wine itself was usually red and was to have an alcohol level of about 10 per cent.

Soldiers were permitted to supplement their half-litre entitlement by buying more from vendors who sold wine behind the front lines, and they could also drink wine in the cafés and brothels that soldiers had access to when they were rotated from the front lines to the rear. In 1917 a French periodical published a photograph of soldiers crowding around a wine wagon. The caption read in part: 'the troopers besiege the wagon, each holding out a 40-sou coin to receive a litre that he will carry off with the greatest care'. If these soldiers drank that litre with the half-litre ration, they would have drunk the equivalent of a magnum of wine that day.

It was not only the volume of wine that French soldiers were permitted to consume (even at only 10 per cent alcohol) that was remarkable, but also the cultural value that soldiers attached to wine. They called their wine *pinard*, a word used before the war to refer to ordinary wine and that is thought to have been a corruption of *pinot*, as in Pinot Noir. The great bulk of the *pinard* drunk by soldiers was certainly not Pinot Noir, as most originated in Languedoc, Bordeaux, and Algeria. Only a small part of the wine requisition, from Burgundy, was made from Pinot Noir. The instructions issued by the army to the mayors of Burgundy's communes for the 1916 vintage specified that 'red, white, and rosé wines will all be equally accepted'.

Most *pinard* was undoubtedly a blend of grape varieties, almost always in the form of red wine, and delivered to the war zones of north-eastern France by train before being taken to the troops in trucks or on horse-drawn carts. Clearly, quality was not an issue. The authorities excluded fine and cru wines, and even the best ordinary wines (*grand ordinaire*) from being requisitioned. But the wine destined for the front lines had to be solid *vin ordinaire* and expert tasters were employed to ensure the quality of requisitioned wines. The guidelines for burgundy wines stated that to be accepted for military use they should be 'well made, with good flavour, free of faults, and having the character of Burgundian varieties'. When three producers challenged the classification of their wines as *vins ordinaires* in 1917, six expert tasters (including the mayor of Gevrey-Chambertin and the Director of Burgundy's Oenology Institute) were called in to adjudicate. They found that one wine, a blend of Pinot Noir and Gamay, was a *grand ordinaire* and therefore excluded from requisition, while the other two were mere *vins ordinaires* and were therefore included.

Although French soldiers had access to better wine when they were rotated behind the lines, they regarded *pinard* with a kind of veneration. It was much more than fermented grape juice. It was called *Père Pinard* (Father Pinard) and *Saint-Pinard* (St. Pinard), songs were written about it, and soldiers were said to salute wine barrels as they passed. It featured on the postcards soldiers sent their families and girlfriends, and after the war, was given credit for its role in the French victory.

The soldiers themselves might have idolized *pinard*, but they had few illusions about the quality of some of the wines accepted by the requisitioning authorities. An ode to *pinard* that became a marching song included the words, 'You may have very little taste or no taste at all … except for the days … you stink of liquid manure. There are even times you smell of petrol.' But it was affectionate criticism, for the song went on, 'it is the whole country that lives in you'. *Vin ordinaire* was an expression of France that was consumed in an almost religious way, as if it were a rite of patriotic communion.

The French army's demand for wine taxed French wine production. The 1914 harvest was a bumper crop, but the following harvests were relatively poor. Algerian wine made up for some of the shortfall, but the army sent officers as far as Napa Valley in California and Mendoza in Argentina to price wine. These plans came to nothing because the cost of shipping wine was expensive and German submarines in the Atlantic posed a serious threat. Without additional supplies, the army consumed as much as 40 per cent of France's annual wine production. By 1916 civilians were being urged to conserve wine for the soldiers, and by 1917 the authorities imposed wine rationing on the civilian population: half a litre a day for adults and a quarter-litre for children.

Some of France's high-end wines continued to be exported during the First World War, but in much reduced volumes: from 200 to 300 million litres a year to less than 50 million. Production of champagne fell dramatically as much of the region was in the battle zone at some time during the war, and other regions (such as Saumur in the Loire Valley) took the opportunity to increase their production of sparkling wine. The war created problems for wine production because labour (human and equine) had been conscripted, supplies such as fertilizers were scarce, and transportation was difficult. By this time the French wine industry depended on the railway, but the military had priority on the use of rail traffic. Attempts to recruit Spanish and Italian vineyard workers fell short of their goals, and although vignerons in the army could in principle return home for a month during the harvest, they could do so only if they were not needed for military duties.

To appreciate the significance of the French wine ration, we need only look at the alcohol served to other forces during the First World War. In many cases the allotment was small and functional, like the tot of dark rum (often served in tea) that British troops received each morning. It was a treat, and it was doubled in difficult circumstances and before soldiers went 'over the top' – charging out of their trenches into the killing fields of the war. But although rum was issued daily, it was not the item of diet that *pinard* was to the French. Nor were all commanders happy with even the small ration of rum, and one general succeeded in banning it in his Division. In 1917 *The Lancet*, the British medical publication, expressed what might have been a more general British view of the French wine rations, noting with a tone of disbelief, 'The reasonable consumption of the wine of the country (*vin ordinaire*) is evidently regarded as beneficial rather than demoralising.' Like French soldiers, their British counterparts had access to wine and other alcohol when they were not at the front lines.

The British approach to alcohol rations was closer to the Russian and American armies, both of which were nominally dry. As we have seen, the Russian government imposed prohibition on military and civilian populations, and by 1917, when the United States also declared war, most American states had adopted prohibition and the country was three years from enacting it on a national basis. With such strong anti-alcohol sentiments at home, it was out of the question for the American army, already dry since the 1830s, to provide alcohol rations in the trenches. A law passed by Congress in 1917 announced that 'it shall be unlawful to sell any intoxicating liquor, including beer, ale, or wine, to any officer or member of the military forces while in uniform'. But, like their European counterparts, American soldiers were able to buy wine and other alcohol behind the front lines.

On the other hand, the soldiers of the Habsburg armies were served wine. The *Volle Portion* (Full Ration), the rations served when supplies were fully available, included two 'luxuries': 36 grams of tobacco and half a litre of wine. But the Normal Portion, the rations provided when soldiers were in battle, included neither, and the Reserve Portion (the 'iron rations' carried for emergencies), included 18 grams of tobacco but, understandably, no wine.

As for the German Army, the alcohol ration depended where units came from. Those from Bavaria were issued beer, while those from the Rhineland were more likely to have wine rations. Needless to say, when the German army occupied parts of Belgium and France they helped themselves to wine. In the first month of the war a unit of the German supply train entered a house in Charleroi (Belgium) that had been abandoned by its owners as the Germans advanced, and discovered 500 bottles of wine in the cellar. Half the unit was reported to be drunk, and they all took dozens of bottles with them. On another occasion the same unit came across barrels holding 15,000 litres of wine. An American war correspondent noted that there was 'considerable drunkenness' among German soldiers as they crossed Belgium 'due to the men looting the wine-cellars in the towns through which they passed'.

Some German soldiers might thus have had sporadic access to plenty of wine, but their first alcohol ration was a quarter litre of brandy to be shared among ten men. The normal daily ration was either a half-litre of beer, a quarter-litre of wine, or 125ml of brandy or schnapps. There were allegations at the time that German soldiers were given a mixture of rum and ether before going into action, but the same war correspondent who noted their wine drinking wrote that he doubted whether it was true: 'If a man's life ever depends upon a clear brain and a cool head it is when he is going into battle ... I am convinced that intemperance virtually does not exist among the armies in the field.'

The alcohol ration, whether it was the generous serving of wine that French troops enjoyed or the modest allowance of dark rum served to their British counterparts, was extraordinarily important to soldiers. It was a morale booster and provided a moment or more of pleasure, and it was prominent in soldiers' memories of the war. The German artist Otto Dix, who served as a machinegunner, recalled the war trenchantly: 'Lice, rats, barbed wire, fleas, shells, bombs, caves, corpses, blood, Schnapps, mice, cats, gas, artillery, filth, bullets, mortars, fire, steel.' It was not just alcohol. As we have seen, *pinard* was almost venerated by the French, and we find a similar sense in Erich Maria Remarque's comment in *All Quiet on the Western Front* that 'Schnapps has soul'.

Still, there was continued criticism of wine or any kind of alcohol being distributed to soldiers. Jane Addams, the American campaigner for women's suffrage and temperance, claimed that soldiers of all countries were given alcoholic stimulants to give them courage before bayonet charges – including absinthe in the French army. The American war correspondent E. Alexander Powell contested these claims: 'Not only have I never seen a glass of absinthe served in France [production was banned in 1915], but I have never seen spirits of any kind in use in the zone of operations … The regular ration of the French soldier includes now, just as in time of peace, a pint of *vin ordinaire* – the cheap wine of the country – this being, I might add, considerably less than the man might drink with his meals were he in civil life.'

The First World War is sometimes said to have been critical for extending wine consumption in France because it exposed young men from all over France – from regions that drank wine, beer, cider, or distilled spirits – to *pinard*. It was not that *pinard* was necessarily a delicious drink – quality was a matter of luck, a question of where any particular batch came from – but it gathered cachet and appeal from its associations with camaraderie and shared dangers. The expectation and hope of the wine industry was that demobilized soldiers would take their love of *pinard* home, spread the word, and drive up demand for wine. Pierre Viala, a noted professor of viticulture, was confident not only that soldiers from cider-drinking Normandy and Brittany would remain true to wine after the war, but also that all the foreign soldiers fighting with the French 'will take back to their countries, along with victory, the healthy habit of consuming wine and the appreciation of its value for moral and physical wellbeing'. The French temperance movement was on board because it regarded wine positively and supported conversion to wine from other forms of alcohol.

Undoubtedly many soldiers who had not been wine drinkers before the war were exposed to it for the first time and perhaps some were converted. The word 'plonk', meaning inexpensive wine of mediocre quality, was coined during the conflict, and it is thought to be a corruption (by Australian soldiers) of *vin blanc* – although since *pinard* was almost always red (there were sometimes problems when producers delivered white wine) it is not clear why it became a generic word for wine. Nor is it possible to say whether wine consumption made advances in French regions that had historically been primarily consumers of beer, cider, or spirits. Alcohol consumption in France was affected by the deaths of about 10 per cent of the adult male population during the war. More than a million soldiers would have had to convert to wine simply in order for overall wine consumption to remain steady.

Whether or not the war expanded the wine-drinking population in France, there was widespread praise for *pinard*'s role in the war effort. A French military newspaper declared after the war: 'No doubt our brilliant generals and heroic soldiers were the immortal artisans of victory. But would they have been without the *pinard* that kept them going to the end, that endowed them with spirit, courage, tenacity, and scorn for danger, and made them repeat with unbreakable conviction, "We will prevail".' (The same was said of rum in the British army, with one medical officer writing in 1922, 'had it not been for the rum ration I do not think we should have won the war'.)

WINE AND THE SECOND WORLD WAR

The relationship between the French and wine in the Second World War was totally different because although both wars began with a German invasion, they unfolded utterly differently. For one thing, there was effectively no French army after June 1940, and far more of France was directly implicated in the war. From 1914 to 1918 the battle zone was confined to a small part of north-east France that included Champagne, it is true, but that left most French wine regions unaffected and able to supply their fighting forces with wine. But between 1940 and 1945 the major French wine regions – Champagne, Alsace, Burgundy, Bordeaux, and parts of Languedoc and Provence – were occupied by Germany. Most of the rest of France was governed by the collaborationist Vichy regime led by Philippe Pétain.

Although there were variations from one region to another, in the appellations occupied by Germany most of the wine production from 1940 to 1944 was seized or bought (at dictated prices) by the German authorities. Within the German economic plan for Europe, France was designated a supplier of agricultural goods, including wine. There is an echo of a much earlier invasion of France from the east: the so-called 'Barbarian invasion' of the western Roman Empire from about 500 AD, which the historian Edward Gibbon attributed partly to the attraction of wine.

Some military events have had disastrous effects on wine, as vineyards were destroyed in order to deprive local populations of both crops and income, while in other cases occupying forces have in various ways protected vineyards so as to ensure that they themselves had a continuous supply. The German occupation of France from 1940 to 1944 falls into the latter category. The aim was to obtain wine, and even though the occupation meant that vignerons were often short of labour and supplies, the Germans had no interest in interfering with wine production. Some French wine was purchased for resale on the German civilian market, some for the officer corps of the various branches of the German military, and some for the SS. Officials with backgrounds as wine merchants were stationed in each wine region to oversee and organize the purchase and shipping of wine to its destination.

The purchaser in Champagne was Otto Kläbisch, the manager of a German sparkling wine company and brother-in-law of Nazi foreign minister Joachim von Ribbentrop – who had himself been a German representative of the Mumm and Pommery champagne houses. Kläbisch oversaw the shipping of some 20 million bottles of champagne to Germany each year of the occupation. It not only represented more than half of each year's production but also cut deeply into Champagne's reserves.

In Burgundy Friedrich Dörrer, the official German wine buyer in 1940–41, invited producers to let him know what they wanted to sell. He was deluged with wine, as he represented virtually the only opportunity for the region's vignerons and *négociants* to sell their wines and remain in business. Unable, he said, to reply individually to so many producers, Dörrer put out a general statement thanking them for sending him samples and assuring them that he had tasted them all very carefully. They had, he wrote, 'made my job easy, all the while showing me their fraternal feelings'. Even so, he complained that some had sent poor wines, especially from the big 1934 and 1935 vintages – they clearly wanted to get rid of inventory – and that some of those wines 'did not even have acceptable colour'.

Beyond these requisitions, much French wine was simply stolen by German (and later by Allied) forces during the Second World War, just as champagne cellars had been looted by French and German soldiers in the previous conflict. But in the second of these wars almost all France's wine regions were occupied and many more cellars vulnerable to soldiers who wanted to help themselves.

There are countless stories of cellars ransacked by occupying troops and of attempts by owners to protect their stocks of wine. In Vouvray,

Philippe Poniatowsky buried some of his best wines in his yard while at Château Haut-Brion, which was used as a Luftwaffe rest home during the occupation, the entrances to some cellars were hidden behind piles of rubbish. In Beaune, Maurice Drouhin, the Burgundy *négociant*, built a wall in his cellar to conceal his stocks of Romanée-Conti from the 1929 to 1938 vintages. Other communities did not do so well. At the beginning of 1941 the vignerons of the small wine-producing commune of Monthelie, in the Côte de Beaune, recorded their misfortunes of 1940: freezing weather in January, heavy rain in April, occupation by the German army in June, followed by the seizure of all their reserves of wine. Such they concluded, 'is the balance-sheet of a particularly catastrophic year'.

There was, however, no single experience because some French wine regions were occupied by Germans, some by Italians, and others fell into the jurisdiction of Pétain's Vichy government. In some respects Pétain's government, centred in the spa town of Vichy – with an unpromising emphasis on the virtues of water – was an ordinary administration. Its rationale was that by agreeing to govern much of the interior of France (the coasts being controlled by the Germans for strategic reasons) it would prevent the occupation of the whole of France. Under its watch, for example, a number of new *appellations d'origine contrôlées* (AOCs) were established. They included Bordeaux Mousseux, a sparkling wine, and Bordeaux Supérieur, a category that had a slightly higher minimum alcohol level than generic AOC Bordeaux.

But the Vichy regime was anything but conventional. It cooperated with the anti-Jewish policies of the Nazi government and implemented a series of reactionary measures in the parts of France under its control. A number affected wine and most aimed to reduce wine production and consumption because Pétain was convinced that over-indulgence in wine had sapped the French of their moral strength and that widespread alcoholism was a symptom of his country's decadence. He was in power, after all, because the French armed forces had been unable to hold back the German invasion in June 1940, and because France had capitulated within weeks. That was evidence enough of the decline of France, and it was clear that much of the blame could be laid at the feet of the French adulation of their national beverage.

The rules introduced by his regime included restrictions on the bars and cafés that served alcohol, so much so that their number declined by nearly 40 per cent – from half a million to barely 300,000. The volume of tax-free wine that vignerons could keep for their family's consumption was reduced. Wine was included on the list of rationed goods (it had not been in the First World War): in 1940 the ration was two litres of wine per adult each week, and that was later restricted to males. There was talk the next year of cutting the ration to one litre per adult male each week, but the German authorities opposed it for fear that it would turn public opinion even more against Pétain's government. The ration was put in place not because there was a shortage of wine but because the government wanted to distil it for fuel.

Ironically, supporters of the Vichy regime, or people and associations that wanted to curry favour with it, often sent gifts of wine to Pétain. In 1942 the association of Burgundy *négociants* sent sixty-six six-bottle cases of their best wine to 'the Saviour of France', and the town of Villefranche-sur-Saône, in Beaujolais, sent thirty cases of their wine. A far more flamboyant gift, from civic officials of Dijon and Beaune, in Burgundy, was a complete vineyard that was renamed Le Clos du Maréchal Pétain. Formerly a vineyard called Les Teurons, it was bought from the Hospices de Beaune for this purpose. It is unlikely that Pétain ever drank wine from his vineyard, which was returned to its previous owner at the end of the war, and these gifts of wine seem out of step with Pétain's critique of wine drinking.

Some of the German soldiers who were stationed in France during the war availed themselves of the wine that was available. We have to be aware that the French regarded Germans as boorish drinkers at the best of times, and occupation in the Second World War was not the best of times. Contemporary French accounts of German soldiers' drinking need to be read with this in mind, but there are plenty of reports of heavy consumption. Observers frequently noted that German officers were intoxicated late in the evening. A historian living in Dijon during the war noted in his diary that on one occasion German soldiers stationed in Côte de Nuits drank the local wine all day long in Volnay and beat up an officer. Saying they had had enough, they left him for dead.

As for the German army in the Second World War, it was not so much served alcohol rations, as it had been in the First World War, as hard drugs such as methamphetamine. In his remarkable book *Blitzed: Drugs in Nazi Germany*, Norman Ohler has documented the extent to which the German soldiers were fed drugs that kept them awake for long periods and gave them extended bursts of energy. The tanks that invaded the Netherlands and France in 1940 were driven by soldiers who were able to stay awake for days at a time, thanks to the chemicals coursing through their veins. Maréchal Pétain could not have known this at the time; no one did, and they were stunned by the incredibly rapid progress the Panzer forces made. Had Pétain known the truth, he might not have been so quick to blame wine for France's military weakness. It was just that wine was no match for methamphetamine.

Wine has been involved in war in various ways over the centuries. At times it has been a staple of military rations, and at times been seen as harmful to military efficiency. Wine villages have been targeted by passing armies as sources of badly wanted alcohol, while vineyards have been destroyed as part of attempts to degrade supplies of basic goods. But the impact of wine on war, and vice versa, has been largely confined to Europe, where wine was more integrated into economies and diets.

8

WINE AND CRIME

In March 1751 the Lieutenant-General of Police of Paris published a pamphlet outlining the offences committed by Étienne Corrot, a wine merchant charged with wine fraud on what was then probably a considerable scale. At the request of the guild of wine merchants of Paris, the police had raided Corrot's establishment (a shop, cellars, and a bar) and a panel of five 'expert tasters' (*Experts-Dégustateurs*) had tested the contents of the barrels in his cellar. There they found eight barrels containing what they identified as a mixture of wine and pear brandy, two more barrels containing a liquid made from water and wine lees and then fortified with pear brandy, and another barrel containing pear brandy diluted with water.

Corrot was a licensed wine merchant who was permitted to sell wine but not distilled alcohol. Moreover, it was forbidden to mix wine with anything, and certainly forbidden to dilute it with water or to make 'wine' by adding water to wine lees – what later became known as a *deuxième cuvée*, or second batch. For concocting these illegal beverages, Corrot was condemned to pay fines and damages totalling 650 *livres* (a sizeable sum), and forbidden to sell wine for a year. His establishment was boarded up for that period, the offending contents of the barrels were poured into a stream that ran near his establishment, his barrels were burned, and the bottles found in his shop were smashed. The judgment was published and posted on the door of his bar and his house.

This case shows how seriously the authorities of eighteenth-century Paris took wine fraud. Even though it was not possible until the nineteenth century to test food and drink chemically so as to ascertain what they were made from, trusted tasters could sniff out additives and adulterants that were not permitted. (Such tasters, known in England as ale-conners, or ale-knowers, performed the same service for ale and beer.) Just how common this kind of wine fraud was, we have no idea. Wine merchants and tavern owners were prosecuted on a fairly regular basis throughout France at this time, but the number of cases does not necessarily give us any precise insight into the extent of fraud. We have no idea if the authorities caught half, a quarter, a tenth, or one in a hundred of the offenders.

Even so, wine fraud – the addition of illegal substances to wine – is historically one of the most common forms of crime associated with wine. The other is wine counterfeiting, the representation of a wine as something that it is not: such as (today) putting the label of a first growth wine from an excellent vintage (why make it from a mediocre vintage when you're cheating, anyway?) on a bottle that contains ordinary red wine. In the past – before the nineteenth century, let us say – wine fraud was probably more common than counterfeiting because place of origin and vintage were less important than they are today. But there are modern examples of wine fraud, such as the artificially sweetened wines that are frequently sold as Canadian Icewine on some Asian markets. In fact many of these cases involve both fraud and counterfeiting, as the bottles not only contain wine that has been adulterated by the addition of artificial sweeteners, but also have fake labels declaring they are Icewine.

Counterfeiting is more common than wine fraud today because fabulously high prices are often paid for some wines from Bordeaux and Burgundy, not to mention prestigious wines from elsewhere, such as Australia's Penfolds Grange. It is not clear how far counterfeiting goes back in historical terms, although there is no reason to think that it did not occur in classical times. When wines from certain Greek islands or regions of Egypt and Italy were prized – and priced – above others, it does not stretch credulity to think that there must have been merchants who sold their mediocre wine as coming from the places that had a reputation for quality. But such practices at those times lie in the realm of speculation, not the historical record.

WINE ADDITIVES IN THE ANCIENT WORLD

Wine fraud has a longer documented history, but it is a complicated history because the definition of wine has changed over time and the list of permitted ingredients and additives has been anything but constant. Scores of additives are permitted in modern wine (they vary according to wine law) the most prominent including sulphur, tartaric acid, sugar, and tannins. But some of these additives have been contested over time. The addition of sugar to grape must to increase alcohol content in the finished wine (a process now known as chaptalization) was practised by some producers in the eighteenth century, well before Jean-Antoine Chaptal promoted it in a publication in 1801 and it became associated with his name. But in the nineteenth and twentieth centuries some producers in France and Germany condemned the adding of sugar to must. They referred to chaptalized wine as fraudulent and 'industrial' and their own unchaptalized wines as 'natural'. Current German wine law embodies the distinction, with unchaptalized wines occupying a higher tier than chaptalized wines in its wine classification system.

There was no sugar in ancient Europe, but there was honey, and it was liberally added to wine – but generally after fermentation was complete so as to sweeten the wine, rather than before fermentation to raise its potential alcohol level. And honey was only one of the substances commonly added to wines in the ancient world. There was no wine law as such that permitted some additives and prohibited others, although there appear to have been acceptable and unacceptable practices. Among the additives that were widely employed, depending on region and the desired style of wine, were sea water, tree resin, ashes, roots, herbs, and spices. Some were added during fermentation but for the most part they were added after the wine had fermented so that what we might think of as pure wine – fermented grape juice – was merely the base for a more complicated beverage. At the very least, wine was diluted with water, as it always was at symposia, the gatherings of elite men in Greece, where the ratio of water to wine was decided by the host. Water was always the greater part, with common water-to-wine ratios being 3:1, 5:3, and 3:2. A mix that was three parts water to one of wine would have produced a beverage that was very low in alcohol, as appropriate for an occasion that went on all night and where the participants were expected to remain reasonably sober.

In ancient Greece and Rome all these beverages – pure wine alone or pure wine with added substances – were referred to simply as wine, and in his *Natural History* Pliny the Elder described some of the common ways in which wines were made. A frequent additive was resin, or pitch, usually from the terebinth tree, but also from cypresses, cedars, and other varieties. Pliny discussed the qualities of the resins – terebinth resin was the best quality, while cypress resin had a more acrid flavour than any other – and the modes of using them. The method for seasoning wines 'is to sprinkle pitch in the must during the first fermentation ... so that a bouquet is imparted to the wine'. Resin also gave body to thin wines and mitigated any harshness in the flavours, Pliny wrote, but he noted that resin might give wine a bitter, smoky flavour if the resin had been over-cooked.

Other winemakers added gypsum (plaster) and ashes, especially ashes from the wood of vines or oak trees, while sea water was commonly added after the wine had completed fermentation. Pliny recommended collecting it far out to sea, at night, while the north-east wind was blowing. Sea water was an important ingredient in a recipe that Cato suggested for making wine suitable for farm labourers. It involved blending specific volumes of grape must, sharp vinegar, boiled must, and fresh water, and stirring them three times a day for five days before adding old sea water. This wine, Cato declared, would last most of a year, and what was left over would be very sharp and excellent vinegar.

Pliny's descriptions of the various substances that were regularly added to wine (water, resin, ashes, and so on) were written in a factual and morally neutral way. But although the flavours and textures of these wines depended on the additives, Pliny deplored the use of any substance to deepen the colour of wines. The implication here is that darker-hued wines had particular cachet and Pliny not only noted that some winemakers added pigments as colorants but also implied that they were harmful to the consumer: 'By such poisonous sophistications is this beverage compelled to suit our tastes, and then we are surprised that it is injurious in its effects.' He called out the wines from the region around modern Narbonne for particular criticism: 'the growers of that country have absolutely established manufactories for the purpose of adulteration, where they give a dark hue to their wines by the agency of smoke; I only wish I could say, too, that they do not employ various herbs and noxious drugs for the same purpose; indeed these dealers are even known to use aloes for the purpose of heightening the flavour and improving the colour of their wines.'

On the surface, these seem odd criticisms, given the common practice among the Greeks and Romans of flavouring wines with all manner of additives, but perhaps Pliny's complaint was based on a distinction between wine before and after it was modified. Perhaps consumers had a right to expect to purchase wine in a pure form so that they could flavour it themselves to their personal taste preferences – even though resin was typically added to wine during fermentation, as we have seen.

It is difficult to get a clear sense of wine fraud – for that is what Pliny was alleging of producers who artificially deepened the colour of their wines – in a culture where it was normal to add myriad substances to wine, and where what we might think of as pure wine was rarely, if ever, consumed. The bias against pure wine is shown in one allegation sometimes made to justify prohibitions on wine drinking by women in Rome – that instead of drinking it diluted with water, as men did, women were prone to drinking wine undiluted. There seems no reason why this should have been true, but it clearly shows a bias against drinking wine straight and probably a fear that women would become easily intoxicated.

As Pliny's example shows, we must have a sense of what was permitted and what was not before we can discuss wine fraud at any period. The difficulty of pinning down the rules and conventions makes any discussion of fraud very tentative unless we have clear indications, such as Pliny's warning against artificially colouring wine.

WINE FRAUD

More precise regulations governing wine, often set down by guilds, began to emerge in the Middle Ages and Early Modern period (about 1500 to 1800). As we see in the case of Étienne Corrot which opened this chapter, there were laws regarding diluting wine with water and mixing wine with other beverages. Even so, plenty of recipes circulated that involved adding a wide range of suspect substances to wine. One prominent genre of writing concerned ways of fixing 'broken' wine, wine that had gone off, mainly (one supposes) by becoming oxidized as barrels gradually emptied or by being spoiled by brettanomyces, a yeast sometimes found in barrels and that beyond a certain threshold gives off-odours and -flavours to wine.

The *Ménagier de Paris*, a fourteenth century work on household management, suggested treating spoiled wine with various additives. A bad smell in wine could be corrected by adding elder wood and powdered cardamom; cloudy or muddy wine could be clarified by suspending in the barrel bags containing egg whites that had been boiled and then fried; unwanted colour in white wine could be removed by adding holly leaves or, if that did not work, a basketful of sand washed in water drawn from the River Seine. If individual householders made their bad wine more drinkable in this way, it would not be an offence, just as it would not be if they added water to their own wine. But it was a different matter if a tavern keeper or wine merchant did the same thing and sold the result as pure wine.

Clearly there were regional variations in what constituted wine and therefore what constituted adulteration and fraud. Resinated wine remained popular in the eastern Mediterranean (as Retsina still is) long after resin ceased to function as a way of making amphoras impermeable. When barrels replaced amphoras and began to be used in the making, storing, and transporting of wine, the flavours from new barrels must have been tolerated as the price to pay before a barrel had been used often enough for the wood to become inert and not affect the flavour of the wine. (It was centuries before barrel fermentation and barrel ageing were deliberately used to modify the flavour and style of wine.) Despite a few exceptions such as these, throughout most of wine-drinking Europe wine became what we now understand it to be: fermented grape juice. It might sometimes be diluted with water, warmed, or used as a base for spiced beverages, but wine-based beverages were not called simply 'wine'.

From the 1500s, starting with the wines of Jerez in Spain and the Douro Valley in Portugal, distilled alcohol began to be widely used to fortify wines so as to prevent their spoiling during shipping. But these wines were called sherry (or sherry-wine) and port (or port-wine), respectively, not simply wine. Nor were beverages made from wine and other ingredients. They included hippocras, a (usually) warm beverage of wine that was mixed with a little distilled alcohol and infused with spices and sometimes fruit – what is often called glühwein or mulled wine. Sangria, a blend of wine, sometimes brandy, and fruit juices that dates in some form to the eighteenth century, was not called wine.

'He is very wise. He puts water in his wine.' An innkeeper waters down his wine while his wife distracts his customer, a baker's son, by kissing him. Engraving c.1660 by J. Lagnier.

We can see, then, that the meaning of the word 'wine' has evolved over time. In all languages it has always referred to fermented grape juice, although occasionally there has been some slippage and the fermented juice of other berries and fruit have been referred to as wine. The point here is that in the classical period, wine was more than that, and the definition was broad enough to encompass beverages that included many other ingredients. Since the Middle Ages, however, wine took on the more limited meaning that we use today, and it was embodied in legislation in many countries in the nineteenth and twentieth centuries. This tightening of the definition of wine widened the definition of wine fraud. We shall return later to the irony that in the last few decades winemakers have been permitted to add to wine scores of substances that are not considered to constitute fraud.

FRAUD IN THE DOURO VALLEY

As early as the 1750s, however, a major case of wine fraud came to light. In the preceding decades port, the lightly (at that time) fortified wine from Portugal's Douro Valley, had become a hugely popular drink among middle-class English men. Exports of port to England rose quickly, reaching 12 million litres in 1728. But before long the producers were unable to keep up with demand. The weather in some years led to smaller than average crops and the area under cultivation on the steep and difficult slopes of the Douro Valley was small and could be expanded only very slowly. Many port producers in Portugal and merchants in England began to resort to fraudulent methods to make enough wine to fill the orders that rolled in relentlessly. The problem lay with the success of port, but the eighteenth-century wine merchant John Croft blamed the English port dealers for the fraudulent solution. The port shortage, he wrote, 'induced the English factors [merchants] and Wine coopers to try the expedient of adulterating, and teaching the Portuguese to sophisticate [tamper with] the wines'.

The adulteration of port took place both in the Douro Valley itself and in England. In the Douro, producers began to blend the wines made from their own grapes with inferior wines from elsewhere – a practice that probably fell in the category of counterfeit rather than fraud, although the distinction would have been a fine one to consumers. Some producers added sugar to give their ports more sweetness, while others fortified theirs with more alcohol to give them additional strength. (At that time port contained relatively little distilled alcohol – it made up about 3 per cent of the total volume, compared to about 20 per cent today.) Yet other port producers turned to out-and-out fraud. They used crushed elderberries to give their ports deeper colour, and added spices such as pepper, cinnamon, and ginger to give them more flavour.

In England, merchants manipulated port in a variety of ways and even fabricated 'port' from scratch. In addition to the existing manuals on how to fix wine that had spoiled, new publications provided guidance on increasing the volume of imported wine by adding local (that is, English) ingredients and on using local products to make wines that appeared to be foreign. One recipe included the juice of elderberries, wild mulberries, and cider, with the result then being blended with real wine.

Such practices, together with widespread smuggling, produced a situation where merchants were selling far more wine than they were paying duties on. In 1733 the government proposed legislation that would have given excise men, agents of the department that oversaw the payment of import duties, the right to inspect the cellars of wine merchants so as to identify wines that had entered England illegally, as well as barrels containing adulterated wines. The wine trade vigorously opposed the bill and it was defeated, but the publicity drew attention to the corrupt state of the port business. Many English port consumers, unwilling to pay good money for what was clearly a product of dubious authenticity and quality, turned away from port in favour of other beverages. In 1754 the merchants were warned that port had a worse reputation than any other wine and that the English thought it was 'injurious to health – an opinion so strong in the minds of many, that some even account them as poisonous'. The 12 million litres exported to England in 1728 plummeted to less than half that by 1756. Moreover, the bottom fell out of the port market, and the price of a barrel fell from £16 in the 1730s to £2 10s in 1756.

In an exchange of letters between the English merchants and the producers, each blamed the other for ruining the port business. The merchants accused the producers of shady production practices that resulted in ports that had no longevity. They also condemned the adding of brandy during, rather than after, fermentation – the current practice in port production but one the merchants alleged led to unpleasant flavours. This calls into question the style of port that the merchants had in mind, because adding brandy during fermentation has the effect of stopping it before all the natural sugar has fermented out, leaving the sugar that gives port its characteristic sweetness. Adding the brandy only after fermentation was complete ran the risk that the wine would ferment to total dryness. The reality was that eighteenth-century port came in many more styles and levels of sweetness and alcohol than it does today.

The producers replied by blaming the merchants for encouraging the adulteration of port so as to produce a wine that 'should burn in the stomach; that, thrown in the fire, it should flash like gunpowder; that its colour should be as deep as ink; that its sweetness should be like the sugar of Brazil, and its aromatic flavour should be like the spices of India ... It was by these DIABOLICAL INSTRUCTIONS of the Factory [the wine merchants], that the wine growers were compelled to load their wines with elderberry, brandy, and sweets, or run the risk of not selling their wines except for common use.'

The English market was the single most important for port exports and the prosperity of the Douro region was threatened by the adulteration scandal. The Portuguese government acted swiftly to restore the wine's reputation. A royal decree created the General Company of Vineyards of the Alto Douro to regulate the industry, delimited the geographical area where port could be made, and created a mechanism for supervising all phases of production. The blending of wines from the demarcated region with outside wines was prohibited and the cultivation of elderberries in the Douro Valley was banned (even though an enterprising port producer could easily find elderberries elsewhere). Additional measures included identifying areas within the broader region that were higher quality, and limiting the use of fertilizer there.

These measures, which were vigorously resisted by the English merchants, had the intended effect of restoring confidence in port, and by the late 1770s – as the popularity of port spread from the middle classes to the English elites – exports of port to England had more than rebounded. From about 6,000 casks in 1756, they rose to more than 12,000 in the 1770s, and to more than 20,000 casks in the early 1790s. These figures are impressive in themselves, but what is really astonishing is that such an increase in exports – and these related to England, alone – could be managed and sustained without recourse to fraudulent production methods. It is an open question how much fraud persisted, despite the new rules. A nineteenth-century English cartoon showed an industrial street in the middle of which a vat labelled 'Genuine Port' was being filled by three casks labelled Brandy, Cyder, and Red Cape (red wine from the Cape of Good Hope, South Africa). Lying by the vat are sacks labelled Rum Dragon, Red Sanders (a tree with medicinal properties), Alium, and Tartare, as well as – for good measure and to suggest the goodness of the concoction – a human skull.

THE NINETEENTH CENTURY: A GOLDEN AGE OF WINE FRAUD?

It was in the nineteenth century, when the definition of wine had tightened and was beginning to enter legislation, and when the development of organic chemistry began to provide more certainty as to the composition of foods and beverages, that the authorities and consumers began to focus more closely on wine fraud. There was also increasing concern about public health and sanitation – it was called the 'hygiene movement' in some places – and governments began to adopt regulations to ensure the safety of these goods. Integral to it were campaigns to ensure that the foods and drinks available to the public were healthy. Moreover, the temperance movements attacked alcoholic beverages as dangerous to human health, and even though they focused on distilled spirits, wine came under closer scrutiny than ever before.

The adulteration of food and beverages engaged the attention of authorities throughout Europe and North America from the middle of the nineteenth century to the beginning of the First World War. For these and other reasons, the nineteenth century might well appear to have been a golden age of wine fraud, not necessarily because wine fraud was more extensive at that time, but because it was more often detected and even more often suspected. One of the most influential wine writers of the period, Cyrus Redding, argued that adulteration was widespread in the wines imported into England, especially fortified wines whose 'spirituous strength', he wrote, could easily mask adulteration and deceive even experienced tasters. Redding blamed the victims – English consumers – for the ease with which wine producers and merchants deceived them. They so much preferred distilled spirits and fortified wines that their palates were dulled and they could hardly tell genuine wine from the fraudulent beverages they were sold: 'As the fondness for spirit increases, that for wine diminishes. The cuticle on the hand of a blacksmith is hardened by the hot iron, and cannot distinguish objects by the sense of feeling; in the same manner the stomach of the spirit drinker is lost to the healthy freshness of wine, being too cold and unseasoned for his seared stomach, while adulterations or coarse mixtures of the grape remain undiscovered.'

There was a class perspective in play here, as Redding was essentially describing working-class drinking habits. As for the better-off, the wine connoisseurs, Redding thought they would easily see through 'any attempt to fabricate Romanée-Conti … because the fineness, delicacy, and perfume of this wine are not to be copied'. It was an optimistic view underpinned by class confidence, for there is plenty of evidence over time and in recent years that many experienced wine connoisseurs have been persuaded by a label to believe that a fraudulent or counterfeit wine was the real thing.

The nineteenth century also saw the practice of 'Hermitaging' – adding Syrah from the Rhône Valley, especially from the Hermitage district – to Bordeaux wines to give them more complexity and aromatics. This would now be forbidden, although multi-regional blending is permitted in many parts of the New World, and it was permitted in nineteenth-century France before appellation rules were adopted. It was, moreover, publicly acknowledged, and it is another example of a practice that was not considered fraudulent or problematic until changing rules made it so.

PHYLLOXERA AND WINE FRAUD

Just as the conditions were right for the unprecedented examination of wine that writers such as Redding represented, the European wine industry was thrown into a crisis that led to a concentrated phase of wine fraud in Europe. In the last decades of the 1800s phylloxera, the aphid that generally kills *Vitis vinifera* vines, destroyed vineyards throughout Europe. France, the world's biggest wine producer, was the first to be affected, and between 1875 and 1890 more than three-quarters of its vines died. The immediate result was a steep decline in wine production – and a wine-fraud industry soon sprang up to supply the robust demand that gave France the world's highest per capita rate of wine consumption at the time.

Undoubtedly the most common form of fraud was the easiest and most banal: diluting wine with water. This was not done at the winery because producers were taxed by the volume of wine they shipped and paying more taxes on the increased volume of diluted wine would largely cancel out any additional revenues it would generate. Rather, water was added by merchants and retailers, who could enjoy the benefits of selling more wine than they bought. By being not too greedy and diluting their wine minimally, they could profit from stretched supplies without the fraud being too obvious to their customers.

But watering down was not negligible: according to the tax authorities in Paris, in the early 1880s water accounted for one sixth of the volume of wine consumed in the capital – the five million hectolitres of wine consumed each year was stretched to six million by the addition of water. As taxes were paid on the undiluted wine, merchants and retailers were able to evade taxes on one sixth of the wine they sold as well as profit from sales of the extra wine. Ordinary wine had only about 10 per cent alcohol at that time, and dilution on that scale (it would bring the alcohol level to a little over 8 per cent) might have been noticed, so the practice developed of fortifying wine with distilled spirits before diluting it with water, thus maintaining the alcohol level but adulterating the wine even further.

Yet other fraudulent wines were made from raisins and currants imported from the eastern Mediterranean. Raisins, it is true, are dried grapes, but they are made from varieties not suitable for making wine. And while some genuine wines are made by drying the grapes before they are pressed, raisins are dried far more and lose about 85 per cent of their water, compared to 30 to 40 per cent for grapes used in winemaking. For this reason, water had to be added to wine made from raisins and currants, another reason why it was an example of wine fraud. A popular book on making raisin wine that appeared in 1880 (and went through twelve printings in the next six years) provided a simple recipe: soak raisins in warm water, let them ferment for twelve days, then press the liquid off the pulp. The resulting pale-coloured 'wine' would have an alcohol level of 10 to 11 per cent, and it could be transformed into red wine by adding some genuine red wine, elderberries, or a chemical dye harmless to humans.

The production of raisin wine became a big business during the 1880s and 1890s, especially in Bordeaux and parts of Languedoc. Bordeaux became a major import point for raisins and currants from Greece and Turkey. The French government declared that raisin wine could be sold as long as it was labelled as such, but that any labelled simply 'wine' was considered fraudulent.

The other major category of fraudulent wine was *deuxième cuvée* (second batch), which was made by adding warm water and sugar to the solid residue (mainly skins, but also seeds and stems) left over from winemaking. After fermentation was complete, the colour was fixed and tartaric acid was added. It is estimated that hundreds of millions of litres of raisin wine and *deuxième cuvée* were made during the phylloxera period in France, and that together they made up a tenth of all the wine sold in 1890.

The shortage of wine and allegations of widespread wine fraud during the phylloxera crisis drew attention to other practices. Many producers added plaster (gypsum or calcium sulphate) to their wines because it made them a brighter and clearer colour and raised the level of acidity, an important preservative against temperature fluctuations during shipping. It was practised mainly in the warmer wine-producing areas, such as the south of France and Spain. French scientists determined that 'plastering' wine moderately (2 grams per litre of wine) was not harmful to human health, but in the 1880s permission to plaster was suspended and in 1891 it was banned entirely, partly because of concerns about its effect on health, partly because Bordeaux wine producers argued that plastered wines had an unfair advantage over their non-plastered wines. Even after the prohibition came into effect there were continuing allegations that producers in southern France and Spain persisted with the practice.

Chaptalization, the addition of sugar to must in order to raise the alcohol level in finished wine, also came under attack. It was a widespread practice in Burgundy and northern regions where grapes did not accumulate as much sugar during the growing season, and it was attacked by producers in warmer regions. Their grapes accumulated more sugar and they had no need to chaptalize. Adding sugar and removing acid from wine were the subjects of a vigorous debate conflict in some of Germany's wine regions in the 1800s, leading to a distinction being drawn between 'natural' and 'artificial' wines. High acidity was a recurrent problem in wines from many German wine regions because the cool and variable weather often failed to ripen grapes fully to the extent that sugars and flavours increased and acids declined.

In the early and mid-1800s the wine producers of the Mosel River Valley faced many challenges selling their wines. They were more expensive to produce than in other regions because of the notoriously steep slopes that made vineyard care and harvest slow and expensive, but a major marketing problem was the trademark acidity of Mosel wines. Johann Philipp Bronner, a German wine expert of the time, wrote pithily that 'If we praise the distinctive Riesling that grows along certain parts of the Mosel ... we must then recognize that the greatest share of Mosel wine remains simply a sour drink'. In 1821 Karl Graff, the German religious scholar, wrote that 'It is only too true that Mosel wines compare unfavourably with those from other German wine regions ... there is a terrible mass of Mosel wine that originates from around Trier and Koblenz ... which no doubt damages the reputation of all Mosel wines among non-experts. In this mass of wine there is an excess of acidity that even in the best vintages they cannot be sweetened by nature.'

As Kevin D. Goldberg has shown, by the middle of the nineteenth century it was possible to measure acidity, sugar, and alcohol in wines. An 1853 paper presented to the Royal Society of London, detailing the respective composition of the eight wines most commonly imported in England, showed that Mosel wines had 10 per cent more acidity than wines from Burgundy, which were the next highest in acid. Mosel wines had 20 per cent more acid than wines from the Rhine River Valley. As far as alcohol was concerned – and alcohol was regarded as a surrogate measure for grape ripeness – Mosel wines were the lowest of the eight, and 28 per cent lower than the levels in Rhine wines. There seems no doubt that Mosel wines at this time were seriously unbalanced in favour of acidity.

Karl Graff's statement that grapes in much of the Mosel region 'cannot be sweetened by nature' seemed to suggest the solution to the Mosel wine that was low in fruit and high in acid: add sugar. Cheered on by a different Karl – Karl Marx, whose father owned a vineyard in the Mosel region – Mosel producers adopted a winemaking method devised by another German socialist, Ludwig Gall. This involved adding a carefully calibrated solution of sugar and water to the must before fermentation. This did not increase the sweetness of the wine but diluted the acidity, thus giving the perception of sweetness and riper grapes. Gall insisted that his method was 'improvement' not 'falsification' because it did not add to the wine anything not already naturally there. Moreover, wine was made by humans, not nature: 'Wine is as other foods, which are not provided in a finished state directly from nature, but only made so through the assistance of man … nature offers to us from our vineyards not wine, but only grapes, which even in a completely ripe condition are still not finished. They only contain the necessary material for winemaking.'

Once Mosel producers began to use Gall's method, their fortunes – figuratively and literally – began to rebound. Their more balanced wines began to win awards at exhibitions, and wine prices and sales rose. It is almost unnecessary to say that this success and the new competitiveness of Mosel wines on export markets drew the ire of wine producers in Germany's other wine regions. Some were clearly motivated by what they considered a shady practice that gave Mosel wines a commercial advantage – the sort of argument that was used in France against wines that had plaster added to them. Others worried that once *Gallisierung*, as Ludwig Gall's process was called, was widely known, it would undermine the reputation for purity that wines from other German regions had. Others feared the slippery slope of falsification. As one wrote: 'If we decide to allow artificial improvement only for competent winemakers, there will soon appear other participants who will bring the greatest shame and discredit to vintners and wine merchants … the original idea of rational-artificial improvement [will be brought] into the realm of affectation, cover-ups, and deceit.'

Other regions carried out a sustained campaign. They invoked the idea of terroir, arguing that the taste of their 'natural' wine derived from the growing conditions of the grapes and was present in the must, and that interfering with the must by adding sugar and water to it produced unnatural aromas and flavours. An 1879 German law on foodstuffs made Gall's process illegal, but later wine law allowed it. Modern

German wine makes a distinction between wines that are made with added sugar and those are not. The irony was that as German wine producers debated the ins and outs of the process, what was natural and what was not, the addition of sugar to wine was a winemaking practice throughout most of Europe.

COUNTERFEITING WINES

It was also in the modern period that wine counterfeiting became more common. As with wine fraud, there is a contextual history to consider because counterfeiting involves misrepresenting a wine's provenance – for example by labelling it as a wine from the Graves region of Bordeaux when it was actually made from grapes grown in less prestigious areas. Clearly, the effort that goes into counterfeiting is worthwhile only when some wines have a higher reputation than others and when reputation can be translated into monetary value. This means that the potential for counterfeiting goes back as far as the Greek and Roman world, where some wines were singled out as being desirable because of their particularly high quality. In Greece, for example, wines from the island of Thasos were highly esteemed. It might well have been worthwhile for some Athenian wine merchant to claim that his mediocre wine from (let us say) Crete was from Thasos. It would help if he had poured the wine into a Thasian amphora; each island used a distinctively shaped amphora with recognizable designs etched into it. Anyone who bought this speculative wine might well have been convinced that it was from Thasos.

There are suggestions that wine fraud might have been rife in ancient Italy. Falernian wine, often considered the best wine produced on the peninsula, appears to have been available in limitless volumes and at low prices in the bars of Rome. Examinations of seals on amphoras have shown that a number purporting to come from Pompeii, the major export point of quality wines, were counterfeit. As in Greece, it was probably fairly easy to counterfeit wine in Italy because wine was diluted with water and infused with various additives before being consumed, and there were no quality controls to ensure any level of consistency in flavour and style from batch to batch.

It is also quite likely that most counterfeit wine has historically not been discovered because the purchasers had never before tasted the wine it claimed to be and therefore had no point of comparison. Even if purchasers had tasted the wine that the counterfeit purported to be, they would be comparing the wine with the memory of an earlier tasting, rather than tasting two wines side by side. Comparison is complicated by the variations that occur quite naturally among bottles, barrels, or presumably – in the ancient world – among amphoras.

Pliny the Elder, who had a lot to say about wine and a little to say about wine fraud, was silent on counterfeiting, and in fact the earliest unambiguous reference might come from the late 1300s. The English poet Geoffrey Chaucer, who was the son of a wine merchant and presumably knew what he was talking about, wrote in his *Canterbury Tales*:

> Keep clear of wine, I tell you, white or red,
> Especially Spanish wines which they provide
> And have on sale in Fish Street and Cheapside.
> That wine mysteriously finds it way
> To mix itself with others – shall we say
> Spontaneously? – that grow in neighbouring regions.

The reference here is not to fraud, the addition of unacceptable or illegal ingredients, but the blending of Spanish wine into wines from elsewhere. It is likely that the 'neighbouring regions' Chaucer was referring to included Bordeaux. The merchants of claret, the light red wine from Bordeaux that was extremely popular in England from the thirteenth century onwards, are known to have sourced and blended wines from a number of regions, including Spain, and sold them as claret. The practice seems to have been common enough that the authorities in London eventually banned tavern keepers from cellaring barrels of wine from France, Spain, and Germany together.

We have no idea how common wine fraud was in earlier times, but it seems likely to have been infrequent. Virtually all wine (champagne is an obvious exception) was shipped in bulk until the twentieth century, and even by the middle of the 1900s only a small percentage of wine (high-end wines from prestigious regions such as Bordeaux and Burgundy) was shipped in bottles. It is possible, probably likely, that unscrupulous wine merchants in the 1600s and earlier tried to pass off their barrels of ordinary wines as coming from regions that were becoming known for high-quality wines, but there is no evidence of it. As for misrepresenting wines as coming from particular estates or producers, that was not likely until the late 1600s and 1700s, when regions such as Graves and properties such as Haut-Brion and Lafite began to become well known for their wines.

The shortage of wines during the phylloxera period in France led not only to wine fraud, as we have seen, but also to suspicions of counterfeiting, as the well-regarded wine regions fell on hard times and had to resort to various means to meet continuing demand for their wines. Huge volumes of Spanish and Portuguese wines were imported through Bordeaux – the barrels being off-loaded from ships that lay alongside vessels carrying raisins and currants. Although much of the foreign wine was sold as such, as France became a net importer of wine for several decades, some of it disappeared into the *chais*, the warehouses at Bordeaux's port that held the region's wines.

In 1885 the London newspaper *The Telegraph* reported that 'An immense proportion of the wine sold in England as Claret has nothing to do with the banks of the Garonne [a river running through Bordeaux], save that harsh, heavy vintages have been brought from Spain and Italy, and dried currants from Greece. There to be manipulated and re-shipped to England and the rest of the world as Lafitte [sic], Larose, St. Julien, and St. Estèphe.' The demand for luxury wines in Britain declined because of uncertainty about their authenticity. *Ridley's*, the leading British alcohol trade periodical, noted in 1891 that 'blends with Spanish Red, South of France, and other wines are sold, occasionally under their true designation, but generally under the usurped title of "Claret".'

So critical were the effects of counterfeiting and adulteration on French wine exports that the government intervened. In 1889 French law defined wine as a beverage made only from fresh grapes, and forbade the addition of water and alcohol. Similar laws were adopted in Germany in 1892 and Italy in 1904. Wine made from raisins had to be labelled as such. Some retailers tried to sell wine labelled as containing added water or alcohol, on the legal precept that sellers were indemnified as long as buyers were aware of what they were buying. But in 1894 a new French law stopped the practice so that the ban on adding water and alcohol could be enforced.

These issues came to the fore in 1905, when the French government tried to enact a comprehensive law on wine. A prime target was fraud, which was thought to be rampant, and the parliamentary debate included allegations that the substances being added to wines were variously toxic and killing people or driving them mad and filling up the asylums. In England, a journal suggested various ways for testing the safety of the substances used to deepen the colour of wines, substances that ranged from benign elderberries to dye made from coal tar and arsenic. One suggestion was gun cotton, a fluffy white substance and low-level explosive, that could be used to determine if the colour of wine was natural or had been deepened with artificial dyes. The writer suggested that 'by carrying about a supply of gun-cotton to test one's *vin ordinaire* at a hotel restaurant, it would be possible to avoid being poisoned, but one might come within the penal clauses of the Explosives Act.' To read these accounts, drinking wine around the turn of the twentieth century could be a high-risk undertaking.

THE PROBLEM OF CLARET AND BURGUNDY

The British, so often portrayed as the victims of French deceit, were often complicit in wine fraud and counterfeiting, as they had been in the port scandal of the eighteenth century. Some British wine merchants were adept at blending prestigious Bordeaux wines with cheaper wines to increase their profits. *Ridley's*, an important whistleblower of the period, noted in 1906 that 'people drink so-called "Claret," composed of one-third of the genuine article and two-thirds of the British imposition, and condemn, not the latter, but Claret.' We might note that the 'genuine article' itself might have been blended with Spanish wine, making the proportion of claret in the blend even smaller. Claret, indeed, suffered a very bad press as a result of fraud and counterfeiting. *Ridley's* wrote scornfully 'The Public, who unfortunately know more about Growths, than Vintages, receive circulars offering Château this or Château that at apparently extremely low rates, and on the strength of the name, purchase Wines, which can but prove intensely disappointing. They then are apt to argue that, if wines bearing the names of the best estates of the Médoc be so inferior, then those of the lower grade must be bad indeed. Thus their faith in Claret, instead of in the merchant, who has sold it to them, is shaken, and an inducement is at hand to try wines from some other districts.'

In order to give consumers some confidence that they were buying wine that came from the estate they wanted, some Bordeaux producers began to bottle their own wines on their estates, rather than shipping them to merchants for bottling where they might be blended with other wines. The producers who began to do this – starting with Châteaux Mouton-Rothschild, Margaux, and Haut-Brion – began to note on their labels *mis en bouteilles au Château* ('Bottled at the Château'). That is now such a common element on Bordeaux wine labels that most consumers ignore it, but it derives from a period when fraud and counterfeiting were widespread.

Some of the practices we would now consider counterfeiting were permitted until clearly defined appellation laws were adopted. A wine labelled by one of Burgundy's communal appellations, such as Volnay, Meursault, and Monthelie, must now be made only from grapes grown in the appellation, but until rudimentary appellation rules were adopted in 1920, *négociants* – brokers who bought wine from a number of vignerons, blended them, and sold them under various brands – had considerable leeway in the way they labelled wines. They could label a wine by the name of a commune even if the wine did not come from there, as long as the *négociant* believed that the wine had the character of a wine from that village. Thus a wine that was a blend of wines from several districts could legally be labelled 'Pommard' if the *négociants* believed it tasted like a wine from Pommard. The result was that many wines tasted like those from Burgundy's more prestigious villages; of the twenty-nine villages in Burgundy's Côte de Nuits region, only twelve gave their names to wines before the 1920s. The other seventeen tasted like one or more of the select dozen.

This practice was known as *équivalence* as it was based on the principle that wines from some parts of Burgundy were equivalent in style and quality to wines from other parts. The practice would now be considered counterfeiting because French wine law closely regulates labelling, but before 1920 the name of a Burgundy village on a bottle of wine was understood not to mean that the wine necessarily came from that village (although it might), but rather as an indication of style and quality. The underlying rationale was that if consumers wanted a wine that tasted like a wine from Pommard, any wine that tasted like a wine from Pommard would be satisfactory. It is a compelling argument. In fact, only people in the wine business would know what a genuine Pommard tasted like because consumers could not tell which 'Pommard' wines really were from Pommard and which were not. Village names, then, were not to be understood literally. They represented styles, and as long as *négociants* were good at their jobs and their 'Pommard' wines from other districts really did taste like Pommard wines, there was no reason for consumers to complain.

The English physician and wine writer Robert Druitt drew attention to *équivalence* in the mid-1800s: 'What do the names given to wines really mean? ... with retail dealers the name is often a mere conventional sign of the quality of the wine. Thus, we may see in a wine merchant's list, the names of half a score of villages or towns; Moulin à Vent, Savigny, Beaune, Pommard, Nuits, Volnay, etc., etc. This merely means that there is a certain standard of goodness, which a wine ought to have when it is called by these names; but if anybody thinks that all the wine ticketed Pommard or Volnay, etc., etc., comes from those places – why, he may be complimented on his faith.'

The practice of *équivalence* shows clearly how the idea of counterfeit wine must be contextualized historically. It would have been quite legal to label a wine blended from several villages as 'Pommard' in 1918, but to have done so in 1921 would have been illegal, an example of counterfeiting. The difference is simply a shift in the meaning of the communal appellation from a representation of a style to an indication of provenance.

A different practice in Bordeaux also ended as appellations were interpreted literally and strictly. In 1911 when the Bordeaux appellation was first defined, it followed the boundaries of the *département* (the administrative region) of the Gironde. This had been opposed by many of Bordeaux's *négociants* because they regularly included wines from outside Gironde in their Bordeaux-labelled wines. In 1913 and 1914 a compromise was reached that allowed 'small quantities' of non-Gironde wine to be added to wines labelled 'Bordeaux': 'In Gironde it is local, authentic, and long-standing practice to maintain the appellation of origin of the finished wine, when the light addition of another wine simply has the result of making it conform better to the taste of the consumer, while respecting the distinct qualities that are common to all the wines of the origin indicated.'

This is a variation on the principle of Burgundy's *équivalence:* that wines from outside Bordeaux could be added to wines labelled 'Bordeaux' as long as they contributed to their tasting like wines from Bordeaux. Again, inter-regional blending was open and accepted, even though it was not stated on the label. From the modern perspective these labels were deceptive as to the provenance of the wine – although it must be recognized that modern wine laws that allow labelling by region as long as 75 or 85 per cent of the wine comes from there are hardly transparent.

Earlier than this, in the nineteenth century, Bordeaux producers commonly added some Syrah from the Rhône Valley to their red blends. As mentioned above, it was known as 'Hermitaging', from the well-known northern Rhône Hermitage district, and the practice was so common that Syrah should probably have been considered the seventh approved red grape variety of Bordeaux. It was also widely enough known that it was mentioned in a number of publications. The influential English wine writer Cyrus Redding noted in his *A History and Description of Modern Wines* (1851) that all Bordeaux wines destined for the English market were 'worked' (manipulated) in some way: they were blended with wines from Spain and Hermitage, and some alcohol was added: 'Orris root is employed to give the perfume destroyed by mixing, and sometimes a small quantity of raspberry brandy is used, two ounces to a cask, in order to flavour factitiously and replace the natural flavour it has lost.' This, we might note, was the way fine claret was made in what is sometimes called 'the golden age of Bordeaux'.

WINE AND CRIME IN THE TWENTIETH CENTURY

There is no doubt that there has been more certainty of detecting wine crimes such as fraud and counterfeit from the mid-twentieth century onwards. Chemical analysis of corks and labels is more sophisticated than ever, and so is the analysis of wine itself – although anyone owning a bottle of suspect wine would rather have its authenticity verified by its packaging than by having to open the bottle. Opening and resealing bottles without leaving evidence has become straightforward. Among the tests that can be run on wine is analysis of pesticide residues, because pesticide formulations – and thus their footprint in the wine – change almost every year. Improvements in detection probably explain what appears to be a higher incidence of wine fraud in recent decades than in earlier times.

At the same time that detection has become more certain, making fraudulent wines has in some respects become easier. It is possible, for example, to digitize labels and make them far more difficult to identify as counterfeit. Like counterfeiters of bank notes, forgers of wine labels no longer have to create labels from scratch, with the risk of making errors. Fake labels were key to a 2014 case where an Italian oenologist obtained counterfeit Brunello di Montalcino and Rosso di Montalcino labels and was preparing to put them on more than 200,000 bottles of mediocre red wine that had been aged to give some semblance of being Brunello or Rosso. He had also been able to penetrate the database of the Consorzio (the appellation's authorities) to falsely certify his bottles. The operation was discovered by the police before any of the counterfeit bottles were released onto the market.

Although this and other examples often involve representing mediocre wines as being prestigious and expensive, there is also money to be made in representing poor-quality as merely mediocre and somewhat more expensive. In Canada a large-scale fraud discovered in 2015 involved several prominent wine industry figures. They were instrumental in importing millions of litres of Italian bulk wine, adulterating it with various flavouring agents, and then bottling the fabricated wine as a range of twenty different brands. One was a brand from Montepulciano d'Abruzzo and another was a Barbera d'Asti, but others were brands of inexpensive Ontario wines that sell for about $10 a bottle. The adulterated wines were then sold on the black market to restaurants in Ontario and Quebec. A dozen men were charged, some with adulterating wine, but all with tax fraud involving tens of millions of dollars.

Examples of fraud such as these become well known within the wine industry but generally attract little attention from the wider public. An exception was the adulteration of some Austrian wine with diethylene glycol (an ingredient in antifreeze) in the 1980s because it seemed to pose a serious risk to health. Most Austrian wines at that time were sweet whites and their main market was Germany, where sweeter wines were more popular than they are today. Sweetness is achieved by harvesting grapes late so that they accumulate sugar and lose water, and fermenting them only to the point where they retain enough sugar for the desired degree of sweetness. When some vintages, notably 1982, were not suitable for a good crop of late-harvested grapes, some producers began to look for ways of compensating for what nature had failed to provide in the way of sugar. Chaptalizing (adding sugar before fermentation) was an option to increase sweetness, as was adding unfermented, sweet grape juice (Süssreserve). But diethylene glycol in small measures added not only sweetness but also some viscosity to the texture, giving adulterated wines a closer resemblance to many late harvest wines.

Some of these adulterated Austrian wines were exported to Germany where they were (illegally) blended with German wines, and the adulteration was discovered during routine quality testing in Germany. In almost all cases the level of diethylene glycol was far below the level of immediate danger – a lethal dose is about 40 grams, while most affected bottles contained only a few grams – but its very presence was enough. The wines were ordered off the German market and the German Ministry of Health warned against consuming any Austrian wines. A total of 27 million litres of wine was destroyed by the German authorities.

Needless to say, the warning about Austrian wines was heard well beyond Germany, and the result was a crisis for Austrian wines generally. Exports fell from 45 million litres a year in 1985 to under 5 million in 1986. Exports did not reach 1985 levels again until 2001, meaning that it took Austrian wine fifteen years to recover from the fraud – despite rapid action by the Austrian authorities. The German ban was announced on 9 July 1985, and within seven weeks, on 29 August, the Austrian parliament passed a new wine law so that it could be applied to the 1985 harvest. Since that time, Austrian wineries have focused on making dry wines rather than the sweeter styles. As for the individuals responsible for adding the diethylene glycol, they were variously sent to prison for short periods or fined.

RECENT AMERICAN CASES OF COUNTERFEIT WINES

Two well-publicized examples of counterfeiting involved fine and rare wines sold to collectors in the United States. One scandal involved four bottles of wine that were sold by a German collector, Hardy Rodenstock, as being wines that had belonged to Thomas Jefferson, the third president of the United States (1801–09). Jefferson was well known as a wine aficionado and left diaries of his visits to numerous French wine regions while representing the United States in Paris in the 1780s. When he returned to America, Jefferson ordered wine from France, but the four bottles that were sold in the 1980s were said to have been found in a walled-up cellar in Paris. They were engraved 'Th. J.', which was considered firm evidence that they had belonged to Thomas Jefferson. It was common practice for the well-to-do to have wine put in their own bottles, often engraved with their names or coats of arms. In 1988 Bill Koch, a wealthy American art and wine collector, bought four bottles of 'Jefferson wine' from two auction houses for a total of about half a million dollars. The four were all from Bordeaux, 1784 and 1787 vintages from Lafite and Branne-Mouton. These estates were later known as Château Lafite and Château Mouton-Rothschild, the first classified as a Premier Cru in the 1855 Bordeaux Classification, the other originally classified as a Deuxième Cru but elevated to Premier Cru in 1973.

Almost two decades later, when they and other items from Koch's collections were to be exhibited at the Boston Museum of Fine Arts, the museum asked for evidence of their provenance. Research showed that the auction houses had obtained the bottles from Rodenstock, who was already suspected of dealing in counterfeit wine, while the curator at Monticello (Jefferson's home in Virginia) advised that, based on Jefferson's records, it was unlikely that the bottles had ever belonged to the president. A forensic examination of the wines and bottles revealed a number of problems, including the high probability that the letters 'Th. J.' were engraved with a power tool (which clearly did not exist in the 1780s).

Koch sued Rodenstock for fraud in 2006 but Rodenstock refused to acknowledge the American court's jurisdiction. In 2008 Koch filed a new suit alleging that nine other bottles in his possession, and also originally from Rodenstock, were fakes. Rodenstock has continued to insist on the authenticity of the wines, but has never divulged the name of the person who sold them to him, the address in Paris where they were said to have been discovered, or the total number of bottles involved. (The number given at various times has ranged from 'a dozen or so' to thirty.) Some certainty was offered when three tests (tritium, carbon-14, and caesium) dated the wine in two of the bottles to the early 1960s.

This case drew a great deal of publicity. In 2008 a book on the subject, *The Billionaire's Vinegar*, was published and English wine critic Michael Broadbent sued the publisher for libel for misrepresenting his role in selling the wine. That suit was settled out of court and the publisher agreed not to sell the book in the United Kingdom. In 2010 Bill Koch sued Christie's auction house, but the suit was dismissed. In the end, despite the compelling evidence that at least some of 'Jefferson's wines' (and other eighteenth-century wines handled by Rodenstock) were fake, there was no definitive judgment on the origins and extent of the counterfeiting.

An even more infamous example, involving tens of millions of dollars' worth of counterfeit wines, was also one of the most brazen. Rudy Kurniawan, who was born in Jakarta, Indonesia, in 1976, travelled to California in the late 1990s on a student visa. He studied for a while before his visa expired and was ordered to leave the US in 2003, but he remained in California as an illegal alien. In the early 2000s, just as wine was becoming a popular commodity for investment, Kurniawan began to buy and sell large lots of rare wines, especially from Burgundy and Bordeaux. Unlike many other collectors, who bought wines almost purely as an investment, Kurniawan began to host tastings and dinners for wealthy wine collectors – including Hollywood personalities and some of America's wealthiest CEOs – where he opened some of the world's most expensive wines. He opened so many bottles of Domaine de Romanée-Conti that some people called him 'Dr Conti'. It is estimated that by 2006 – when he was only thirty – Kurniawan was spending $1 million a month on rare wines at auctions. This was a period when the stock exchange was high, when fabulous executive bonuses were paid out, and when the dot.com businesses produced a stratum of highly paid young people who were willing to spend tens of thousands of dollars for trophy wines they were told were rare and of exceptional quality. The bubble in wine prices burst when the recession began in 2008, but until then the financial and cultural environments were very favourable for counterfeit wines.

In addition to buying rare and expensive wines, Kurniawan began to sell substantial quantities through established auction houses. Two lots sold through Acker Merrall & Condit in 2006 fetched a total of more than $35 million, not only bringing Kurniawan huge wealth but also catapulting the minor auction house to being a major dealer in fine wines. As these auctions were going on, Kurniawan offered for sale eight magnums of Château Lafleur from 1947, often regarded as the best Bordeaux vintage of the twentieth century.

But starting in 2007, some experts began to question the authenticity of some of the wines that Kurniawan tried to sell. In that year he consigned several magnums of Château Le Pin from 1982, another stellar Bordeaux vintage, to Christie's in Los Angeles. But the producer contacted the auction house, concerned that these bottles were fakes, and they were withdrawn from sale. The same year, the former head of wine auctions at Sotheby's cast doubt on the authenticity of the 1947 magnums of Château Le Pin that Kurniawan had sold the year before, because only five magnums in total had been bottled.

A turning point came when in 2008 Kurniawan consigned a number of bottles from various vintages of Domaine Ponsot, a prestigious producer in Burgundy's Morey St. Denis appellation. One bottle was a Clos de la Roche Grand Cru 1929, and there were thirty-eight bottles of Clos St. Denis Grand Cru from vintages between 1945 and 1971. But an eagle-eyed wine collector knew that the first vintage of Clos de la Roche was 1934, while the first Clos St. Denis was made in 1982. He alerted the producer and Laurent Ponsot, the head of Domaine Ponsot, attended the auction. At the moment the bottles were to be auctioned, Ponsot stood and demanded they be withdrawn from sale. Ponsot met Kurniawan to find out where he had obtained the bottles, but he was unable to give a satisfactory explanation. Ponsot was left unsure whether Kurniawan was knowingly selling counterfeit wines or was merely the person who happened to own them when the counterfeit was discovered. These wines, especially very old vintages, can change hands many times over the decades.

The Ponsot affair, together with the earlier problematic wines, convinced many collectors and auctioneers that Kurniawan was knowingly dealing in counterfeit wine. Bill Koch, the billionaire who had purchased what were claimed to be Thomas Jefferson's bottles of wine, sued Kurniawan for selling him and other collectors counterfeit wine at auction and in private transactions. He hired an investigative team to learn more about Kurniawan's background and to try and estimate the extent of wine fraud. Koch found in his own cellar some 400 fraudulent bottles, for which he had paid a total of $4 million. From that point, Kurniawan found it increasingly difficult to sell or consign any more wine, although he might well have done so through an intermediary: in 2012 a London auction house withdrew wines worth three-quarters of a million dollars when it was discovered that they were consigned by Kurniawan through a third party.

In 2012, well after serious doubts arose about Kurniawan's activities, the FBI raided his Los Angeles house and found what looked like a wine factory. There were thousands of bottles on storage shelves, in boxes, on the floor, and even several bottles lying in water in the kitchen sink so that their labels could be removed. Kurniawan's computer showed that he had scanned and printed labels. There were old corks, bundles of labels, and wax, as well as a stamps and a corking machine. There was, in short, all the paraphernalia needed for counterfeiting. There were also ordinary wines from Napa Valley with notes indicating which older Bordeaux vintages they could be passed off as, as well as bottles marked up to show that Kurniawan had been blending wines to achieve a result that was as close as possible to the wines they would be sold as. It turned out that Kurniawan also bought older wines from Burgundy and relabelled them as coming from more prestigious (and lucrative) producers and vintages.

But photographs from the scene (which are shown in *Sour Grapes*, a 2016 documentary on Rudy Kurniawan) suggest that Kurniawan's house contained an artisanal operation where bottles were counterfeited one at a time. There might have been thousands of fake labels, bundled together with rubber bands, but two bottles in the sink having their labels soaked off suggests a small-scale operation. Laurent Ponsot estimated that it would take an hour to produce a counterfeit bottle of wine – to fill it with a wine that would pass muster, stamp and insert the cork, apply the wax or capsule, and glue on the labels and dirty them to give them the appearance of age – not to mention the time it took to create labels. Kurniawan is thought to have produced a total of some 15,000 bottles of counterfeit wine. Working fifty hours a week, it would have taken six years to produce that many bottles. The scale of the operation seemed disproportionate to the scale of the sometimes alleged production, but there was no evidence of anyone helping Kurniawan or of another production location.

In retrospect, when the extent of Kurniawan's counterfeiting activities was revealed, it is more than fair to ask whether any of the wines he put on the market were genuine – although some people are convinced that most were and that his counterfeits represented only a small part of the wines he handled. At the same time, there is general recognition that many of the wines that are bought and sold on the secondary market – not coming directly from the producers' cellars, but sold by auction, retail, or privately – are not genuine. In these cases, sellers might be well intentioned and sincerely believe that they are dealing with genuine wines. Clearly, a counterfeit wine was fabricated by somebody who profited at the very beginning of the chain of exchange and the person caught trying to sell it might have bought it in good faith.

Kurniawan was not given the benefit of the doubt – there was plenty of evidence of counterfeiting, however extensive – and he was convicted of a number of offences, including mail and wire fraud. There were also charges related to specific wines, such as selling a counterfeit jeroboam of Château Mouton-Rothschild 1945 in 2006 for $48,000. But although such specific examples of Kurniawan's activities came to light, the extent of his counterfeiting is unknown. *Sour Grapes*, the 2016 documentary based on the story, speculated that there might be 10,000 bottles of Kurniawan wine in private collections. Kurniawan was sentenced to ten years' imprisonment in 2013, and he is due to be released in 2021. If there are that many of his fake wines undiscovered, some collectors will be enjoying his fake wines long after Kurniawan is set free and deported to Indonesia.

THE ROLE OF CHINA

Although some sensational wine frauds have taken place in Europe and the United States, a lot of attention has been paid to China, which for the last decade has possessed conditions likely to foster wine fraud: a fast-growing stratum of extremely wealthy people, many of them millionaires and billionaires, who are willing to pay high prices for rare and prestigious wines; a culture in which these wines are highly prized; and a regulatory regime which was, until quite recently, very lax and permitted the counterfeiting of designer-branded goods of many kinds. (On a more restricted level, the coexistence of sudden wealth and a desire to own 'trophy wines' was the culture that initially enabled Rudy Kurniawan to be successful in the United States.)

Quite how common and extensive wine fraud is in China is anybody's guess, and there is no doubt that some of the suspicion reflects ethnic or racial prejudice – the same prejudice that underlies the stories that often circulate of wealthy Chinese mixing Pétrus and first-growth wines with Coca-Cola. Stories such as these underline the perceived failure of Chinese people to be as sophisticated as Western connoisseurs. Estimates of extensive wine fraud in China are buttressed by centuries-old images of Chinese people as untrustworthy (the 'wily Oriental' stereotype), and they ignore how widespread wine fraud has been at similarly propitious times in Europe and elsewhere in the Western world. The fabrication of claret in the early twentieth century is only one example.

That said, the producers of Canadian Icewine have been especially concerned about adulterated wines, labelled as Canadian Icewine, for sale on Asian markets. In many cases the contents of these bottles are artificially sweetened, generic white wines that are not made from any of the approved grape varieties and certainly not made from grapes frozen naturally on the vine before being pressed. As for the labels, they tend to be not copies of genuine brands, which is odd in itself, but labels designed from scratch and sporting names such as Maple Dew, Silver Maple, and Toronto Icewine. Some feature photographs of Ontario vineyards taken from winery websites and many include other recognizably Canadian elements, such as Niagara Falls and maple leaves. Some Icewine counterfeiters have been prosecuted in China, but the industry has taken action – such as training Chinese and other Asian sommeliers and wine merchants to recognize the sensory and stylistic character of the genuine product. Some producers are adding security features to their bottles to distinguish them from counterfeits.

Small and massive examples of wine fraud and counterfeiting will undoubtedly continue to crop up. The profits – either large profits per unit on a small number of highly sought-after wines or small profits per unit on large numbers of wines that can be sold on the mass market – can be substantial. Wine, in this sense, is a commodity that is no different from other branded goods such as sunglasses, bags, and watches. Like these sorts of counterfeit goods, the success of wine fraud depends upon a market. At the level of rare wines, there seems to be no end of people willing to pay high prices for wines that are hard to obtain, even though they have no guarantee of authenticity. These wines have cachet and give prestige to their owners, who might well have never tasted them before and therefore have no point of reference when they do (if they do) drink the wines. And unlike a new watch, there is no guarantee that a bottle of older wine will be in good condition. If a bottle of a Cru Classé 1961 does not taste sublime, it can be attributed to bottle variation or the way it was stored in the intervening years.

There is, today, more definition as to what constitutes wine fraud. What goes into wine is closely regulated and chemical analysis easily identifies forbidden additives or excessive levels of any component. Appellations and brands are legally protected as never before, making the definition of counterfeiting more straightforward than ever. The longer history of wine and crime, when anything could be added to wine and when there was (shall we say?) a flexible approach to labelling by provenance, has now disappeared.

But a new discourse on wine fraud has arisen in recent years, as some of the promoters of 'natural wine' seek to distinguish it from what we might call conventional wines. There are echoes here of nineteenth-century Germany and early twentieth-century France, as partisans of particular wine regions called their wines 'natural' and denounced others as 'artificial', 'industrial', 'commercial'. What are referred to as natural wines today are made with minimal intervention, and some enthusiasts denounce wines made using some of the scores of additives and techniques available to winemakers. Such wines are routinely criticized in such ways as to imply that they are fraudulent. Fraudulence and adulteration are now closely defined by law, but they remain potent cultural charges to lay against any wine.

BIBLIOGRAPHY

This bibliography lists only the main works mentioned in the book and consulted while writing it.

General

Garrier, Gilbert, *Histoire Sociale et Culturelle du Vin* (Paris: Larousse, 1998).

Johnson, Hugh, *The Story of Wine* (London: Mitchell Beazley, 1989).

Lachiver, Marcel, *Vins, Vignes et Vignerons: Histoire du Vignoble Français* (Paris: Fayard, 1988).

Nourrisson, Didier, *Histoire du Vin* (Paris: Perrin, 2017).

Phillips, Rod, *9000 Years of Wine: A World History* (Vancouver: Whitecap Books, 2017).

Phillips, Rod, *Alcohol: A History* (Chapel Hill: University of North Carolina Press, 2014).

Phillips, Rod, *French Wine: A History* (Oakland: University of California Press, 2016).

Phillips, Rod, *The Wines of Canada* (Oxford: Infinite Ideas, 'Classic Wine Library', 2017).

Chapter 1

Curth, Louise Hill, 'The medicinal value of wine in Early Modern England,' *The Social History of Alcohol and Drugs* 18 (2003), 35–50.

Curth, Louise Hill, and Tanya M. Cassidy, '"Health, strength, and happiness": Medical constructions of wine and beer in Early Modern England,' in Adam Smyth (ed.), *A Pleasing Sinne: Drink and Conviviality in Seventeenth-Century England* (Cambridge: D.S. Brewer, 2004), 143–60.

Deuraseh, Nurden, 'Is imbibing *al-khamr* (intoxicating drink) for medical purposes permissible by Islamic law?' *Arab Law Quarterly* 18 (2003), 356–60.

Grieco, Allen, 'Medieval and Renaissance wines: Taste, dietary theory, and how to choose "the right" wine (14th –16th centuries),' *Mediaevalia* 30 (2009), 15–42.

Leake, Chancey D., *The Old Egyptian Medical Papyri* (Lawrence: University of Kansas Press, 1953).

Lucia, Salvatore P., *A History of Wine as Therapy* (Philadelphia: J.B. Lippincott, 1963).

Paul, Harry W., *Bacchic Medicine: Wine and Alcohol Therapies from Napoleon to the French Paradox* (Amsterdam: Rodopi, 2001).

Prestwich, Patricia E., *Drink and the Politics of Social Reform: Antialcoholism in France since 1870* (Palo Alto: The Society for the Promotion of Science and Scholarship, 1988).

Chapter 2

Britland, Karen, 'Circe's cup: Wine and women in Early Modern drama,' in Adam Smyth (ed.), *A Pleasing Sinne: Drink and Conviviality in Seventeenth-Century England* (Cambridge: D.S. Brewer, 2004), 109–26.

Ludington, Charles, '"Claret is the liquor for boys; port for men": How port became the "Englishman's wine", 1750s to 1800,' *Journal of British Studies* 48 (2009), 364–390.

Martin, A. Lynn, *Alcohol, Sex, and Gender in Late Medieval and Early Modern Europe* (Basingstoke: Palgrave, 2001).

Roberts, Benjamin, 'Drinking like a man: The paradox of excessive drinking for seventeenth-century Dutch youths,' *Journal of Family History* 29 (2004), 237–52.

Roller, Matthew, 'Posture and sex in the Roman *convivium*,' *American Journal of Philology* 124 (2003), 377–422.

Tlusty, B. Ann, 'Drinking, family relations and authority in Early Modern Germany,' *Journal of Family History* 29 (2004), 253–73.

Tlusty, B. Ann, 'Water of life, water of death: The controversy over brandy and gin in Early Modern Augsburg,' *Central European History* 31 (1999), 1–30.

Chapter 3

Deurasch, Nurdeen, 'Is imbibing *al-khamr* (intoxicating drink) for medical purposes permissible by Islamic law?' *Arab Law Quarterly* 18 (2003), 356–60.

Heskett, Randall, and Joel Butler, *Divine Vintage: Following the Wine Trail from Genesis to the Modern Age* (New York: Palgrave, 2012).

Kennedy, Philip F., *The Wine Song in Classical Arab Poetry: Abu Nuwas and the Literary Tradition* (Oxford: Clarendon Press, 1997).

Kreglinger, Gisela H., *The Spirituality of Wine* (Grand Rapids: William B. Eerdmans, 2016).

McNeill, John T., and Helena M. Gamer, *Medieval Handbooks of Penance* (New York: Octagon Books, 1965).

Seward, Desmond, *Monks and Wine* (London: Mitchell Beazley, 1979).

Woodruff Tait, Jennifer L., *The Poisoned Chalice: Eucharistic Grape Juice and Common-Sense Realism in Victorian Methodism* (Tuscaloosa: The University of Alabama Press, 2011).

Chapter 4

Dickenson, John, and Tim Unwin, *Viticulture in Colonial Latin America: Essays in alcohol, the vine and wine in Spanish America and Brazil* (Liverpool: University of Liverpool, Institute of Latin American Studies, Working Paper 13, 1992).

Guy, Kolleen M., 'Silence and savoir-faire in the marketing of products of the terroir,' *Modern and Contemporary France* 19 (2011), 459–75.

Maltman, Alex, 'The role of vineyard geology in wine typicity,' *Journal of Wine Research* 19 (2008), 1–17.

Matthews, Mark A., *Terroir and Other Myths of Winegrowing* (Oakland: University of California Press, 2015).

McGovern, Patrick E., *Ancient Wine: The Search for the Origins of Viticulture* (Princeton: Princeton University Press, 2003).

Parker, Thomas, *Tasting French Terroir: The History of an Idea* (Oakland: University of California Press, 2015).

Rice, Prudence M., 'Wine and brandy production in colonial Peru: A historical and archaeological investigation,' *Journal of Interdisciplinary History* 27 (1997), 455–79.

Robinson, Jancis, Julia Harding, and José Vouillamoz, *Wine Grapes: A Complete Guide to 1,368 Vine Varieties, including their Origins and Flavours* (New York: Ecco/HarperCollins, 2012).

Sereni, Emilio, *History of the Italian Landscape* (Princeton: Princeton University Press, 1997).

Szabo, John, *Volcanic Wines: Salt, Grit and Power* (London: Jacqui Small, 2016).

Unwin, Tim, *Wine and the Vine: An Historical Geography of Viticulture and the Wine Trade* (London: Routledge, 1991).

Wilson, James, *Terroir: The Role of Geology, Climate, and Culture in the Making of French Wines* (Berkeley: University of California Press, 1999).

Chapter 5

Druitt, Robert, *Report on the Cheap Wines from France, Italy, Austria, Greece, Hungary and Australia* (London: Henry Renshaw, 1873).

Gargantuan Wine, 'On Wine and Gender: A Critical History' http://gargantuanwine.com/2017/02/on-wine-and-gender-critical-history/

Grieco, Allen, 'Medieval and Renaissance wines: Taste, dietary theory, and how to choose "the right" wine (14th—16th centuries),' *Mediaevalia* 30 (2009), 15–42.

Johnson, Hugh, 'From earnest bud to exotic flower,' *The World of Fine Wine* 44 (2014).

Redding, Cyrus, *A History and Description of Modern Wines* (3rd edn., London: Henry G. Bohn, 1850).

Chapter 6

Albala, Ken, *The Banquet: Dining in the Great Courts of Late Renaissance Europe* (Urbana: University of Illinois Press, 2007).

D'Arms, John H., 'The culinary reality of Roman upper-class convivia: Integrating texts and images,' *Comparative Studies in Society and History* 46 (2004), 428–50.

Grieco, Allen J., *The Meal: Themes in Art* (London: Scala, 1992).

Malaguzzi, Silvia, *Food and Feasting in Art* (Los Angeles: J. Paul Getty Museum, 2006).

Strong, Roy, *The Feast: A History of Grand Eating* (London: Pimlico, 2003).

Chapter 7

Bennett, Norman R., 'The vignerons of the Douro and the Peninsular War,' *Journal of European Economic History* 21 (1992), 7–29.

Harari, Yuval Noah, 'Strategy and supply in fourteenth-century Western European invasion campaigns,' *Journal of Military History* 64 (2000), 297–334.

Johnson, Nicholas K., Five-part blog for Alcohol and Drugs History Society on alcohol and tobacco in World War One: https://pointsadhsblog.wordpress.com

Keegan, John, *The Face of Battle: A study of Agincourt, Waterloo, and the Somme* (Harmondsworth: Penguin Books, 1987).

Lucand, Christophe, *Le Pinard des Poilus: Une histoire du vin en France Durant la Grande Guerre (1914–1918)* (Dijon: Editions Universitaires de Dijon, 2015).

Ridel, Charles, *L'Ivresse du Soldat: L'alcool dans les tranchées, 1914–1918* (Paris: Editions Vendémiaire, 2016).

Chapter 8

Sour Grapes (documentary, Faites Un Voeu/Met Film Production, 2016).

Goldberg, Kevin D., 'Acidity and power: The politics of natural wine in nineteenth-century Germany,' *Food and Foodways* 19 (2011), 294–313.

Holmberg, Lars, 'Wine fraud,' *International Journal of Wine Research* (2010:2), 105–113.

Phillips, Rod, 'Wine and adulteration,' *History Today* 50 (2000), 31–37.

Stanziani, Alessandro, 'Information, quality and legal rules: Wine adulteration in nineteenth-century France,' *Business History* 51: 2 (2009), 268–91.

Steinberger, Michael, 'A vintage crime,' *Vanity Fair* (12 June 2012).

Wallace, Benjamin, *The Billionaire's Vinegar: The Mystery of the World's Most Expensive Bottle of Wine* (New York: Crown, 2008).

INDEX